The Uncovered Head

The Uncovered Head

Jewish Culture
New Perspectives

Yedidya Itzhaki

Translated by Nahum Steigman

UNIVERSITY OF DELAWARE PRESS
Newark

Published by University of Delaware Press
Co-published with The Rowman & Littlefield Publishing Group, Inc.
4501 Forbes Boulevard, Suite 200, Lanham, Maryland 20706
www.rlpgbooks.com

Estover Road, Plymouth PL6 7PY, United Kingdom

British Library Cataloguing in Publication Information Available

Library of Congress Cataloging-in-Publication Data

Library of Congress Cataloguing-in-Publication Data on file under LC#2010013174
ISBN: 978-1-61149-036-7 (cl. : alk. paper)
eISBN: 978-1-61149-037-4

⊗ ™ The paper used in this publication meets the minimum requirements of American National Standard for Information Sciences—Permanence of Paper for Printed Library Materials, ANSI/NISO Z39.48-1992.

Printed in the United States of America

"There will be no victory for light over darkness until we take in a simple truth—we should not be battling the darkness but redoubling the light."

—Aharon David Gordon

Contents

Preface

Wнат is it that has turned Jewish identity—the product of such a long history, a commonplace the world over—into a problem that has preoccupied Jewish thinkers and Hebrew authors for over two hundred years now? Is it true that the core and substance of Judaism is the Jewish religion and that, divorced from the religion, Jewish existence is meaningless? Is a religious Jew "more Jewish" than a non-religious one? Has the line and the continuity of Judaism, from its origins to the present day, been sustained only by Orthodox Jewry? If so, what do we make of Reform Judaism and Conservative Judaism? Is there such a thing as *secular* Judaism? How are Jewish and Israeli identity related? And what are the interrelationships between Israeli and Diaspora Jewry?

These are the questions that beat at the heart of this book and they are posed and answered from the point of view of a secular humanism. I have written this book with educated secular readers in mind, who have asked themselves the questions I have posed above and who want to examine what it means to be both Jewish *and* secular and what the implications of their secularism are. The book is not an attack on religion or on religious life, nor is it an argument against organized religion. Its purpose is to explain the secular view of the world and to consider how to live in it. In one direction, these views are rooted in the long evolution of Jewish civilization and culture, in all its components, values, variants, contradictions, forms and facets; in the other direction, secular Judaism is an offshoot of Western European humanism, a civilization with its own values and a culture that has expanded and ramified over the last six hundred years. The book also offers a secular perspective of the historical evolution of Jewish culture and examines how the attitudes and thinking of this culture have responded to the encounter with European humanism. It traces the emergence of Jewish pluralism and of secular Judaism during the nineteenth and twentieth centuries and considers the consequences of these two developments, consequences with which we are currently coping.

If there is one premise at the core of the book's conception, it is that there is no need to devise compromises or build bridges between the

9

many worldviews within Judaism. If we could learn to appreciate how many views and groups co-exist within "Judaism," each of them could be accorded the respect and understanding all deserve. It is common knowledge that Judaism has permitted and even cultivated a diversity of opinions and a variety of textual interpretations, that its great rabbis developed a fertile culture that depended upon controversy and mutual criticism for its vitality, even in periods when strict solidarity was demanded. If controversy was permitted even then surely it should be encouraged even more now, at a time when this communal solidarity is no longer necessary.

The current calls for Jewish unity should be neither meant nor taken as calls to supress controversy or to make concessions on matters of ideology or lifestyle; rather they should be construed as calls for coexistence and understanding, for the mutual acknowledgement of a diversity of opinions, outlooks and practices within Judaism and Jewry, for the maximum possible respect and tolerance for each opinion, outlook and practice, as long as it does not infringe upon the right of others to have their own opinions, outlooks and practices. This book is intended to contribute to this general acknowledgement of the rich diversity of Judaism and Jewry. As I have indicated, I write from the standpoint of a secular Jew, a standpoint that views secular Judaism as an authentic form of Jewish life, rooted in and sustained by hundreds of generations of Jewish tradition.

In the course of this book I shall also try to construct a clear picture of the nature and materials of Jewish identity, in all the forms and apparel in which it had appeared throughout the ages, from the biblical to our own. I shall examine what constitutes Jewish civilization and culture and how secular-minded Jews have interpreted it and practiced it. I will discuss how contemporary Jewish culture represents a renewal and an extension of received tradition. The lifestyles and the boundries of secularism are examined and described and suggestions are made that would help secular Jews sustain a full and enduring dialogue with other parties of the Jewish people.

～

This book evolved during a sabbatical at Stanford University's Program in Jewish Studies and at the Oxford Center for Hebrew and Jewish Studies at Yarnton, England. It began as a research study into changes in perceptions of Jewish identity and what impact they made on modern Jewish literature. My study uncovered how perceptions of Jewish identity had fragmented and multiplied over recent generations; this revealed the need for a deeper examination of the problems raised by Jewish pluralism in the modern period, in particular, the problems of the legitimacy and authenticity accorded to secular Judaism. I felt that this deeper examination needed comprehensive, precise and coherent treatment.

In my research study, literary matters were foremost, but in this book they have been reduced to illustrative excerpts, quotations and passing references. Sometimes a passage from a great author can clarify an issue more precisely and vividly than reams of analysis. The quotations cited here are drawn from all periods of history and from all schools of Judaism, and serve to demonstrate that the question of the nature of Jewish existence, in its many possible forms has troubled Jewish thinkers for a very long time, in fact from the time that the entity called "the Jewish people" first came into being.

In all quotations from the Bible and references to the "personality" of the Israelite or Jewish God, whose name will be written here as "Yahweh," which is as near as we can get to the actual vocalization of the unvocalized "Y-H-W-H" of the Bible (the combination in the Hebrew Bible of the consonants y, h, v, h and the vocalization of "Adonai" gave rise to the misnomer "Jehovah"). No provocation or defiance is intended. I can see no reason not to call God by His name; I do no believe in the holiness of the four letters. To my mind, to distort the name is a greater insult than to pronounce it or write it out in full. In any case, anyone who is upset by seeing the Ineffable Name written out in full can simply not pronounce it out loud when it appears, for the prohibition applies only to pronunciation, not to writing. The book draws on numerous sources, most of them cited in the footnotes as recommended further reading for those interested. Quotations from the sources are identified in standard fashion—for the Bible: book, chapter, and verse (e.g., Lev. 18:28); for the *Mishna:* tractate, chapter and paragraph (each paragraph is also called a *mishna*) (e.g., *Yadaim* 4:6); for the *Gemara* or the *Babylonian Talmud:* tractate, page, side (*BT Sanhedrin* 91a–b). Passages from the *Midrash* are referenced by Midrash, biblical portion, and paragraph (*Tanhuma, Vayakhel* 1). Canonical and famous works are cited by name of author and work (e.g., Bialik, *Metei Midbar*); other books are cited in accordance with standard bibliographical forms. Translation of excerpts from the Bible are based on the King James version.

I take this opportunity to thank the many friends who took an interest in my work and provided encouragement along the way: to my friend, Nitza Ben-Dov, who conceived the idea of the book and supported its publication; to my friends and colleagues, Yaakov Malkin, Shneur Einam, and the late Bubby Tzervanitzer, who, having read the manuscript, drew on their great breadth of knowledge to make constructive comments; to my editor, Nili Landsberger, to the translator, Nahum Steigman, to my English editor, Glendyr Sachs, and to Felix Posen for supporting the English version of my book. Most of all, thanks to my family, Rina my wife, and Tal and Raviv our children, who were put to a great deal of trouble and bother but who all read the book at every stage and contributed numerous helpful suggestions and corrections. To all of the above my gratitude, affection and love.

∼

Throughout the phrase "R." denotes Rabbi

Introduction

IN THE PAST, A NON-RELIGIOUS JEWISH PERSON WAS CONSIDERED TO BE a "free-thinker," an appellation that had certain approbatory connotations, deriving from the positive values thought to be implicit in a worldview and lifestyle that were not religion-bound. However, the appellation was used negatively by religious people, for whom Judaism was inherently "the yoke of the Torah and the commandments." Thus, to them, secularism involved the repudiation of that yoke to be "free of the Torah and the commandments." More recently, "free-thinker" has been replaced by religious people with "secular," which is even more negative in intent, for implicit within it is the assumption that the religious way of life possesses a sacredness that is completely lacking in the non-religious lifestyle. To be secular is to lead a life totally devoid of the sacred and the holy. The implications of this dichotomy between "holy" and "secular,"[1] however, depend on how one understands and to what one applies these two terms.

This dichotomy is very ancient and can be traced back to the biblical period when Hebrew paired the word "secular" (in Hebrew *khol*) not in antithesis to the "religious" but to the words of "holy" or "sacred": "You may put difference between holy [*kodesh*] and unholy [*khol*]" (Lev. 10:10). In Hebrew, *khol* designated all that bore no connection to religious rite and ritual, to "*kodesh*" or holiness. For example, weekdays are called "*yemei khol*" ("secular" days), in distinction to *shabbat kodesh* ("Sabbath of the Holiness") and the days between the Holy Days that mark the beginning and the end of the Passover and Sukkot festivals are called "*khol hamo'ed*," "secular days of the festival." *Khiloni* is the Aramaic translation for *zar*, an outsider, someone who is not a *Cohen*, a descendant of the High Priest Aharon: "There shall no outsider [*zar*] eat of the holy things" (Lev. 22:10). Onkelos, the second century translator of the Pentateuch into Aramaic, translates *zar* into the Aramaic *Khiloni*. For the sages of the Talmud as well, a secular Jew (*khiloni*) was merely one who was not a priest: ". . . a high priest [*Cohen Gadol*] who met a *khiloni* on the road" (Lev. Rabba 24).

It was only much later, when "secular" was applied to anyone who was not religious, that we get the antithetical pairing "secular-religious," which takes for granted that, by its very definition, religion is bound up with the sacred and that whatever is not religious is secular. Lately, in Hebrew, the concept of *kedusha*, holiness, has taken on new connotations and is even used synonymously for "values": for example, the phrase *kedushat hakha'im* (the holiness of life) implies that a non-religious way of life, being empty of the holy, must also be empty of values and that a life of values is inconceivable outside a religiously-observant lifestyle. This is a claim that is often made explicit, particularly in the field of educational values. I shall address this assertion more fully later, when I will argue against it. At this stage it suffices to say that the value-content of secular humanism is nothing less than that of any religion, even if we do not attribute to it the quality of holiness, as that understood by religious followers of Judaism.

Despite certain reservations, therefore, this book will use the terms "secular" and "secularism." They are already commonly used to refer to a non-religious way of life, and the original meaning of "secular" in ecclesiastical Latin—"the world" (as opposed to the Church)—has all but disappeared. Etymologically, it may sound somewhat strange to talk about the sacred values within secularism, but the apparent paradox is an extraneous dichotomy that has been imposed upon secular and sacred. Secularism is a worldview that is based on the humanist concept that human beings are sovereign over their world, their bodies, their acts and their thoughts; this is in contrast to the religious worldview which delegates this soverenity to a supernatural entity, God, who exists beyond the grasp of human capacity and comprehension. To be secular, therefore, is to hold to a humanist worldview and to lead a life that does not derive from any religious worldview or any religious organization or religious organizing principle and that owes no obligation to any such organization or principle. Religious organizations and movements are usually voluntary bodies, or are centered within an institution or community, but they can also be part of a state, regional, political, educational, or social apparatus. All of them, however, function by dint of the religious affiliation of the people who participate in them, whether they are "members" in the strict sense or belong in some other way.

Our appreciation of secularism depends to some extent on our appreciation of religion. As a worldview and as a way of life, secularism stands in part as an antithesis to religion, as the repudiation of religious worldviews, ways of life and ways of organizing people. This does *not* mean that the origin and essence of secularism is in opposition to religion or that secularism therefore has no value content of its own. Nor is secularism merely an attempt to lighten the practical burdens of religion, "to throw off the yoke of the Torah and the commandments," as the religious would have it. It is an autonomous worldview, possessing its own values, a single strand of which is repudiation of the religious way of conceiving our world. For all that, in secularism there is no quarrel with religion itself. The historical importance of religion in the shaping of human society and in the development of human thought is appreciated and the right of religion to exist, as long as religion is not imposed upon those who do not want it is recognized. After all, one central tenet of humanism is the right to freedom of religion.

In essence, secularism and religion are separated by the assumption that religion has sole access to absolute truth, dismissing all alternative conceptions of our reality and in so doing disqualifying secularism out of hand. Yet religion, although it may meet real needs, is not an essential constituent of human existence. It is a complex of conceptions of the world, characteristic of human thought during a certain period in history, that has clothed itself in the mantle of absolute, universal, and binding truth. Yet fundamental to every religious system is the stipulation that a supernatural "revelation" occurred that bestowed on humankind the gifts of faith and religion—what religion calls "the knowledge of God"—and which *humankind did not have before that revelation.* By contrast, secularism regards the sovereignty that human beings exercise over themselves and over the conduct of their life as an essential ingredient of their status as free humans, and thus it seeks to give them back the universal primal sovereignty. The freedom that contemporary seculars enjoy is perceived and understood from the standpoint of contemporary human beings, who, within limitations, know themselves and their world by virtue of the work of modern scientists and philosophers.

Most western religions are inherently total, that is to say they encompass their followers' total being, concerning themselves with every facet and element of their existence. They determine their primary identity, and this is especially true of the Jewish religion. Religious Jews are first of all adherent of the Jewish faith and only afterwards members of the people to whom they see themselves as belonging or citizen of the state in which they live. Religious identity often takes precedence over family identity: for many religious people the commitment to their faith certainly comes before any family obligations. To be secular, on the other hand, is to accept a primary identity that is individual and not bound up with any faith or religion. As we have seen, the fundamental tenet of secularism is the worldview and values of humanism that acknowledge the sovereignty of free human beings over themselves, their bodies, and behaviors, within the framework of a social contract to which they have freely consented.

A secular worldview does not restrict itself to any one area of life, nor does it bind the secular individual to any one vision of the world and its human inhabitants. It respects a range of interpretations and viewpoints and encourages a broad and multifaceted understanding of reality and of the ways in which human beings can live. It is a paramount value of humanism that people embrace a wide spectrum of outlook and opinion, of points of view and lifestyles and conceptions, with an openness towards them all. In a nutshell, secularism recognizes people's right to be different. It has tolerance and sympathy for what appears to be outside the mainstream and it refuses to intervene in areas it deems personal to the individual. While it recognizes no duty to religion as such, it has no objection to people observing traditional practices, including those inherited from organized religion, for it sees such practice not as personal or communal religious duties performed at the behest of supernatural command, but rather as the maintenance of tradition, which is a part of cultural values, and so a matter of individual free will and subject to a degree of understanding.

Secularism is neither a religion in competition with existing religions nor is it a substitute for religion. It is not a comperhensive system of ideas; it does not posit any absolute truth and it offers no redemption, whether individual or collective. As discussed above, it is based upon a willingness to consider to the broadest possible spectrum of ideas and opinions, which is why seculars feel no need to preach their ideas in halls and streets in order to win souls. It has respect and understanding for those who stand by their faith and the ways of their religion, this being one expression of self-sovereignty. It will always strongly defend the rights of religious people, of all faiths and religions—within the framework of state law—to practice their own way of life and culture as they see fit and free from outside intervention. The obvious corollary is that seculars demand the right to live their own lives in their own homes and communities according to their own fashion, free from impositions and even symbols that are drawn from a religious worldview and way of life and that are incompatible with the secular vision of the world.

I have been arguing that secularism is a personal standpoint, that it is the way in which individuals conduct themselves at home, at work, in society, and so on. If that is the case how can we postulate a secular Judaism, for the very concept supposes a collective secularism? Further, isn't there in Judaism an essential religious constituent whose repudiation negates the very possibility of Judaism? And what can be called

Jewish in a worldview that rejects the Jewish religion? In the final analysis, can a secular individual also be "Jewish"?

If we accept the premise that Judaism is in essence a religion only, it certainly follows that secular Judaism, like any "secular religion" is an impossibility. There is no such thing as secular Christianity, or Islam, or Hinduism, or Buddhism; not even Voodooism has a secular version. Indeed, there are secular Christian or Moslem individuals, but there is no secular Christianity or Islam. Judaism, for centuries, was more than a religion; it stood for an entity and a content of great complexity than that. In medieval and modern history Judaism was the exception among all contemporary religions in that it was the religion of a single people, that is, it fused religious faith and religious lifestyle with a definition of itself as a people. To be a Jew by religion was to declare oneself one of the Jewish people, and vice versa: to be born into the Jewish people was to be born into the Jewish religion. For many centuries there was no other way of being a Jew. The host nations in which Jews lived would not accept them as full nationals or full citizens until they abandoned Judaism and converted to Islam or Christianity. Likewise, the Jewish communities preferred segregation, in the belief that the Jews were a seperate nation.

This state of affairs changed in the late eighteenth century when the Jews of Central Europe were granted equality of civil rights, or Emancipation,[2] and thousands rushed to take on their new national identity, while continuing to observe the Jewish religion, that is, the Jewish faith and way of life. For these Jews who disowned the national component of Jewish identity, Judaism was a religion like any other. In direct contrast, towards the end of the nineteenth century movements sprang up within European Jewry that gave precedence to the national component in Jewish existence and consigned the religious component to a secondary, historical status. For these groups, religion was the lesser ingredient in Jewish identity; it was nationality that was the essential one.

We can see then why twentieth-century Judaism exists in such a variety of forms. Some Jews identify themselves as Jews by religion only; their nationality belongs to their home state. Other Jews define their Judaism in terms of Jewish nationality and disown connection to the Jewish religion. Yet other Jews, particularly those in Conservative and Reconstructionist communities, while celebrating the relationship tying Judaism to the Jewish peoplehood, understand that it is carried on in the Jewish communities settled within a host nation, as we shall see later. The Orthodox alone, now a small minority of world Jewry, cling to the traditional conception of the unity of religion and peoplehood.

Judging by the facts, a non-religious Judaism clearly exists because there are many people who do not profess to follow Judaism or its articles of faith, do not observe its commandments and even repudiate its institutions, insofar as these touch upon their personal life, and yet nonetheless define themselves as Jews. Their Jewish identity is Jewish *and* secular. In general, they are not organized in social structures whose defining quality is the members' secularism. The secularism of these Jews lies in their worldview, in their personal repudiation of religious beliefs and modes of organization, and in a lifestyle totally untouched by obligatory religious practice. Their Judaism consists of their self-definition as Jews.

The argument has been made that there is no such thing as "secular Judaism," there are only "Torah-and-*mitzva*-observant Jews" and "Jews who have thrown off the yoke of the Torah and *mitzvot*."[3] Only the mindset of a religious Jew could produce such an idea. Although the Hebrew word "*mitzva*" (plural, *mitzvot*) has acquired the meaning of "a good deed," its origin is in the root of the verb "to command," that is, to give an order from on high that cannot be questioned. A *mitzva* is "a commandment" and thus refers to any one of the mythological six hundred thirteen *mitzvot* dictated on Mt. Sinai by Yahweh for Moses to inscribe and hand down to the Children of Israel *plus* any of the numberless supplements and circumscriptions issued by the sages of *halacha* (Jewish law) in the course of hundreds of subsequent generations. The *mitzvot* are thus halachic rulings that have, over time, fashioned the way of life of an observant Jew into a finely planned and detailed, all-encompassing structure. Secular Jews, having no "Torah and *mitzvot*" to structure the way of life they have chosen for themselves, should not be regarded as failing to observe the *mitzvot,* but rather as having taken their "command" from elsewhere—from a humanist value system and from state law in the context of a sense of responsibility to the whole of society. Seculars respect the Torah and its commandments as a cultural tradition of supreme importance. Many of the commandments regulating relations between people derive from exalted universal values and as such are accepted by seculars too—not by virtue of having been dictated by Yahweh from Mt. Sinai but by the virtue intrinsic to them. This is not the case with archaic commandments whose time is long past, nor it is applicable to commandments that—with all due respect—are concerned only to regulate rite and ritual, or commandments that enact inhumane concepts, such as fanaticism, racism, sexism, of which Judaism's code of commandments is certainly not free. This latter category of "commandments" quite simply negates the humanist vision that is at the core of secularism: such *mitz-vot* may be of historical and anthropological interest, as they are part of our culture, but they should certainly not be part of our way of life today.

Nevertheless, many non-observant Jews do observe some of the ritual commandments. Almost all Jews have their sons circumcised, many celebrate a son's bar mitzvah in the traditional manner, are married by a rabbi, fast on Yom Kippur, or light Sabbath candles. Does this make them religious? And if not, where are the boundaries of secularism? We will find answers to these questions if we remember that the heart and soul of secularism lie within a humanist worldview and a way of life, that refuse to be dictated to by the *halakhic* code. Jews who observe a few of the ritual commandments in the belief that they are of direct divine decrees is certainly a religious person, even if they allows themselves considerable laxity in the matter. But if their mitzva-observance is a feeling for tradition or a reverence for cultural values or respect for their parents or ancestral loyalty, but they do not believe in the existence of any God-given code of law, then the choice to observe the *mitzva* is a human choice and thus an act of secularism, pure and simple.

Another key question concerns the Jewishness of a secular life and outlook that disowns the Jewish religion. What makes this life and outlook Jewish? What is the nature and substance of Judaism-as-nationality? These are the issues that will be considered in this book. For now, let me say that in Israel the self-expression of secular Judaism is part of the daily life that takes place within a Jewish, Hebrew-speaking environment, and that secular Jewish life in Israel and all over the Jewish world, throughout the course of Jewish history, has always been nourished by Hebrew and Jewish culture. Secular Judaism and its culture is based upon the Hebrew language and its culture and literature, a literature that has been both sacred *and* secular ever since it first emerged. It embraces the essential tenets of Jewish religion, which form the central pillars of all Jewish culture, including secular Jewish culture. It also embraces the Jewish way of life; the Bible and its endlessly rich literature of commentary; religious and non-religious Jewish philosophy; and Jewish culture of the modern period, including that of our own generation, in Hebrew and other languages. These are just some of the elements that constitute our national culture upon which our Jewish identity stands—a superb inheritance that has come down to us from our history.

Another key question that I will address in these pages relates to the issue of whether the existence of a secular Judaism might split the Jewish nation and spell the end of its unity, won't secularism sever a tradition that reaches back hundreds of generations? True, for centuries Judaism preserved a measure of unity as the religion of a single people, excluding any lifestyle that diverged too much from those formulated by its spiritual leaders, but it paid a heavy price by losing large sections of the Jewish people who were ejected from the body of the Jewish people by excommunication and total ostracism. Despite this, Jewry has always contained a diversity of opinion and an incompatibility of conceptions, just as lifestyles have varied deeply between communities separated by geography and ethnicity. Jewry's unity was never based upon uniformity. Now and for the last three hundred years, Orthodoxy has been too weak to expel those whom it considered to be flouting the rules. The mainstream has split into multiple currents, religious and secular. Even observant Judaism is far from monolithic: within it there are sectors such as the Orthodox, Reform, Conservative, Reconstructionist, among others. Orthodoxy itself is a complex of multiple sects many of which are mutually hostile, some even to the point of banning all intercourse with other Orthodox sects. Contemporary Judaism is pluralist, multi-faceted, multi-opinioned, multi-practicing. There is little uniformity. Each of us can select from a wide spectrum of belief-systems and lifestyles and still be considered a Jew. Secularism is just one option upon which to base a Jewish life. In my opinion, this is all to the good. Multiplicity enriches the nation's mind, spirit and creative energy. I see the Jewish people united in its three-thousand-year-old culture, which in itself forms the predominant component of our identity. In fact, far from secularism severing the tradition of generations, it, more than any other grouping in Jewry today, is pouring energy into expanding and invigorating contemporary Jewish culture, building all the while on the foundations of our long inheritance and tradition. Today, it is secular Judaism and secular Jewry that are holding the line and maintaining the continuity of the Jewish people.

The Uncovered Head

1
Identity

EACH MAN HAS A NAME

THE MIDRASH SAYS THAT "DURING HIS LIFE A MAN IS KNOWN BY THREE
names; one, what his father and mother call him, one, what other people
call him, and one, the name he makes for himself, and the best of them
is the one he makes for himself" (Tanhuma, *Vayakhel* 1). A poem by
Zelda, "Each Man Has a Name," takes up this idea, elaborating on each
source and adding God to the list of those who share in making a man's
name. "The hills," "the stars," and "the sea" are places in man's world
that are given to him by God, as is his death. "His stature and way of
smiling" are gifts from his father and mother; "his neighbors, his enemies, his love" are the other people who call him by name. All the rest
he acquires by himself. All the names given to a man and all the ones
he makes for himself, especially the ones he makes for himself, together
indicate the nature of the man. So say the Midrash and the poem:

> Each man has a name,
> One God gave,
> And one his father and mother . . .
> Each man has a name,
> One his sins gave
> And one his yearnings.
> Each man has a name,
> One his enemies gave
> And one his love. . . .
> Each man has a name,
> One the seasons of the year gave
> And one his blindness.
> Each man has a name,
> One the sea gave
> And one his death.[1]

We first introduce ourselves to others by offering our forename and surname. The first name, one would think, says nothing of our actual identity, our mother and father choose it before we form any opinion, any personality, or any attitude. Some first names represent a parental wish invested in the baby: we know many a Rose who has turned out to be less than beautiful, and many a Leo who is anything but lion-hearted. For all that, first names do carry several hints as to the owner's identity. We tend to seek—and to find—linkages between name and personality; we treat the name as an aspect of the person and even use it to express our feelings for them, as the poet Sha'ul Chernikhovsky did when in one of his poems he chose a special name for his beloved, a name no one else had ever called her by:

> Ill-il . . . !
> When it's just the two of us I shall call her Ill-il . . .
> You know why? Because this is a name
> She has never heard from mother or father;
> No man has ever whispered it in her ear; . . .
> It has never trembled delightfully on the lips of a lover,
> Or been silenced by a kiss,
> It has never enfolded the fondness of brother or sister
> Or been bandied about the streets of the city:
>
> Ill-il. . . ![2]

Many biblical names are explained in the biblical text as commemorating the time, place, or circumstances of the baby's birth. For example: ". . . and [Eve] conceived and bore Cain [in Hebrew *ka'in*], and said, 'I have gotten [*kaniti*] a man from the Lord'" (Gen. 4:1); "Behold, you [Hagar, maidservant to Abraham's wife, Sarah] are with child and shall bear a son; and shall call his name Ishmael ['God shall hear'] because the Lord has heard your affliction" (Genesis 16:11); "And she [Tzipporah, Moses's wife] bore him a son and [Moses] called his name Gershom, for he said, 'I have been a stranger [*ger sham*] in a strange land'" (Exod. 2:22); "And [Hannah] named him Shmuel [in English, Samuel] meaning, 'I asked the Lord for him'" (*sha'ul mi'el*, "asked of God"; 1 Sam. 1:20). Other names tell us of cherished hopes: "And [Lamech] called him Noah, saying, 'This one shall comfort us [*yenahem*] concerning our work and toil of our hands" (Gen. 5:29). Yet other biblical namings foreshadow their bearers' fate and are presumably bestowed by the author of the text. This is the case with Makhlon and Kilion, Ruth's husband and brother-in-law, whose deaths set the plot of the book of Ruth in motion (*makhala*, illness and *kilion*, destruction) (Ruth 1:2). One

character who is "churlish and an evil in his doing" is given the name
Nabal (vile; 1 Samuel 25:3). The same technique of "loading" a name,
to indicate the nature or presage the fate of characters, or to signal their
function in the plot, is often employed in literature through the ages. A
Naomi (my pleasant one) or an Akhituv (brother of goodness) will of
course be friendly and positive characters; an Akhan (snake) or an Izevel
(*zevel*, dung) are all despised by the biblical author, as well as in Hebrew
fiction of the nineteenth century. Thousands of years after the books of
the Bible were composed, Jewish fathers and mothers would still not
name their sons Zimri, Nimrod, Omri, or Ahab, or their daughters
Athaliah or even Hagar, mindful of the verse in Proverbs (10:7): "The
memory of the just is blessed, but the name of the wicked shall rot."

Names can also reflect parental political allegiances or national and
social perspectives including at least the politico-ethical values that
might govern the child's upbringing. Parents who name their son Zion
or Washington are displaying their national pride. Daughters have been
named Maya because their parents are socialists and May Day is a traditional working-class holiday. Other children bear witness to their parents' love of a poet or novelist or for one of an artist's creations, Byron
or Harold, for instance. A name that commemorates a dead grandfather
or grandmother, indicates a family that values its tradition and honors
its past. More than anything else, however, a name tells us the bearer's
ethnic, cultural and linguistic roots. Johnny is sure to come from an
Anglo-Saxon background and Ivan from a Slav one, even though both
names originate in the Hebrew Yokhanan.

Among Jews, first names and their diminutives and familiar forms
may identify the ethno-geographic branch of Jewry to which one belongs. A Zechariah, Mazal, or Saadiah are almost without exception Ye-
menites, while a Yossele or Ha'imke are equally certain to be Ashkenazim
from Central or Eastern Europe. Our sages tell us that the Children of
Israel merited deliverance from Egypt by virtue of not having ex-
changed their Hebrew names for Egyptian ones (Lev. Rabba 32), implying their disapproval of those numerous Jews, Mishna sages not
excepted, who in the Second Temple period took on Greek names such
as Alexander, Aristobulus, or Hyrcanus in tribute to the Greek culture,
then in ascension throughout the Near and Middle East. The Talmud
tells us: "Most Jews outside the Land [of Israel] had the same names as
the heathen" (*Gittin* 11b BT). Are things any different today? When
people move to a new cultural environment they often exchange their
origin-betraying name for one that fits in. When Eastern European Jews
sought a new life in the United States, the Mikhails became Mikes,

Shoshanas became Susies, and Abrahams became Abes. The opposite occurred when they moved in the other direction, to Palestine–Israel: Irenas became Ornas and Grishas Gershons. Later generations of Israeli parents would give their sons and daughters names celebrating the Jewish people's renewal in its own land. Names such as Zalman, Mendel, Baile, and Devosha, which had been popular in Europe, were disowned in favor of biblical or new Hebrew names never used in the Diaspora, such as Ehud, Itai, Dalia, Anat, and Carmit, or even names, such as Nimrod and Hagar that had previously been avoided, because of their negative associations in biblical tales. Aharon Megged protested against this trend in his short story "Yad Vashem":

> What is a bond if not memory? . . . A Russian keeps his bond to his people by remembering his forefathers. He's called Ivan, his father is Ivan and his grandfather is Ivan, right back to the first generation. . . . But you—you're ashamed to call your son Mendele, so as not to remember that once there were Jews called Mendele. You think the time has come to wipe the name off the face of the earth. To leave no trace of it . . . no continuity, no witness, no memorial or name, not a trace . . .[3]

In Israel, fashion is also part of naming, sufficiently pervasive in its time to be able to date a person's birth by the name they carry. The early Jewish pioneer immigrants to Palestine, from say, 1880 to 1920, brought with them the names of their Russian origins, such names as Manya, Fanya, Sasha, and Avrasha; but the sons and daughters born to them in the new land were welcomed with newly-minted Hebrew names— Tushia (resourcefulness), Ivria (a Hebrew girl), Asael (God made him), Yigal (he will be redeemed)—names free of taint of the Diaspora. Then tastes moved on and new names were coined: Uri, Uzi, Dalia, and Rina were the names of choice in the 1920s and 1930s. By the 1950s and 1960s, names such as Itai, Omri, Tal, or Anat were the fashion. In the 1970s, Sigal, Sarit, Gil, and Tom became popular.

It is clear, then, that first names do have something to say about identity after all. Nevertheless, surnames remain more immediately revealing. If you lived in Central Europe and your surname was Moscowitz or Kowalski, you were a Jew of, respectively, Russian or Polish descent. If you lived in Eastern Europe and your surname was Rosenberg or Appelbaum you were a Jew of German descent. Of course, names such as Cohen, Levin, or Rabinowitz (son of a rabbi), gave the game away completely. The linguistic origin of a name was also informative. An Eisen or Eisenberg was almost certainly of European ancestry just as a

Hadad had roots in the Arab world. And once in Israel, both would become Barzilai (*barzel, eisen,* and *hadid* all mean "iron" in, respectively, Hebrew, German, and Arabic) to demonstrate their proud identification with the national rebirth of the Jewish people and the Hebrew language. Nowadays the process is reversing itself: many are taking back their old family surname to restore continuity with earlier generations and to preserve the memory of families annihilated in the Holocaust. In the 1940s, the novelist Yitzhak Auerbach translated his surname to Orpaz; in the 1980s he took the Auerbach back, and now he is Yitzhak Auerbach-Orpaz. Some surnames stand as a memorial to one individual, a family matriarch, or patriarch: Mozes (son of Moses), Yakobson (son of Jacob), Rivkin (son of Rivka), Beilin (son of Beile) are examples. Other surnames, as in other languages, state an ancestral trade or profession, such as Banai, Katzav, Dayan, or Khazan (in Hebrew: "builder," "butcher," "judge," "cantor," respectively), Smith or Carpenter. Even some talmudic sages were known by their trade, two famous instances being Rabbi Yokhanan the Cobbler and Rabbi Yitzhak the Smith. So we can see that, far from being arbitrary accessories, names can say quite a lot about identity. Of direct relevance to the development of this book is that a person with a Hebrew or typically Jewish name is making open declaration of a Jewish identity.[4]

OUR IDENTITY

Our individual identity consists of the place we occupy in the social structures and groupings of which we make ourselves part, or of which circumstances make us part, and is a complex of many factors and components. Some of them are inborn—skin color, build, length of nose, hair and eye color, temperament, certain abilities, and other such givens genetically transmitted to every child from their ancestral stock. Gender—girl, boy, woman, man—is, of course, another inborn factor that goes a long way to determine our place and role in the family and also, to a lesser but still considerable degree, in social structures—at school, in the workplace, in leisure-time activities, and so on. Family connections and bonds are both a primary layer of identity: "I'm one of the Boston Cabots"; "That's Judge Fielding's son"; "You know Meg Green, the actress—she's my daughter"; "My family arrived here at the beginning of the century." In some contexts, family connections are wide enough to encompass a whole village or even a wider grouping such as the large extended families that make up whole Bedouin tribes, or the family clans of Scotland and Ireland, the tribes of central and southern Africa, and the Pacific Islands.

With Jews, the family connection stretches as far as the *"eda,"* the ethno-geographic communities of birth into which Jewry has been divided for many years. In the Middle Ages, Jews named the nations of Europe after the descendants of Noah (Genesis 10) and towns in the biblical Land of Israel. Thus, Hispania was *Spharad* and the Kingdom of the Franks *Tzarfat*, and that is what Spain and France are called in Hebrew to this day. Until the very beginning of the twentieth century, the Jews' name for the land of the Germans was *Ashkenaz*, and since it was believed that most of Europe's Jews hailed from that region they were known as Ashkenazim. Most of the Jews of the Mediterranean basin are descended from the Jews expelled from Spain and Portugal (*Spharad*) at the end of the fifteenth century, thus they are called Sephardim. By the same process, Jewry has a Babylonian *eda* originating with the exiles to Babylonia (modern-day Iraq), a Yemenite *eda*, a Bukharan *eda*, and so on. To the citizens of the medieval Islamic world any member of a Christian nation was a "Frank," and so the Jewish exiles from Catholic Spain who made their way to Muslim lands were also called Franks; and to this day, "Franks" is a derogatory term that Ashkenazim use for Eastern Jews.

Where one lives or has lived is another part of one's identity: "I'm a Jerusalemite," sings Israeli Yehoram Gaon with pride. "I'm a kibbutznik," novelist Amos Oz used to declare. Many surnames retain the name of the town from which an ancestor came: the Vilners hark back to Vilna in Lithuania and the Toledanos to Toledo in Spain. Trade and profession contribute their part too: consider how often we introduce our friends or ourselves by saying: "This is Judy Brown, she sells agricultural machinery" or "Please meet Professor Smith from the Math Department at the university" or "I'm Colonel Merom of the Paratroopers." Profession and qualification may determine how we address people. We might call a teacher or army officer, "Sir," "Ma'am," or "Major," while the hospital specialist we might address as "Doctor." Occupation and seniority locates one on the socioeconomic map or hierarchy and go a long way toward establishing identity.

Organizational affiliations can be significant identity markers—from the political ("I vote Republican" or "He used to be a member of the Communist Party") to the social ("We're regular Rotarians" or "Why don't you join us at B'nei Brith?"), to the sporting-tribal ("We've been Lakers fans all our lives" or "The Mets-Yankees World Series is setting the whole of New York alight!"). Most people are proud of their identity and happy to display it. They have business cards printed to announce their trade or profession, they wear the lapel pins of their political party, social organization, or club, they attend conventions of fellow emigrants from their town of birth and they go to school and college and army unit reunions. The symbol of their religion is on a chain around their neck and a sticker of their national flag adorns their car bumper.

There is no harm in wearing one's identity with pride—quite the reverse—but the other side of the coin must be respect for the other's identity, and this we know is variable. Hostility and violence are common, particularly when identities compete, such as in sporting rivalries. Violence is also the frequent outcome of racial or ethnic discrimination and arrogance. Primitive traditions and prejudices impel males to try to keep females in an inferior status. The worst kind of violence is not uncommon in the political sphere. Violence occurs between one party and another, or between the state and its opponents; such violence finds its extreme expression in mass murder or genocide—the ultimate disrespect for and annihilation of the other's identity.

Throughout history, the most terrible collisions of identity have been driven by nationalism and religion. The bloodiest wars between peoples have usually been impelled by a fanatic nationalism, the overweening certainty that the perceived superiority of one national group gives it the right to suppress others. In the record of blood and slaughter, religious fanaticism comes a close second. We may say without exaggeration that what may be among humanity's most exalted emotions—love of homeland and religious faith—have no rival in human history for being responsible for generating the cruelest and the most horrific slaughter.

Religion: Its Nature and Sources

Every religion rests upon a faith and a code of law. The faith proclaims the pillars of the religion's philosophy and mythology while the code lays down a way of life and rules of conduct derived from the faith to meet societal needs. Originally, the message of the Hebrew word which is used now for "religion," *dat*, was law, as the book of Esther explicitly confirms: Reporting about the Jews to his king, Ahasuerus, the Persian Haman says, "their laws [*dateihem*] are diverse from people; neither keep they the king's laws [*Datei hamelech*]" (Esther 3:8). Only later did religion assume a meaning that included both law and faith.

Faith is a profound inner persuasion of the truth of certain things, even in the absence of real proof. The root of the Hebrew word for faith, *emunah*, is *a–m–n*, common to many Semitic languages and meaning "strength and stability"; in European languages it is used to form the word "Amen." *Emunah* is also closely related via the same root to *imun*, in the sense of education and study. In the Bible, we frequently hear the injunction to have faith or trust (*emunah*) in God, in his messengers and in his *torah*, the latter meaning both law and teaching. After Yahweh promised Abraham that his seed would be as numerous as the stars in the sky, it was said of Abraham that "he had faith in Yahweh, and He counted it to him for righteousness" (Gen. 15:6). Once the whole people of Israel saw "the great work which Yahweh did upon the Egyptians . . . they had faith in Yahweh and His servant Moses" (Exod. 14:31). Time passes and we are told that Yahweh is now angry with the people of Israel: "How long will these people have no faith in Me despite all the signs which I have shown among them?" (Num. 14:11). Religious faith, persuasion of the truth of tenets of a religion, is in fact to have belief *in*—in this case, in Yahweh, in His messengers, in His prophets, in his law and teaching, in the corpus of tales about God's or the gods' deeds and exploits, about the feats and adventures of the people's primal heroes and ancestors. Against "belief *in*" we must contrast "belief *that*," which is a matter of assuming, accepting, or agreeing that a certain statement is true. For example, in trying to wiggle out of the mission to the Israelites that Yahweh has thrust upon him, Moses says: "they will not believe me, and not listen to me?" (Exod. 4:1). In other words, what if the people neither accept the truth of what Moses tells them nor agree to act accordingly? Years later, Moses says to the people: "you rebelled against the commandment of Yahweh your God; and you believed Him not nor listened to His voice" (Deut. 9:23). Although the Children of Israel believed *in* Yahweh, they did not believe *that* He would keep his promise to give them the land.

Christianity and Islam define themselves as faiths and their followers as believers: non-Christians and non-Moslems are unbelievers. Judaism also possesses articles of faith, but the usual term for Judaism's faithful is not "believers" but "those who keep the Torah and the Commandments," which goes to show that the heart of Judaism is not faith but law and upholding the law. Much has been said and written about the contrast between faith and knowledge; for instance, knowledge about something removes the need for faith. Or further, that while the fundamental quality of faith is indeed a profound persuasion, or even a certainty, in the truth of particular things, nonetheless implicit in the very essence of the concept is an immovable measure of doubt, no matter how slight. Endeavors to remove that doubt have been frequent and numerous, and have been attempts to prove—logically, philosophically, even scientifically—that the articles of a religion are true and that God exists. All such proofs are circumstantial. Generalizing across the whole field, the commonest argument is that neither experience, nor science, nor even logic, allow us to posit that the beauty of the world and the marvelous ordering of it are a matter of chance, and if they are not chance, they must be the work of a higher power or a higher intelligence that created the universe and bestowed upon it the order and lawfulness it requires to survive. The secular view of the world argues that this order and lawfulness are the way human beings explain perceived regularities. The "laws of nature" are no more than a theory that provides a satisfactory explanation for natural phenomena, one that will remain satisfactory only until a better one is found. Religious thinkers reply that science too is constructed on faith and not on absolute knowledge, to which seculars respond that while science indeed has no absolute knowledge, the difference between scientific theory and religious faith is that theory is not binding but constantly subject to modification, updating and correction, not to say total eclipse, whereas religious faith claims for itself absolute and unalterable truth.

And there is another difference between faith and scientific knowledge. Science bases its postulates on demonstrable experimental evidence, repeatable at any time under the appropriate conditions. The religious also claim an experiential basis for their faith in that many people have reported mystical experiences and communication with a higher world, with angels, even with God Himself, or they report miracles that have happened to them or in their sight. The crucial difference between religious experience and scientific experiment is the element of control. An experiment is held to be corroborated and valid only when it can be replicated under identical conditions at any time or place; this is not the case with religious experience, which is always a unique phenomenon and impossible to corroborate under controlled conditions. Not that this has stopped every religion from passionately promoting the articles of its faith as ultimate truths that exist beyond question and beyond appeal.

Religious zealotry proceeds from the assumption, fundamental to every monotheistic religion, based upon the belief in a single unitary God, that it and it alone has a monopoly on the truth and that anyone refusing to accept its tenets in their entirety is an infidel or heretic who merits the most terrible penalties—to be roasted in the everlasting hellfire of the next world or, in this world, to be burnt alive at the stake or stoned to death, among other such outlandish methods. Worse still, the infidel or heretic loses all title to the benefits and rights that followers of the "true faith" enjoy. In such a situation, honest citizens and true believers are duty bound to do their utmost to save the infidels and their soul by leading them to the "true faith," if possible, by kindness; if necessary, by compulsion. Extreme violence, deceit, and fraud are all condoned or even rendered praiseworthy by the sanctity of the goal. Given the one-eyed zealotry of the premise, violence and compulsion follow, indeed they are inevitable, in the absence of tolerance and of a worldview that recognizes that different people may and can hold different opinions, faiths, and ways of life and that different religions can coexist peacefully. Given the dogmatic conviction that one's own religion is the one, single, and true faith, religious tolerance appears nothing less than social irresponsibility; after all, if one knows the "truth," how can one allow others, whether they are believers in another faith or people of no religious belief, to live according to such an immense "error," knowing the terrible penalty that will be meted out to them by Heaven itself in due course? The concept that another religion—or irreligion—is neither a repudiation of true belief nor false belief but simply another truth, different but of equal value with one's own, is a notion of religious tolerance that few deeply religious persons can accept. No religion can possibly accept the postulate that its own truth is a relative one, neither absolute nor exclusive. And this means that even in circumstances of religious tolerance, be it individual or that decreed by the law of the state, religious persons and groups will always perceive themselves as superior to people and groups who profess another religion or no religion at all.

Research into aboriginal societies still existing in our own time has generated a number of theories as to the origins of religion, all of which locate it in the lifestyle of early tribal people.[5] Frightened and threatened by the natural phenomena he could see and experience but not understand, primitive man supposed that every object and force in nature had a soul and consciousness like his own, and that natural phenomena represented the will of these objects and forces. This being so, the way to influence them was by dialogue or negotiation or by appeasing them with food and other gifts. Rites and rituals were devised to give order to relations with the forces of nature. Certain individuals made this mediation their especial skill and concern—they were the first priests, primitive man's rabbis. In the course of time, these forces of nature were given human form and stories and legends grew up around their characters and their interactions with humans. Told and retold, passed down from generation to generation, eventually written down usually by gifted poets, these bodies of legend at last rose to the status of Holy Writ. They constitute our primal myths, the central pillars of early religion. Here, for example, is a passage from the Babylonian myth, *Enuma Elish* (*When on High*), recounting the creation of the world:

> When on high the heaven had not been named,
> Firm ground below had not been called by name,
> There was nought but primorial Apsu, their begetter,
> And Mother Tiamat who bore them all,
> Their waters commingling in a single body . . .
> Then it was that gods were formed within them.[6]

Before the world came into being, before it came to be called by its name, only the gods of the waters, Apsu and Tiamat, lived in it and from their copulations, from the mingling together of their waters, all the other gods were conceived and born, and from them, in the course of time, came humans. According to the Greco-Roman tradition the world was created by an anonymous god who imposed order on chaos, the primeval formless void that was the state of nature then, by separating the pre-existent but formless elements, and bringing the world into a state of harmony. Here is Ovid's rendition of that myth:

> God, or some such artist as resourceful
> Began to sort it out.
> Land here, sky there, And sea there.
> Up there, the heavenly stratosphere.
> Down here, the cloudy, the windy.
> He gave to each its place.[7]

The descriptions and conceptualizations of natural phenomena vary from locality to locality, because of variation in the phenomena themselves and because human beings are so diverse. For the same reasons, rites, rituals and legends differ from place to place. They also evolved over time and underwent modifications as experience accumulated and new knowledge was acquired. People performed the rites and believed in the myths that had evolved to fit the environment in which they lived. The myths were altered to reflect their different environments, just as particular climatic or geographical conditions gave rise to a specific calender of rites. Each locality-defined groupings, consisting of the off-spring of one family or of a group of related families all speaking a common language had its own local mythology and ceremonials, which helped to consolidate the sense of familial, group, or tribal identity and eventually the identity of a whole people. The narratives of the book of Genesis take us through just such a process, as one family, the family of Jacob, expands into a grouping of tribes, which then coalesces into a people, the people of Israel.

Each tribe, and later each people, chooses one of the powerful forces of nature and anthropomorphizes it into a protector, who will guard the well-being of the group and defend it from the ravages of nature and of other tribes. This is how territorial gods came into being, gods who wielded power over only the parcel of land held by the tribe or people who had placed their faith in them. The Bible mentions several of them: Dagon of the Philistines, Chemosh of Ammonites, Ba'al of Canaan. Yahweh also started out with this status, His jurisdiction limited to the land of Israel, the territory of His people. Numerous records of this phenomenon have been preserved in Biblical lore: When the Israelites and Ammonites both claim rights to the land of Gilead, Jephthah the Gileadite says to the Ammonite king: "Will not you posses that which Chemosh your god gives you to possess, so whomsoever Yahweh our God shall drive out from before us, them will we possess" (Judg. 11:24); after Saul has expelled David from his kingdom, David says to Saul: "For they have driven me out this day from abiding in the inheritance of Yahweh, saying, 'Go serve other gods'" (1 Sam. 26:19); the prophet Elijah taunts the king of Samaria's emissaries: "Is there no God in Israel that you go to inquire of Baal-Zebub, the god of Ekron?" (2 Kings 1:3). Verses such as: "and against all the gods of Egypt, I will execute judgement, I am Yahweh" (Exod. 12:12), and "Who is like you, Yahweh, among the gods" (Exod. 15:11) and many others show clearly that the existence of other gods besides Yahweh, although sometimes inferior to Him, was taken for granted in this period of history. Early religions were ethnic possessions, as resolutely defended as the territory that each ethnic group guarded as its own.

It was common for the tribe's leader, usually bearing the title of king, to proclaim his kingship as a personal gift from the gods, or himself to be a descendant of gods, or even that he was himself a god. This instantly made his leadership absolute and his will the law. In more than one kingdom the law, promulgated and inscribed in the name of the king, possessed divine validity by right of the king's standing as a divinity or divine emissary. In Israel, the books of the Bible tell us, its leaders, mentors, prophets, judges, and kings were all selected for their roles by Yahweh, who was also deemed to be the giver of the law, which we know as the Torah, and which to this day is the basis of the religious Jewish way of life. The Torah is a code of law comprising rules for daily life, bodies of civil and criminal law, that regulate dealings between men, ritual regulations and religious practices, and injunctions covering the interaction between man and God. The enforcement of religious law was in the hands of the *Cohanim*, priests, descendants of Aaron the Priest, Moses's elder brother; the enforcement of the civil law was in the hands of judges and officers of the law.

It was considerably later in Israel's history, around the sixth century BCE, towards the end of the period of the First Temple, that the idea of monotheism, the idea that there was only one god, was born in Judea and proclaimed to the people by the prophets of Israel. Yahweh was not one god among many but a universal god, one and alone, master of the world. His was not an authority that could be stopped at the borders of any land: His dominion was the universe and all that was in it. He was, moreover, a transcendental god; that is, He was not part of the universe, nor even *in* the universe, but existed above and beyond the universe, on some other level. The early gods, as we have seen, were very much part of the world, either one of its natural forces or understood by men as representing these forces. Men and gods lived within the same scheme of things, just as Yahweh did according to the early books of the Bible. Recounting the myth of Sodom and Gomorrah, Genesis says: "Then Yahweh said, 'Because the cry of Sodom and Gomorrah is so great, and because their sin is very grievous, I will go down and see whether they have done altogether according to the cry of it, which is come to me; and if not, I will know" (Gen. 18:20–21), whereupon Abraham argues with Yahweh over the fate of the two cities and in the end, we are told, "Yahweh went his way as soon as he had left communing with Abraham" (Ibid., 33). This account tells us that Yahweh, as any other interested "person" would do, comes down from Heaven to Earth to check out the truth of the rumors reaching Him about the deeds of the Sodomites; face to face with Abraham He argues the matter out and goes on His way. The concept that Yahweh is not a god like all the others, is not even the supreme god over a pantheon of gods, but is the one and only and unique God, and that no others exist, is also the source of the idea of an abstract God, lacking all physical existence in the universe; indeed, the universe is part of His being. As the Sages said: "Why is the Holy One Blessed Be He called 'the Place' [in Hebrew, *Hamakom*]— because the world is not His place, He is the world's place" (Gen. Rabba 68:9). We, for our part, may say that His reality is conceptual.

It was this new idea that Yahweh was the one and only God that brought religious fanaticism into the world. Polytheism, which acknowledged that the world is home to many gods, was conducive not only to tolerance but to accepting that other people's cults and religions had equal status with other cults and religions. I have already noted that in moving from land to land, a man accepted the sovereignty of the local god and bowed his knee to him, as David says in the quotation cited earlier. In conditions of peace or to consolidate an international alliance, people would show reverence to their neighbors' gods, even going as far as bringing the neighboring cult onto their own land. In the period of the First Temple, Israel was no exception to this custom. King Solomon, we are told, having taken wives from the neighboring kingdoms, "went after Ashtoreth the goddess of the Sidonians, and after Milcom the abomination of the Ammonites" (1 Kings 11:5). King Ahab likewise "took to wife Jezebel daughter of Ethbaal king of the Sidonians, and went and served Ba'al and worshiped him" (Ibid., 16:31). These cults were introduced openly into Israel alongside the Yahweh cult, as we learn from Elijah: "How long halt you between two opinions? If Yahweh be God, follow Him; but if Ba'al, then follow him" (Ibid., 18:21). As did the kings of Israel and Judah, so did their subjects:

> Then all the men which knew that their wives had burned incense to other gods, and all the women that stood by, a great multitude, . . . answered Jeremiah saying: "As for the word that you have spoken to us in the name of Yahweh we will not listen to you, but we will certainly do whatsoever thing goes forth out of our mouth, so to burn incense to the queen of heaven, and to pour drink offerings to her, as we have done, we and our fathers, our kings and our princes, in the cities of Judea and in the streets of Jerusalem, and we were well and saw no evil". (Jer. 44:15–17)

In the Second Temple period, the Emperor of Rome customarily displayed his respect for the god of the Jews by having sacrifices offered in his name on every day of sacrifice at the Jerusalem Temple, and he did the same for the gods of all the peoples living under Roman rule. True, there were exceptions to this norm of polytheist tolerance. Athens executed the philosopher Socrates on the grounds that he openly declared his disbelief in the gods, and corrupting of the city's youth. There were periods in Greek and Roman rule over Judah when the Yahwist cult was restricted. But the reasons for such exceptional persecutions were political, not religious. Socrates threatened the very structure of authority in his city; the Jews were flaunting opposition to Greek and Roman imperial policy, which demanded a minimal show of cultural unity.

The Bible leaves us in no doubt at all as to the inevitable consequence of religious zealotry. In his zeal for Yahweh, the prophet Elijah slaughters 450 of the prophets of Ba'al and four hundred of the prophets of Ashera (1 Kings 18), and all the prophets who followed after Elijah insisted that Yahweh alone should be worshiped. Indeed, this is the moment that Israel acquired a religious identity, for their one God, "a jealous God" as the prophets described Him, demanded total and absolute loyalty. Significantly, it was only by force of historical circumstance that the Jews, subsequently living more or less permanently and everywhere as a powerless minority, that their zealotry was turned inwards and vent itself on fellow Jews. On very few occasions have Jews forcibly converted others to Judaism, and even then, as when the Hasmonean king, Alexander Yannai, conquered and Judaized the Edomites, the policy was vehemently opposed by the people's spiritual leaders, the senior rabbis, probably on political grounds, since, generally speaking, the Judaized Edomites turned to be supporters of the king against the Pharisees.

It was the conditions of exile that finally transmuted the Jewish religion into a universal non-territorial faith. Their land captured and their Temple destroyed, the Jews of Israel and Judah fled or were driven into exile to Babylon and Egypt, and from there out to all the other lands of the ancient world. This was the beginning of Israel's history as a people of diaspora. Now that they were living not in one land but in many it became vital to the very continuation of Jewish existence that they develop a non-territorial religion and universal god, for without them the people would almost certainly have conformed to the gods of Babylon and Egypt or of any of the lands they found themselves in. In order to survive the Jewish religion had to become universal and that, in effect, is what happened. Although the religion remained the religion of the Jewish people only, they were exiled to all parts of the known world, and became "scattered abroad and dispersed among the other peoples" (Esther 3:8). Nevertheless, no matter where Jews found themselves, their religious identity was sustained by the premise that their religion was a universal one and their God a universal god, unlimited by any territorial demarcation. Yet, for all its universality, the Jewish religion remained reserved for the Jewish people. To be a member of the religion was to be a member of the people. It was also much more than that. The religious identity that developed during the period of exile was the most all-encompassing identity ever possessed by Israelites and Jews; it determined national affiliation, communal affiliation, and how one lived one's daily life. There are even those who argue that a life of exile was preferable for Jewry, because it put an end to one of its core conflicts, that between prophet and king, or in effect, between the absolute authority of God and the territorial authority of the king. In exile, in the absence of state apparatus, the only king was God and religion was the sole determinant of Jewish life.

It was also during the period of exile that several sects, having removed themselves from the body of the Jewish people or developed alongside it, proclaimed themselves to be the true heirs and bearers of Judaism. Two of these sects expanded into universal religions. Christianity, having begun life as a reformist but still orthodox Jewish sect, very quickly grew into a world religion and a community of many nations and peoples. Islam, also descended from Judaism, having captivated the Arab tribes of the Arabian peninsular, was then carried to the limits of the known world. Both Christianity and Islam in turn split into numerous and even mutually hostile sects, none of which, however, had or sought a single territorial or national base. Both inherited from Judaism the belief in the one god, universal and transcendental, and with this belief the zealotry of "the faithful." Both these great religions and their sects fought each other for hundreds of years, and in the process they wreaked terrible havoc on the Jews who refused to convert to either one. The first and greatestest victims of religious zealotry were its inventors.

This zealotry, however, was extremely useful to the rulers and political systems of the time. In the medieval period, feudal kings and princes, asserting a God-given right to absolute lordship over their subjects, generally found priesthoods very supportive. Under both Christianity and Islam, religious identity became the all-inclusive marker of one's place in the world, the individual's first and paramount identity. It was bestowed at birth: every child was born into its parents' religion, which in most cases was also the official religion of the state. This identity could also be bestowed by force on unbelievers living in lands where Christianity or Islam held sway. Fiercest of all was the zealotry of both faiths against the wayward among their own believers. Monotheism could not allow any deviation from the articles of its creed or from the way of life that this creed dictated. Deviators risked imprisonment or death. In different times and places, tens of thousands died for the sin of holding an opinion that appeared heretical or atheistic to a priest or an imam.

Judaism was not any better. Anyone who tried to change some element of the faith or lifestyle against the expressed rulings of the elders of the faith fell under a ban of excommunication and ostracism and was deemed to have removed himself from the body of Israel. The best known victims were Uriel Acosta and the philosopher Benedictus (Baruch) Spinoza, both expelled by the Amsterdam community in the seventeenth century. Groups, whether large or small, who were guilty of the same sin shared the same penalty. Such was the fate of the Samaritans, survivors of the Jewish population of the northern kingdom of Israel after its destruction by the Assyrians in the eighth century BCE, who believed in the authority of the five books of Moses (the Pentateuch) but dismissed all later books as well as the rulings of the Oral Law; of the early Christians, who regarded themselves, and behaved as Jews; the Karaites, a sect formed in the eighth century CE in Babylonia and which repudiated the authority of the Talmud; and of the Sabbateans, a remnant of the mass movement of Jews in the seventeenth century CE that hailed Sabbatai Zevi as the messiah. This was the method Jewry chose to preserve its unitary structure throughout the centuries of Diaspora existence. Only at the end of the medieval period and with the arrival of the ideas of humanism in the sixteenth century did the powers of the religious establishments of most European states begin to weaken, as did those of Jewry's authorities. Its spiritual leadership no longer commanded the power needed to expel groups and individuals from the body of the people for rebelling against their word by promoting new ideas and new lifestyles. Judaism became a pluralist faith and Jewry a pluralist society. New thinking and new possibilities proliferated.

RELIGIOUS IDENTITY

Religious identity is not just a membership card to a "club of believers," accounting for part, even a large part, of the whole person, it is not just one of many other constituents of identity. Religious identity is a total thing, all-inclusive, leaving no part of men or women and their surroundings unfilled, unpervaded. The whole of their world, their life and lifestyle, their opinions and ways of arriving at opinions, their relations to family and to all other human beings, all should be determined by their religious identity. It is inclusive and demands believers' absolute devotion. To a truly religious person religious identity overrides any other, subsuming or annulling all other components of individual identity. The first requirement for a true believer is perfect faith in the religion's absolute truth, extending to all the articles and sub-articles of its creed, a faith that carries with it utter disdain for all other religions and faiths and for all opinions and knowledge that challenge or are incompatible with the tenets of the creed. Second on the list of conditions is the continual practice of the cult's prescribed rites, almost always performed in a communal setting, so that a believer must also be a conformer. Then comes commitment to a lifestyle, the details of which are minutely prescribed by religious tenet: every action performed by the believer is subject to this tenet, at home and in society, at his lying down and at his rising up, in the bosom of the family and in the marriage bed, at work and at play (see Deut. 6). Some religions and sects go as far as dictating dress and hair codes, occasionally in order to announce the believers' religious or sectarian identity to everyone they meet, more often to disallow certain garments. For example, Judaism forbids crossdressing (see Lev. 19) fundamental Judaism and some Islamic sects demands that men grow beards; while most religions forbid clothing deemed immodest.

Religious identity also tells you what to think, although each religion issues different instructions under this heading. The monotheistic faiths, for instance, reject Darwinian theory, which traces man's development back through millions of years of evolution, as it contradicts the ancient Genesis myths that describe the world being created in six days, almost six thousand years ago. Other scientific discoveries are similarly rejected out of hand. For centuries Roman Catholics were forbidden to believe that Earth circles the Sun, because in the Middle Ages the Church had determined that Earth itself was the center of the universe. The position and role of men and women in family and society is similarly determined by religious codes, as it is regarded as having been ordained during the Creation, when Genesis proclaimed the superiority of the male and the inferiority of his partner: "your desire shall be to your husband and he shall rule over you" (Gen. 3:16, among many other similar statements). Next comes children's education. The key texts are hundreds and thousands of years old. Proverbs 13:24, for instance, warns: "He who spares the rod hates his son," recommending the regular use of corporal punishment. Educational content is delineated by the books that most religions ban, be they "works of heresy and atheism" (that is, they contain anti-doctrinal ideas and materials), or "trivial and frivolous works" that the elders deem not only a waste of precious time but a positive distraction from "words of wisdom and righteousness," (see BT *Sanhedrin 100b*) or the Holy Writ of other religions, a religious Jew will not read Christianity's New Testament or Islam's Koran. None of the three monotheisms, nor any of their denominations or sects, is any more lenient than the others in this respect. Each has closed itself off to innovation and change, preferring to devote its time to sanctifying the truths of hundreds and thousands of years ago, even though each one's truths are very different from the others' and the creed, cult, and lifestyle to which their believers must commit is just as dogmatic and inflexible.

If one stops to think about it, very few people have chosen their professed religion for themselves. It is seldom persuasion or revelation, but rather the faith of their parents dictates their creed. The vast majority of believers are born into a faith, they believe in what their father and mother believe and what they are brought up to believe, and they know very little about any other religion's teaching. Even those who return to the faith from a life of secularism, that is, those who are convinced in one way or another of the "truth" of orthodox belief and conduct, almost always return to their parental religion. In short, religious identity is usually not a matter of choice but of birth. We are born into a family and via the family into a community. From this we must conclude that chance is a key player in our religious allegiance and religious identity. One is Jewish because she was born into a Jewish family and brought up in Judaism; and the other is a Christian because he was born into a Christian family and brought up in Christianity, and what have religious values to do with it? No religion is, or can be, superior to another and none of them possesses the absolute truth that its believers like to think it does.

Religious values are cultural values. All members of a culture, even the secular individuals, are likely to find the particular set of religious values upon which their culture is based preferable to other faiths. We Jews, to the extent that we show interest in our religion, prefer the cultural values of Judaism over those of any other religion. And this is not in any way to dismiss or deny the cultural values of any other people, language, or religion. On the contrary: genuine culture treats other cultures with respect and understanding for, in essence, there is no real opposition between one religion or culture and another. In our own time, the free societies of enlightened democratic states have instituted freedom of religious faith and practice, under which all citizens have the right to live the life they prefer or that their religion or views require. Democratic state law even guarantees the conditions that facilitate these rights, provided that this can be done within the limits of state law.

NATIONAL IDENTITY

Generally speaking, there is no fixed correlation between nationality and religion. Most Irish are Roman Catholics but some are Protestants.

Most Germans are Protestants but many are Catholics. Most Arabs are Sunni Muslims but there are Arabs who are Shiite Muslims and even Christian Arabs of several sects. Not only Irish are Roman Catholics, of course, Italians, French, Poles, and Hungarians have Catholic majorities. Not only Germans are Protestant; so are the majority of English, Dutch, and Scandinavians and some other nationalities. There are non-Arab peoples, Iranians, Turks, Pakistanis, and most peoples of Indonesia, for example, who are in the main Muslim. True, some states define themselves by the majority religion: Argentina designates itself a Catholic republic and Iran an Islamic republic even though Argentina has non-Catholic and Iran non-Muslem citizens.

Very few national groups are the product of a single racial or ethnic stock. From the earliest recorded time we find national groupings intermixing to different degrees and in a variety of ways. Both Greek mythology and early Greek historiography (e.g., Herodotus) recount how Greek men kidnapped Canaanite women and Canaanite men abducted Greek women, which of course blended the two stocks thoroughly. Europa, the mother of the Cretan kings, was a Canaanite princess from the city of Tyre. Even earlier than that, we know that the "Greek people" was an amalgam of all the peoples and races who had inhabited the Balkan Peninsular at different times and that subsequent generations added Romans, Germans, Slavs, Turks, Normans, and others to the racial stew that we in the twenty-first century now call the "Greek people." Four main ethno-racial groups contributed to the composition of the "English" people: Celts, Anglo-Saxons, Danes, and Normans, not to mention the French, Germans, and Spaniards and immigrants from every corner of the British Empire who were later assimilated into the mix. As for the Spanish, to an ancient, diverse base of Semites, Greeks, and Romans was added an early medieval Germanic layer and then, with the conquests of Islam, strong Arab and Berber inputs, and other even later admixtures. "A pure Teutonic-Aryan blood" is as much a fallacy as other "pure-bred" stock: Germans are a mix of Germans, Slavs, Normans, Mongols, and all the other peoples caught up in the wars that have been waged over the "German" homeland throughout history. In Africa and Asia, the tale is much the same. Wars and migrations also confused ethnic and national groups beyond disentangling, even before European colonialism gave the melting pot a few more stirs. As for the peoples of the "countries of immigration," such as the United States, Canada, Australia, the South American states and others, they are the product of a miscegenation of colonizers, immigrants, and aborigines (those, that is, who survived the colonial slaughter and who themselves were immigrants of an earlier era). Their tale of interbreeding is no different in kind and perhaps not even in degree from that of the Europeans. It has merely been too obvious to permit mythologizing. Conquest and the enslavement and migration of individuals and whole peoples have all made a mockery of any pretensions to racial purity anywhere. Certainly, many national groups share characteristic physical features, but these, far from bearing witness to a purity of line, are themselves the product of racial mixings under a variety of historical circumstances. The Talmudic sages acknowledging the phenomenon, ruled that "Sennacherib, King of the Assyrians, has long ago made a thorough mixture of all nations" (Mishna *Yada'im* 4:4). The issue of racial origin was of no relevance to membership of the Jewish or any other people.

Certainly, Jewry does not consist of pure stock. Many contemporary Jewish faces display hardly a trace of their ancient origins. The biblical myths relate that from the moment of its emergence as a people, at the time of the Exodus from Egypt, the twelve tribes, the original Children of Israel, were accompanied by "a mixed multitude" (*erev rav*) who, tradition maintains, were not Israelites but people of other stocks who tagged along with this great expedition. In other words, according to tradition there were multiracial elements at the time of the very founding of the people of Israel. Later, the Bible relates, the Israelites interbred with Canaanite peoples, flouting the strict prohibition pronounced against the practice. King David's line, for one, goes back to Ruth the Moabite. Bathsheba, David's wife and King Solomon's mother, was the ex-wife of Uriah the Hittite, himself one of David's top military commanders. The Hittites, let us remember, were one of the Canaanite peoples the Israelites were supposed to have exterminated. In the Second Temple period, King Alexander Yannai forcibly Judaized thousands of the land's non-Jewish inhabitants and neighboring tribes, in particular the Edomites. The descendants of these forced converts included great sages and leaders such as Shemaya and Avtalyon (BT *Yoma* 61a) and King Herod. Over the centuries of dispersal and exile vast numbers of non-Jews intermarried with Jews. Whole tribes and peoples of totally separate racial stock adopted Judaism and considered themselves part of Jewry, the most famous example being the Khazars, a numerous people of apparently Mongol extraction, who occupied a large swath of the Caucasus region. They voluntarily adopted Judaism in the eighth century CE and within several hundred years they had vanished from recorded history, their numerous survivors assimilating into other parts of Jewry and non-Jewry. There were tribes in Arabia and Yemen who adopted the Jewish faith, and also among the Berbers of North Africa, in Ethiopia, in India. One of the kings of Yemen was a Jew and a Jewish queen, Cahina, led the Berber resistance to Arab conquest. In addition, numerous children were born into Jewry to Jewish mothers raped in riots or pogroms throughout the ages; in this way, too, the genes of every "host" nation among which the Jews ever lived mixed with "Jewish" genes. As noted, Jews from across the world clearly do not share characteristic facial or physical features. Those of European origin are pale-skinned and have the same range of hair color as other Europeans while those of Middle Eastern origin tend to be dark-skinned and dark-haired, like the rest of the population of the Arab world.

Nor can territory be the factor that makes a people, even though there is not a people in the world that was not to some degree formed within a finite territorial context, which it now regards as its "homeland." Here, too, the composition and frontiers of many populations have been changed beyond recognition by war, mass population movements and individual migrations. Today, vast numbers of people live far from the land they call home. The United States holds far more Irish than Ireland; the overseas Chinese have spread by the millions all over the Far East and the United States. Other peoples inhabit more than one state: the Arab people more than twenty, Germans are to be found in Germany, Austria, and Switzerland, and before the Second World War there were large German minorities in Czechoslovakia, Poland, and Russia; today there are substantial German minorities in the United States and several South American countries. Conversely, there are many states populated by more than one people. Spain is home to four: Catalans, Castilians, Galicians, and Basques, each with its own language and culture; Switzerland to three: Germans, French, and Italians, again each speaking its own language. In Belgium, competition between the Flemish-speaking Flemings and the French-speaking Walloons remains fierce to this day. The Republic of South Africa accommodates two white peoples, Anglos and Afrikaners, and six black peoples, plus a large East Indian minority. They share the same territory, but each protects its own language, culture, and character.

So how do individuals of disparate racial stock and diverse ethnic extraction who are scattered over a number of states and embrace more than one religion, nonetheless constitute one people? The consolidating forces are a shared memory of history and a collective cultural tradition rooted in a common language. We place men and women with this or that people by the language they speak and their daily traditional culture, by the books they refer to for pleasure and inspiration, by the songs they know and like to sing and hear, by the ceremonies they maintain and the holidays they celebrate, by the food they prefer and the music they enjoy. All these add up to a feeling of collectivity, identification, and solidarity with the group of which each person considers himself a member.

If we say, then, that "peoplehood" is at root a matter of traditional culture, we are also saying that most people do not choose their group but are born into it; their upbringing merely consolidates it. In recent generations there is a greater tendency for individuals to select their people, which makes "peoplehood" or nationhood more subject to individual decision. Some select by emigration, others by intermarriage, others cross over for cultural or religious reasons. Yet, whether we deliberately select a new people or passively remain with the one into which we were born, in the final analysis this element of our identity can be within our choice.

Most individuals are quite content to belong to the people into which they were born, and most have great respect for its cultural traditions. Most also treat other peoples and their cultures with respect, but it is also very common for one people to elevate its own qualities, and belittle those of others, scorning their natural rights to the point that the "superior" people considers itself to have the right to rule over the "inferior," to enslave it, seize its lands and exploit its resources. Human history is full of stories of peoples who set out to conquer others, since by proving their superiority on the battlefield, they could appropriate the conquered people's lands and possessions. For centuries the nations of Europe claimed right of possession by conquest, simply seizing the land from the "natives," as they dubbed them, and by the same force of arms held it and exploited its riches. Further shows of force and bloodshed were needed from time to time to protect these "empires," as the indigenous peoples would occasionally rebel against their colonial rulers in an attempt to regain their freedom and land, or other imperialistic predators wanting the resources for themselves, would try to wrest the territory from the occupiers. The first half of the twentieth century saw the German nation set out to conquer the world for the "Aryan" race, a project that envisioned the extermination of whole peoples in the firm belief that as a "superior" or "master" race, it was the Aryan destiny to rule all others and "purify" the world of its "inferior" elements. Several tens of millions of people, six million Jews among them, had to die before this vision crumbled to pieces. Human history records many other visions like this one.

PEOPLES, NATIONS, AND NATIONALITY

In the past it was neither as necessary, nor as possible, to make exact distinctions between these three terms, but the modern period has brought far-reaching changes in the forms peoples use to maintain their existence. Consequently, the precise defenition of these concepts has become more important. Continentwide wars provoking massive waves of emigration have brought changes not only in ethnic mix but in the ways peoples organize themselves in terms of territory and governance. Indigenous subjects have won political independence from their former colonial rulers. The First World War divided the Austro–Hungarian empire into nation-states. In the case of the Russian empire, national and territorial rights were redefined within an overall imperial context, renamed the Soviet Union. The breakup of the British, French, Dutch, Spanish, and other empires in Asia, Africa, and the Americas brought into being independent self-governing states whose frontiers bore little or no relation to the boundaries recognized by the local peoples and tribes. People frequently found their ancestral lands dissected by two or three state borders. Over time, the fragment segments lost contact and developed into separate peoples. The reverse also happened: two or three or more peoples were allocated to one newly-defined state, and their shared teritorial framework imposed upon them a degree of unity; occasionally the process was sustained to the extent that a new people was formed out of previous disparate elements, as happened in the United States, Australia, Brazil, Argentina, and other countries of South America, where new peoples were forged by the mass immigration of families and individuals who originated from many other peoples. All in all, we have now reached a situation where peoples' identities are in a process of flux and the old definitions of what constitutes a people are no longer satisfactory. New distinctions must be drawn. From all the kaleidoscopic variety of forms and phenomena now associated with a people's identity, I shall try to impose an order sufficient for our needs on three terms—people, nation, and nationality.

A "people" is a group of individuals and families sharing a historico-cultural tradition rooted in a common language. Most peoples, we may assume, came into being within a single land that they later came to regard as their homeland, motherland, ancestral land, or some similar concept. Over time many were dispersed among a number of lands and states, but in most instances the bonds connecting them were not lost, nor were the traditional bonds to homeland and culture. Consciousness of these bonds was likely to take the form of preserving the language and teaching it to the children, of regularly preparing and eating special foods and dishes, of celebrating certain festivals and holidays, of "return" visits to the land of their ancestors, and occasionally of shows of social, political, and economic solidarity with the members of their people in other countries, and especially in the homeland. To this day, large numbers of United States and Argentinian citizens, for example, regard themselves as belonging to the Italian people, even those who have been settled for generations in these two countries. English-speakers who reside all over the world and have never seen the green fields of England in their lives still identify themselves as English, Anglos, or Anglo-Saxons and consider their local culture to be directly derived from English ways. The Irish, the Germans, and many others maintain their sense of "peoplehood" without needing to inhabit their "mother country." This being so, "people" is a rather loose concept. The heart of "peoplehood" is historical origin and cultural-linguistic bonds: a defined geographical location or state are not essentials.

A single people inhabiting a single country is a "nation," in the basic sense of the word. The members of a nation are by definition the members of one people but the reverse is generally not true: we have seen that one people can be scattered over a number of countries. It is obvious that where the members of a single people inhabit a single country, speak one language, and share a history and a cultural tradition they will also have a common political, economic, and social system. A nation is, thus, a group of people living in one country, speaking one language, maintaining a political and economic system, and sharing a history and culture. Danes, Bulgarians, Egyptians, and other peoples, each inhabiting its own country, are by this definition nations, and their states are nation-states. There are countries that varied historical circumstances have made the home of two or more nations. Belgium is such an instance; Flemings and Walloons share one political entity and the same international borders. The United Kingdom, as its name suggests, is another; it is home to the English, the Welsh, the Scots, and the Northern Irish. In most such cases, each constituent nation tends to occupy one part of the country: Flemings live in northern Belgium and Walloons in the south; most Scots live in Scotland, most Welsh in Wales and most English in England, and these regions are culturally and geographically defined.

Other national groups have settled beyond the borders of their own country without having been incorporated into their host nation's dominant socio-cultural system: we call them "national minorities." Members of national minorities take care to preserve their own tongue and other cultural assets and in terms of national identity consider themselves as belonging to their national country, not to the nation of the host state where they currently happen to live. Before the Second World War there were numerous national minorities in Europe: Germans in Poland, Russia, and Czechoslovakia, Hungarians in Romania, Bulgarians in Greece. They precipitated so many grave international crises that after the war a huge repatriation operation was mounted. The situation is hardly different today: there are Russians in most of the former republics of the Soviet Union and Albanians in Serbia and Macedonia. In some places the territory in which a certain nation lives is divided between two or more neighboring states, and thus they form national minorities in the countries in which they live; examples include the Kurds in Turkey, Iraq, and Iran, and the Basques in Spain and France. In short, the basic sense of the concept "nation" is a well-defined people occupying a recognized political and territorial entity. This entity can be a nation-state, that is, a state populated by one nation, or a bi-national or multinational state, accommodating two or more nations within the one political framework and one set of borders. Nation-states and multinational states can also be "host" to one or more national minorities.

We now come to the problem that in the English language "nation" has also lately been used in a looser sense, as the total citizenry of a uninational or multinational state and inclusive of national minorities. Using the term in this sense, one can talk of the Belgian nation, whereas in the previous stricter sense there is no such thing, or of the American or British nation, or of the nation of the Russian Federation, for that matter. However, nationality, the descriptive category derived from nation, clarifies the issue. The main contemporary meaning of "nationality" is "the status of a citizen or subject of a particular State, the legal relationship by which this is defined, usually involving allegiance by the individual to the State and protection by the State of the individual."[8] To be of a nation or hold a nationality in this sense is thus a matter of citizenship and international recognition, manifested by holding a passport and in fulfilling the obligations and enjoying the rights of a citizen. A citizen may be the son of generations of citizens and regard his State as the political realization and embodiment of his homeland, or he may be a recent arrival, having immigrated only for the purposes of work or study, granted citizenship just yesterday, and having no deep or long-term ties to his new country.

By refering to these three terms—people, nation, and nationality—we can pin down with sufficient precision diverse forms of allegiance to a national entity and also solve certain difficulties of definitions concerning the identity of individuals in complex situations involving a number of countries and peoples. To sum up, persons can belong to a nation, meaning a political-cultural-territorial entity, and as members of that nation be the citizens of and hold the nationality of the state in which they reside, while beyond this they remain bound by historico-cultural bonds to the people they identify themselves with. Gunter, a resident of Zurich, holds Swiss nationality and citizenship, belongs to the Swiss–German nation, and identifies himself with the German people. Harry, an English-speaking resident of the Republic of South Africa, belongs to the global group of English people and South Africa's "Anglo" nation while holding South African nationality and citizenship. Pedro of Madrid, holding Spanish nationality and citizenship and belonging to the Castilian nation, belongs also to the Spanish people who settled in Spain itself, but also in most of the states of Latin America and elsewhere. By Spanish law, for instance, the descendants of Jews expelled from Spain in 1492—wherever they now live—still belong to the Spanish people and are entitled to claim Spanish nationality and citizenship. In some cases, two or even all three of our terms may apply to the same entity. In a state of one nation and one only, with no minority of a size and solidarity to constitute a national community, nation and nationality are coextensive. Similarly, a nation with no national communities overseas is both nation and people. If there were such a thing as a people congregated entirely in one state, containing no members of any other people or nation, then all three terms, people and nation and nationality would coincide. If such a state did exist today, it would be an anomaly, since every state has a national minority in it, and almost all nations have branches in other states. Some argue that there is no point in distinguishing between nation in its narrow and wider senses as the term is in effect a linking up of people and nationality, of ethnicity, and international relations. To my mind, the distinction clarifies an important issue concerning multinational states, an issue that will assume great significance when we come to discuss Israeli identity. The State of Israel is today home to a Jewish nation and an Arab–Palestinian national minority. The members of both groups hold Israeli nationality and together constitute Israel's citizenry. Jewish Israelis belong to the Jewish people, Palestinian Israelis to the Arab people. Yigal is a member of the Jewish people, a Jew by nationhood, and an Israeli by nationality; Izzam is a member of the Arab people, a Palestinian by nationhood, and also an Israeli by nationality.

2

Secular Identity

The "Full Cart" of Secular Humanism

THE METAPHOR OF A "FULL" OR "FULLY LOADED CART" TO STAND FOR the sublime abundance of Jewish religious culture and of an "empty cart" to represent the alleged vacancy of Jewish secular culture are the inventions of R. Avraham Yeshayahu Karelitz, renowned author of the work of *halachic* commentary, *Khazon Ish*. The story goes that David Ben-Gurion, Israel's first prime minister, invited the great rabbi to give his opinion as to the proper scale of priorities that should govern any clash between state law and *halacha*. The rabbi replied that clearly, just as a full cart had the right of way over an empty one, *halacha* took precedence over secular state law. Not only was Karelitz quoting the *halakhic* ruling itself (BT *Sanhedrin* 32b), which regulates the right of way when a fully laden ship, cart, or camel meets an empty ship, cart, or camel, but, in the rabbi's mind, *halacha* stood as a metonym for the whole of "full" religious culture, while secular state law could only represent "empty" secular culture. Ben-Gurion, secular to his bones, responded by elaborating upon the extremely heavy weight involved in directing the affairs of the new state and ensuring its survival.

Even today, many still believe that in terms of Jewish culture and considering the prime sources of that culture, the religious possess a far greater store of riches than that available to the secular. I do not agree. The cultural wealth of secularism is necessarily greater than that of religious Judaism, because Jewish secular culture not only encompasses religious Judaism—including the riches of all its multiplicity of denominations, sects, and sub-sects—but also those parts of our people's civilization and culture that our rabbis never sanctioned and tried hard to repress. Morally and intellectually, secular humanism in no respect falls short of the religious value system while it surpasses it in many aspects. And that is not all: since we secular Jews regard ourselves as full partners in world cultures, we are entitled to claim that the holds of our "ship" are laden to overflowing with a humanist Jewish culture of boundless scope and wealth, only one compartment of which holds the Jewish religion's "full cart."

WHAT IS SECULARITY?

As we have noted, secularism is tied to the humanist view of our world. As a worldview, humanism—which flowered during the Italian Renaissance of the fifteenth century CE—turns the focus of human attention away from theological speculation on the nature of God, towards the nature of humanity and of the human capacities that are revealed in our pursuit of the arts and sciences. Renaissance humanism adopted the premise of the fifth-century BCE. Greek philosopher, Protagoras, that man is the measure of all things,[1] and from that premise the idea of human sovereignty followed.

It is central to secular humanism that humans are sovereign over themselves and their world and not subordinate to any transcendental hegemony issuing from somewhere outside their world. Neither religious doctrine nor religious law, nor the rulings of religious sages decide what is socially acceptable, what is true and what false, what is good and what is evil. Nor should the commandments, customs and practices of religion have any say in the ways they live their lives. Humans should determine all these matters for themselves, according to their own will and to the best of their judgement and knowledge, within the framework of the norms governing a binding social contract.

Atheism

Most people think that secularism is founded in atheism,[2] that is, in the view that posits that God does not exist and that, therefore, there is no divine sovereignty either. It was the Romans who first coined the term and who, in an irony of history, used it against the Jews and Christians who denied the gods of Rome. Later, it was the Catholic Church that labeled as atheistic Christian sects that would not accept the divinity of Jesus Christ and the principle of the Holy Trinity—God who is in His nature both one and three, God the Father, Jesus His Son, and the Holy Ghost. Finally, the term was applied to those who denied the very concept of divinity. It is certainly true that many seculars are atheists who openly declare their disbelief in the idea of a god.

Closely related to atheism is agnosticism,[3] a position found in the writings of Protagoras himself. He opens his book *On the Gods* with the statement: "With regard to the gods, I cannot feel sure either that they are or that they are not, nor what they are like in figure; for there are many things that hinder sure knowledge, such as the obscurity of the subject and the shortness of human life."[4] The term "agnosticism" meaning "to be without knowledge of the existence of God," was coined by the philosopher T. H. Huxley in the late nineteenth century. Huxley considered that the matters dealt with by religion and all matters relating to the supernatural are not susceptible to knowledge since religious faith cannot engender knowable facts and what cannot be known by scientific research and corroborated by experiment is best left to silence. There is no way of settling the question of God's existence or non-existence, or any other religious question; we can never know if He really exists. It is a view that several of our contemporary thinkers have endorsed and seculars as a group are widely identified with agnosticism. Certainly the majority of those defining themselves as agnostic lead a secular lifestyle and profess one sort of humanist worldview or another.

Nonetheless, a distinction must be drawn between atheism and secular humanism. The essence of atheism is its denial of the existence of God, but it offers no alternative belief or value system, while secular humanism is no less dismissive of the idea of divine sovereignty than is atheism, its vital advance is to replace the sovereignty of God with the sovereignty of man. Agnosticism too, built on doubt about divine existence, is not entirely compatible with a secular humanist position, for it could lead to the idea that perhaps it would be better to stay loyal to *Torah* and *mitzvot* on the off-chance that there is a God after all. Indeed, the French philosopher Pascal argued that in a strict calculation of the benefits and losses entailed, it was clearly preferable to maintain faith.[5] A Hasidic tale tries to debunk enlightened Jews with the same idea, it tells that an enlightened man had heard of the rabbi Levy Yitzhak of Berditchev, and looked him up in order to debate with him. When he entered the zaddik's[6] room, the rabbi looked at him and said: "My son, the great Torah scholars wasted their words on you. They could not set God and His kingdom on the table before you, and I cannot do this either. But, my son, think! *What if* it is true, after all!" The enlightened man tried to reply, but the words *What if* beat on his ears again and again and broke down his resistance.[7]

But this still leaves us with a problem, ignored by both Pascal and R. Levi Yitzhak of Berditchev. Of all the gods and of all the religions available, in which one should we invest our belief, in case "it's true after all?" Pascal, of course, had Catholicism in mind; R. Levi Yitzhak was certainly thinking of Judaism, but who is there to guarantee beyond the limits of doubt that the absolute truth is not held by another religion, perhaps Hinduism, in which case that would be the sensible choice for the repository of our beliefs?

Denial or doubts of God's existence are far from new ideas. Even in antiquity, there were several thinkers who cast doubt on the reality of God and on the truths pronounced by religion. Protagoras was not alone among Greek philosophers in thinking as he did, and there seem to have been skeptics even among the great Jewish thinkers. The book of Psalms twice repeats the verse: "The fool has said in his heart, 'There is no God'" (Psalms 14:1; 53:1), sure evidence that denial of Yahweh's existence occurred from the earliest times, even if the author of the psalm describes the deniers as "fool." The Talmudic sages dubbed non-believers "epicures," after the Greek philosopher Epicurus, who was held to have denied divine providence and man's possession of an immortal soul, and to have advocated a life devoted to pleasure. So often did the sages have to find answers to the epicures and the difficult questions they raised that they equipped themselves with ready-made retorts, a sort of "How to Deal with an Epicure" kit (Mishna *Avot* 2:19; BT *Sanhedrin* 38b). It is evident, then, that there were more than a few unbelievers. The sages certainly saw them everywhere: even in Adam, the world's first man, of whom R. Nakhman said, "He denied the existence of God." Heretics and unbelievers of all kinds and categories left their strong imprint on Judaism from its earliest days and continue to do so, even though in nearly all cases religious "censorship" made sure that their writings did not survive for us to inherit. But the rabbis' frequent denunciations of atheism and skepticism have survived and can mean only that there were many atheists and skeptics who were willing to raise their voices loud and clear.

In the second century of the Common Era, in the aftermath of the Bar Kokhba revolt, Elisha Ben Avuya, one of the greatest *tannaim* (*Mishnaic* scholars) of his time, reached a point where he could no longer accept the reality of Yahweh's providence and rebelled openly against Judaism. For this his fellow *tannas* refused to call him by his name, and referred to him only as "that other one" ("Aher," BT *Hagiga* 14). In the Persian city of Balkh, in the ninth century CE, a Jew, Khivi by name, who persisted in posing questions about faith and existence of God, displayed enough competence to demonstrate logical contradictions in the biblical text and in the articles of Judaism as then formulated. His writings, enumerating two hundred points of doubt about the biblical text, have not come down to us, but one of the greatest minds

in the history of Jewish thought, R. Saadiah Gaon himself, found that
he had to refute Khivi formally. In fact, but for Saadiah's refutations and
some other writings against Khivi we would not have known that he had
ever existed and had ever put forward his public challenge to the word
of the Bible and its rabbinic interpreters.[8] In the centuries after Saadiah,
medieval Jewish philosophy makes several determined attempts, de-
ploying a variety of strategies, to prove the existence of God, from which
we must conclude that openly expressed skepticism and atheism by Jewish intellectuals had developed to proportions that made such counterattacks necessary. Maimonides called these doubters "the perplexed"
and for them he wrote his famous *Guide.*

A few hundred years later, in the seventeenth century, the Jewish philosopher, Benedictus (Baruch) Spinoza, advanced an idea called pantheism. This holds that God is everywhere and in everything, the
universe is God, the world and God form one unity, and divine law is
no more and no less than the laws of nature. Doing away with the idea
of a transcendental divinity, existent in some way on some non-human
plane, the conception of Spinoza returns to the premise of the early Israelite faith that humankind and God co-exist in a single scheme of
things. In effect, so close is Spinoza to the vision that humans are sovereign over their own world that his teaching laid the foundations on
which the humanist secularity of the modern period was subsequently
built. In his own time, Spinoza had to face the accusation that he himself was an atheist. Found guilty as charged by the leadership of the
Amsterdam Jewish community, where he lived and worked, he was sentenced to ostracism, and the sentence remains in force to this day.[9] Yet
Spinoza's contemporary, the English philosopher Thomas Hobbes,
went much farther than him in this respect: from start to finish, Hobbes'
system is void of any trace of religion and divinity and may be considered atheist.

In the nineteenth century, the Danish philosopher Søren Kierkegaard, a religious man and a firm believer in the reality of God, nonetheless argued that since the nature of that reality is hidden from us, we
have no way of knowing what God wants from us and what we must do
to serve His will. A divinity so totally impenetrable that no understanding can pass either to or from Him is in effect, from humankind's point
of view, non-existent—just as a buried treasure hidden in a place that
no one knows and that no one knows how to find would also be, to all
intents and purposes, non-existent. In such a situation, humans have no
choice but to take responsibility for their lives. By so removing God
from any kind of intervention in human life, Kierkegaard heralded the

Existentialist school of philosophy and this premise of his remained fundamental to the philosophy as it was developed and elaborated by his heirs[10] Martin Heidegger, Jean-Paul Sartre, Albert Camus, and others. Friedrich Nietzsche, a German philosopher also of the nineteenth century, went so far as to proclaim "the death of God." Our world has no God in it, he said.[11] Nietzsche, too, placed the responsibility for issues of existence and morality solely and exclusively in human hands.

In the aftermath of the Second World War and the Holocaust, doubt and denial of the existence of God proliferated among Jews and non-Jews alike. They could find no adequate answer to the question of how God could allow such horrors into His world. Not that this was the first time the question had been raised. Every time a calamity has struck humanity, whether war, plague, earthquake or some other disaster, the religious establishment's stock response has been that the calamity is the punishment for sinfulness. Yet the priests and rabbis have always failed to demonstrate the direct relation of the sin to the penalty, paid also by children innocent of sin, and to explain the lapse of time between cause and effect. Inevitably, after every catastrophe visited upon Jewry, misgivings appeared, giving rise to questioning and loss of faith in Yahweh's guardianship. This occurred after the destruction of Jerusalem and the quelling of the Bar Kokhba revolt in the second century CE, after the Crusader slaughters of the eleventh to thirteenth centuries, after the great expulsion from Spain at the end of fifteenth century, after the pogroms in Eastern Europe during the seventeenth century, late nineteenth century, early twentieth century. Almost all the writings giving voice to such questioning of divine providence have disappeared, but the counterattacks and the counterassurances of "trust" in Yahweh prove that the questionings were widespread enough to be well-known and were probably printed and distributed. After the final defeat of the revolt led by Bar Kokhba and Rabbi Akiva in which hundreds of thousands of Jewish lives were lost (132–135 CE), the *tanna* Elisha Ben Avuya,"'the other one," saw Khutzpit the Translator's tongue being dragged around by a pig; Khutzpit was one of the ten revered elders the Romans selected for exemplary execution. The Talmud tells us that Elisha went and sinned (BT *Kiddushin* 39b). Even R. Shimon Bar Yokhai, a disciple of Rabbi Akiva and revered as the saintliest Jew of his generation, found a singular way to cast doubt on the nature and justice of Yahweh's guardianship. He made the Cain and Abel episode into a parable that implies that God could have prevented the slaughter but chose not to do so: "It is hard to say and impossible to understand. It is as though two athletes had come to wrestle before the king. Had the king wanted

he could have separated them but he chose not to. One of them was
stronger and killed the other, who cried out: 'Who will obtain justice for
me before the king?'" (Gen. Rabba 22:22).

After the massacre of Jews in Kishinev in 1903, Chaim Nahman Bialik
composed his "Al Hashchita" ("On The Slaughter,") a poem of an-
guished protest that, since Heaven had been shown to be empty and
abandoned, the Jews had no road left to God:

> Heaven, beg mercy for me!
> If there be in you a God and through you a way to this God
> —One I have not found—then pray for me!
> For my own heart is dead and prayer has died on my lips;
> Strength is gone and even hope is no more.
> How much longer, how much longer, till when?

In his poem "Harugel tiramoni" ("The Dead of Tiramoni)" Sha'ul
Chernikhovsky, writing in the aftermath of massacres of Ukrainian Jews,
expressly denies the existence of God, and questions the possibility that
any God could ever exist:

> There is no God because there isn't—and that's all!
> There is no God, not Hebrew, not Christian!
> Could anything have prevented God from answering us?
> Could anything have stopped His mercy? . . .
> Could there be a God on this Earth and He not have seen
> The terrible wrongs, the huge evil being done in His name
> And to His name, done by man to man?

After a pogrom against Polish Jews during the First World War, Uri Zvi
Greenberg, in his poem "Kfizat Haderech" ("Leap Forward") puts
some essential questions about God's involvement in the atrocious murders, even going so far as to deride faith in God and trust in His aid:

Is there a God up there who is any better for us than Titus,[12]
Or than soldiers on thresholds of frontiers?
If He is there he's a whiner and coward,
Nice and cozy as a sick granddad, hiding away
Up in the clouds from the terrors of the pogroms in Jews' villages.
What does it matter! Hey, you, God, you whining coward, our very own
    Yahweh in Slav-land, making himself a swamp of His tears in Canaan!
If He only knew that He could come down to us, slake His thirst and restore
His worn-out carcass with blood from the Hebrew winery—going real cheap
    now!

Then He would come down, get as drunk as a "goy" and then tell the
  "goyim",
Don't they know He's in fact the father of Christ,
And also knows the words to the Sacrifice Song . . .

Humanism and Democracy

Since the humanist worldview is apolitical, secularism entails no particular political or party-political stance, although certain political views
and social ideologies certainly have a humanist basis. It is true, however,
that most humanists tend to be democratic in their sociopolitical outlook. Belief in humanity and the human spirit tends to make people
exalt freedom as a supreme value from which other values follow and
this scale of priorities is also the basis of democratic thinking. On the
other hand, it does not follow that adherents of a worldview, government, or lifestyle that is democratic must be secular. There are many
religious people who support democratic government and society. Although the religious and democratic value systems are essentially contradictory, the one regarding God as the source of authority and law and
the other locating this source in the people (considered for this purpose
as the collective embodiment of individual humankind). The contradiction is usually resolved by the separation of religion and state. This can
be a matter of both statute and practice, as in the United States and
Mexico, or merely one of practice, as in the United Kingdom, whose
king or queen, by statute both Head of State and Head of the Church
of England, does not in practice intervene in politics. The premise at
the basis of this separation is that religion is the concern of the individual and the religious community and has nothing to do with how the
state is governed.

For religious Jews who want to support democratic government in
spite of their religious doctrine, the following reading of Jewish doctrine
is a reasonable option. God, in bestowing freedom and sovereignty on
humankind, has entrusted each person with the authority and responsibility to act towards other persons in accordance with the spirit and
principles of social justice and personal moral judgement. This is a reading that, by and large, Maimonides endorses and which is corroborated
by a number of textual sources. The best known is the tale of the dispute
over the issue of the Akhnai Oven,[13] between R. Eliezer ben Hyrcanus
and a group of other sages, led by R. Yehoshua ben Khananya, whether
finding a small ritually unclean animal in the oven made the whole of it
unclean:

That day Rabbi Eliezer brought forward every imaginable argument but [the opposing sages] did not accept them. Eliezer said: "If *halacha* agrees with me, let this carob tree prove it." Thereupon, the carob tree was uprooted a hundred cubits from its place. . . . They said: "One does not prove anything by the tree." Again he said: "If *halacha* agrees with me, let this stream of water prove it." Thereupon the stream of water flowed backwards. They said: "One does not prove anything by the stream of water." Again he urged: "If *halacha* agrees with me, let the walls of this *beth midrash* [study-house] prove it," Whereupon the walls leaned as though to fall. But Rabbi Yehoshua rebuked them saying: "Sages are discussing *halacha* dispute, who are you to interfere?" . . . Again he said to them: "If *halacha* agrees with me, let it be proved from Heaven!" Whereat, a Heavenly Voice said: "Why do you dispute with R. Eliezer, in all matters *halacha* agrees with him." R. Yehoshua stood up and said: (Deut. 30:12): 'It is not in heaven!" . . . R. Yirmiya said: "Since the Torah has already been given on Mt. Sinai we no longer pay heed to Heavenly Voices, because You have written in the Torah at Mt. Sinai: (Exodus 23:2) "Follow the majority." (BT *Baba Metzia* 59b)

The outlook this passage expresses is very close to humanism. It grants humans the authority to determine their ways and customs for themselves, it declares a sovereignty and freedom sanctioned by a fundamental divine injunction, couched in the imperative, "Follow the majority," one which liberates humans within essential limitations, from the sovereignty of God Himself, as Rabbi Yirmiya says. Divine sovereignty, as Rabbi Yehoshua says, has no place in the decisions we must make about our lives: "It is not in heaven . . ." In a one-time revelation from Mt. Sinai, Yahweh gave us His Torah and, this done, His presence and interventions in our affairs are no longer required or sanctioned. From that time on, by virtue of the very authority He gave humankind, humans have been sovereign over their acts and choices. Certainly, the passage from *Baba Metzia* is not a repudiation of divine sovereignty, it affirms that the source of law and human sovereignty is God, but there is no longer such a great step from the rights and liberties it claims for humanity to a fully developed humanism.

Secular Non-Democratic Ideologies

There have been and there still are political ideologies that profess a secular view of the world but at the same time preach values that are set over and above the freedom of the individual, even negating that freedom. The values can be lofty beyond question, such as the social equality promoted by socialism and communism, for example, but can also be what most people would regard as pernicious, such as chauvinism, fascism, or racism. Several times in recent history, in particular under fascist or communist regimes, these ideologies have claimed for themselves a totalitarian, that is to say, an absolute, unique and all-encompassing, truth that negates any form or possibility of pluralism and have thus set themselves up as something not very far from the absolutism of religion and its claim to higher authority .

As ideologies, socialism and fascism are not to be equated. The ideals of socialism are preeminently humanist. Man is the center of its concern and human freedom its first goal. Fascism, in contrast, elevates the state, nation, and race as supreme values and makes man subordinate, even subject, to them and duty-bound to serve them. Any type of fascism cannot help but be utterly anti-humanist and every fascist regime established in the first half of the twentieth century operated a policy that in the end brought about the total subjugation of the individual to the state and its ruling party. In the Soviet Union, Eastern Europe, China, and elsewhere in Asia, communist parties also imposed totalitarian and anti-humanist regimes that subjugated all individuals to the will and rule of the Communist Party. Ideologically, the Party justified its tyranny as indispensable to the realization of socialism's lofty ideals, in other words the means were justified by the end; once its ultimate goals were achieved, the totalitarian state would dissolve itself. In reality, the freedom of humans in the here and now was subjugated to a promise of equality for all in some abstract future and in the process, both freedom and equality were destroyed, for without freedom, there is no equality. Equality derives from freedom. Communist totalitarianism represents a degeneration and corruption of what are, in origin, genuinely humanist ideals.

Socialism is fundamentally secular: it regards humans as sovereign over themselves and their freedom as a primary value. There have been movements for social equality that were inspired by religion, however,· their objectives were not human freedom, happiness and the material goods of life but equality in a state of humble and virtuous poverty. In the case of chauvinism and racism, on the other hand, society and politics can coexist quite happily with religion and even be supported by religious institutions. The Fascist regime that ruled Spain under Generalissimo Franco from 1939 to 1975 found a close ally in the Catholic Church and drew much of its strength from that alliance. Fascist, racist, and anti-Semitic organizations and movements in Hungary, Poland, Romania, and other countries have found ready support in the same source. Although the German National Socialist (Nazi) government proclaimed itself secular and harried the Catholic Church and religious establishment, its motives were political not ideological, expedient not humanistic. The general picture is that totalitarian regimes, whether fascist or communist, and likewise the military dictatorships in South America, Africa, and Asia, while emphasizing that "man" is the source of their sovereignty, in fact perceive "man" in the abstract or in the collective, as a people, race or class. For individual living humans, there are no rights under these regimes, neither freedom nor the personal and social sovereignty that, in our understanding of humanism, are the inalienable right of all humans by virtue of their humanity. Totalitarianisms place authority in the hands of the party or an autocrat, dispossessing individual citizens of any liberty and sovereignty.

HUMANISM AND ITS VALUES

For all the pleasure that certain religious figures take in claiming that secularism is another form of nihilism,[14] a mere repudiation of others' values, secular humanism as a view of the world is in reality rich in ideals and values relating to human existence and survival, life and morality, beauty and culture. True, its ideals can lay no claim to divine authority, they are the work of sovereign and autonomous humans looking for a guide to life within a binding but freely-accepted social consensus, equal for all.[15] The poet Sha'ul Chernikhovsky gave voice to his faith in humans in his famous Ani Ma'amin ("Credo"):

> Laugh at my dreams, laugh away,
> I, the dreamer, thus speak;
> Laugh at my still believing in man
> That I still have faith in you.

> That my soul still yearns for freedom,
> I have not sold it to some Golden Calf,
> Because in man, in his spirit's firmness
> I still have faith.

> His spirit will slough off the hold of vanity,
> And raise him up on high;
> Workers will not die in hunger,
> The soul will have its freedom, the poor their bread. . . .

The term "humanism" comes, of course, from "human" (Latin, *humanus*), but at different times it has meant different things. There were times when it implied a favorable attitude to humanity in general, a love of humankind, and a recognition of its rights. In Greek and Roman culture, the word differentiated the human from the animal, on the one hand, and from the divine on the other: on the one side, man could boast reason and skills; on the other side, his puniness was mocked by the power of the gods. He suffered from mortality, a feeble body, and the pitfalls into which his limited, partial, and imperfect understanding of the world led him.

Greco-Roman philosophy and art was homocentric, that is, man stood firmly at the center of its worldview: everything was measured in relation to him and evaluated from his point of view. The proportions of Greek and Roman temples were based on the proportions of the human body; their statuary was intended to glorify that body and highlight its beauty and strength. Even the gods are depicted in human form and likeness, though with vastly greater powers. One of the markers of the closing of the Middle Ages and the opening of the modern period is that a scale of values based on a religious theocentric conception of the world yields way to a restored classical humanism, when once again the dominant scale of values has rational, free man at its center.

Secular Humanist Values and Religious Values

Between the values of secular humanism and of religion there is an essential disjunction. The values dictated by religion as it were derive authority from being the word and will of God. As such, they may not be questioned and must be obeyed, for in a religious belief system the paramount values are faith in God, keeping His commandments, and maintaining His worship. True, among the values commanded by different religions (and Judaism is no exception) are some that are similar in essence to humanist values. The *tanna* Hillel teaches that the precept "Do not to others what you would hate done to you" (BT *Shabbat* 31a) sums up the essence of the Torah; such a principle reflects a humanist value *par excellance* (it is found in several other cultures too). Equally humanistic are the *mitzvot* protecting the rights of the stranger and the sojourner, widows and orphans, employees, and others in dependent situations. Other commandments, however, patently contradict humanist teaching; they are inhumane and anti-human and also are to be found in all religions. In Judaism, outstanding in this regard are the *mitzvot* associated with the conquest of the promised land, decreeing total extermination for its current inhabitants, in a word, genocide: "you shall save alive nothing that breathes" (Deut. 20:16) is only one example.

Others, in the name of the alleged superiority of Judaism, permit the exploitation of non-Jews, for example, "to a stranger you may lend upon usury, but to your brother you shall not lend upon usury" (Deut. 23:20), and do not stop short even of excusing killing: "The best among the *Goyim* (gentiles)—kill him" (Pesikta Zutarta). Other unacceptable categories of decrees are the ones discriminating against women and preaching corporal punishment for children: "Withhold no correction from the child; for if you beat him with the rod he shall not die. Beat him with a rod and you will save his soul from hell" (Prov. 23:13–14), and the like.

Humanism does not derive its values from a divine imperative or any other absolute imperative but from autonomous human experience, which of course evolves and changes over time and from fundamental principles of human relations, among them openness to the other, understanding and tolerance for people's plurality, and respect for human rights. The heart and soul of humanism and its teaching is that human liberty stands at the pinnacle of its value-system and all other values derive from it.

Human Liberty

The concept of freedom enters human history for the first time in Israelite myth: the Children of Israel spend four hundred years in slavery to Pharaoh in Egypt to enable them to learn via their own experience the meaning of freedom, both as individuals and as a nation. The concept of freedom is the Hebrew's greatest contribution to Western civilization. It was not, however, a universal freedom, but one granted specifically to the People of Israel, because freedom of choice was essential for the worship of Yahweh, whose followers had the freedom to choose between good and evil but not the freedom to decide what was good and what evil. In other words, their freedom did not extend as far as freedom of conscience and its corollary, the freedom to criticize. True, odd instances are recorded here and there in the sources of bitter reproaches cast against Heaven: Abraham exclaims: "Shall not the Judge of all the earth do right?" (Gen. 18:25); Jeremiah presses charges against Yahweh (Jer. 12:1); Job conducts his questioning of divine justice. In later generations, Hasidim recounted in awe how the *tzaddik*, Rabbi Levi Yitzhak of Berditchev summoned the Holy One Blessed Be He to judgement (*Din Tora*). But these instances and others are all met with the unchanging rebuke that man in his limited wisdom simply does not have in him the capacity to encompass the purposes of divine acts.

On each occasion the human accuser is finally compelled to acknowledge Yahweh's greater justice. Moreover, these instances are so few that they only emphasize the rule: believers are denied the right to criticize the pillars of their faith and the ordained pattern of religious life. The Bible vividly recounts every complaint, criticism, and doubt the Israelites dared utter during their forty years in the wilderness, and Yahweh responded with fury and ferocious punishments. The freedom Yahweh grants does not grant sovereignty. That said, it was a huge advance on the norm in other civilizations of the time, where the concept of individual rights did not exist at all and freedom was reserved for a few privileged persons of power and wealth. Furthermore, in the course of time this limited freedom grew to become the foundation for the concept of human sovereignty, God-granted, certainly, but, within the inherent limitations of the human condition, it gave humans complete autonomy.

As humanism understands human freedom, its core is freedom of conscience. Free humans think independently, they are critical and self-confident. They do not accept a convention merely because it exists, and they do not submit to authority merely because it is such. Neither do they reject them on those grounds. Marshaling their learning and knowledge, the two requisites for making freedom of conscience a reality, they form their own opinions and their own judgements. They know how to present and defend this opinion even when it is out of the mainstream, and yet they know too always to remain open to self-examination and self-criticism and be willing to modify and correct opinions and assessments should the conditions and factors upon which they were based change or should new insights be found. Freedom of conscience is, we have noted, the core and essence of human freedom. It also makes severe demands. It requires not only knowledge but also a temperament willing to listen and reflect and the strength to withstand the powerful forces constantly working to restrict freedom of conscience, forces that are, for the most part, inside us: the force of habit, lazy thinking, prejudices, fear of public opinion, the reluctance to be different, fear of being wrong, of being laughed at, and so on. External forces too, both political and social, are hostile to independent thought and to lines of reasoning not under their direction. Without doubt, this is a freedom that demands courage and endurance, but without it we lack one of the supreme values of our life and a crucial resource in the battle for human rights.

No wonder that totalitarian regimes have done their utmost to curtail this freedom, whether by intensive and ubiquitous propaganda to "brainwash" their citizens into "correct" thinking, or by eliminating democratically minded educators, thinkers and opinion molders, or by persecuting any individual daring to voice the unconventional. Nor does freedom of conscience usually sit well with the standpoint of most religions, demanding as they do absolute, unquestioning assent and obedience. No religion can agree to have its dogmas flouted and the authority of its priests, rabbis, or mullahs challenged or questioned. Freedom of conscience is preeminently a secular and humanist value.

Under the heading of the primary human freedoms are the social and political rights to which every newborn is heir, irrespective of personal identity or place of birth. The right to sovereignty over our body and mind; the right to make decisions to the best of our understanding and knowledge, free of pressure and constraint on our way of life, on our beliefs and opinions, on our social ties and our place in the world at large. The right to live in dignity, free of want and fear, the right to receive the schooling and education needed for making life choices, and all the other fundamental rights that make up the life of a free human. These rights are absolute, unretractable, unquestionable, and irreducible, provided they remain within the limits set by a freely made societal consensus. This consensus sets limits on individual freedom but no more than those required to prevent injury to the freedom of other individuals or of society as a whole. All other humanist values derive from the paramount value of freedom and defer to it. The vital and enlightened value of equality, for example, in particular equality under the law, derives from the premise that every person, without exception, is born to an equal freedom.

Freedom as a universal right has not been a self-evident idea. It only become part of human thinking in the seventeenth century through the work of the Englishman John Locke and other philosophers. In their vision, freedom was a "natural right" to which every human was born, a right that was absolute, irrespective of identity, and not rescindable under any circumstances whatever. The political implications of the idea were huge. Raising this right to the status of an absolute value, above man-made law and beyond the grasp of kings and the apparatus of state, suddenly gave individuals as individuals and "the people" full sovereignty. In the system devised by the French philosopher Jean-Jacques Rousseau, every ruler and regime drew its power from the people and it became the people's natural right to overthrow any ruler or regime that tried to deprive them of freedoms and rights. The "rights of man" and the acknowledgment that all men are born equal and free were first formally promulgated in the United States' Declaration of Independence of 1776, in the constitution that was later drawn up, and in the Declaration of the Rights of Man and the Citizen affirmed by the French National Assembly after the 1789 revolution.

In 1945, with the Second World War only just ended, the United Nations affirmed a universal Declaration of Human Rights, granting broad international recognition to the concept that freedom was every individual's absolute right. It is self-evident that the current implementation of the Declaration is very far from equal and universal. Some states have totalitarian regimes, others have ideological or religious reservations. It took decades, for instance, for Israel to ratify the Declaration because its religious parties could not stomach sexual equality or the equality of Jew and non-Jew and other such clauses. It was only in 1994 that Israel passed its Basic Law[16] on Human Dignity and Freedom, which refers to human rights "within the meaning of [Israel's] Declaration of Independence." Even though it is a partial and faulty piece of legislation, an outcome of all the compromises made to appease religious parliamentarians, it represents a huge step forward. The ratification of the Declaration of Human Rights by the majority of United Nations member states and the sustained worldwide effort to have these rights implemented represent monumental achievement for the concept of human freedom and for secular humanism, without which it would have been inconceivable.[17]

Pluralism

Pluralism, directly derived from the two values of human freedom and the equal value of every individual, is at the core of both humanism and democracy. Pointedly opposed to any totalitarian vision of the world, whether religious or secular in inspiration, it has a dual essence: it totally rejects any demand for an enforced uniformity and, accepting that humans differ widely, it is accepting of those differences. These differences are to be found at the level of every component of human society, from the uniqueness and otherness of the individual, through family, clan and race, to ethnic and national group. Human diversity is evident in the spheres of ideology and ideas, belief and opinion, culture, language, custom, lifestyle, as well as in physical appearance, skin color, and other ethnic-racial characteristics. In a pluralist society, these diversities will form the kernel around which subcultures take shape, each again differing from the other but coexisting in equality of rights in a heterogeneous and accepting society.

In democratic societies composed of a number of immigrant groups, of which the United States and Israel are two prime examples, the "melting-pot" idea was for years the prevailing norm and in its name the authorities (that is, the dominant population group) applied pressure and constraints to bring divergent ethno-cultural groups into line with the ensconced model. It is an old story, of course. The Bible (2 Kings 18) informs us that the King of Assyria planned to transfer the Jews of Judah, once he had conquered them, to one of his other domains and resettle Judah with another Assyrian vassal people, as he had already done many times with other captured territories, the Kingdom of Israel among them. When Judah was finally vanquished by the Babylonian empire, this is exactly what happened. Later, with Judah back in Jewish hands, the Hasmoneans waged their wars to combat Hellenization, the popular adoption of Greek culture then sweeping across all the lands conquered by Alexander and his heirs. The wars that the Jews fought against their Roman rulers had the same purpose—to prevent the cultural-linguistic Romanization of the Jewish homeland. As the Arabs spread Islam across their empire, they tried to make Arabic the ruling language of every people and culture that came under their rule. Likewise, the Russian czars imposed Russification on their multinational empire. Nor were the English, French, and Spanish imperialists any different.

Another very effective device for achieving imperialist unity and control was religious coercion. Locals were pressured or forced into converting to Islam or Christianity, whichever of the two the chance of conquest brought them. Other faiths were persecuted or denied rights. The Hasmonean king Alexander Yannai (second century BCE) forcibly converted the non-Jewish inhabitants of his expanded kingdom to Judaism, but then the tables turned and for hundreds of years it was the Jews living under Christian and Islamic rule who were the victims of the prevailing religio-political anti-pluralism. In Jewish communities the same thinking applied: total uniformity was demanded. Any group challenging the absolute rule of the elders with new ideas was punished root and branch by ostracism and expulsion. Individuals, too, felt the heavy hand of uniformity on them. "Abnormals" of all sorts found themselves repressed, penalized, tortured, or killed, to either make them mend their ways or to "defend" society from them. In different societies, such "abnormals" might be people who were left-handed, people with eyes of an unusual color, albinos, epileptics, homosexuals, and especially those who voiced discordant opinions. The compulsion towards uniformity created savage inequalities. Anyone or any group not of the majority or not deferring to majority norms was invariably penalized economically and socially and had their rights of citizenship suppressed.

For all the resistance offered, and it was often zealous, the forces of religio-cultural coercion usually achieved significant, if not complete, success. The civilizations of Greece and Rome and their languages took root across almost the whole of Europe and to a considerable extent still rule the European roost to this day. Arab culture and language likewise reign supreme across North Africa and the Middle East. The influence of the imperialists of the modern period—the British, French and Spaniards—is equally pervasive. Wherever their armies once marched, the imprint of their civilization and language is strong, even accepted and welcomed, long after the colonial yoke has been thrown off. Christianity and Islam have become religions of worldwide reach. Even the notorious "melting-pot" policy has had a notable measure of "success" in the states of immigration. Sometimes no pressure is needed. Even in pluralist societies some minorities, adapting and internalizing dominant norms, voluntarily opt for assimilation, although we cannot say that in these cases social pressure, overt or covert, has not been a factor.

This predilection of the powerful for uniformity and control brought about the huge bloodlettings of wars between nations and between religions. Individuals and whole peoples were tortured and slaughtered by this impetus for a society that towed one line. In the end, however, from under this enforced singularity, divergence, separateness, and otherness arose to demand their rights. In sixteenth-century Europe, after the wars of religion had failed to impose unity, the outcome was a measure of reluctant tolerance for other faiths. In the eighteenth and nineteenth centuries, a succession of different peoples fought multinational empires for politico-cultural autonomy and most eventually achieved it. Other peoples fought the same fight in the twentieth century and again, most were successful. The twentieth century also saw wars of inhuman savagery for and against the hegemony of one race, nation, or political system. The end result was to push such coercion outside the consensus of legitimate policy.

The second half of the twentieth century was marked by an upsurge of sub-populations demanding the right to be different without being penalized for it by losing their social, cultural, and economic rights. The 1950s and 1960s in the United States, for instance, witnessed a remarkable protest movement and organized campaign of rights for black people that attracted widespread support both in the United States and around the world, while being met by violent opposition from those whose supremacy was directly threatened. It is undeniable that this struggle achieved monumental victories, although it has not yet achieved all its objects. The total equality of opportunity and freedom to which every citizen is entitled, is still withheld from certain groups, and racism and its heritage is by no means a past phenomenon. Crucially, it turned world opinion against racism, a victory that subsequently brought international pressure to bear on the world's most racist regime, the Republic of South Africa, and eventually contributed to that country's abandonment of the apartheid system of state-imposed racism. The struggle for black equality was part of a general overturning of the United States' "melting-pot" policy. Multiculturalism became the new watchword, the right of ethnic groups to retain and nurture their own cultures within a pluralist national society and culture. Children were entitled to be raised in the traditions within which their parents had been brought up and it became accepted that the larger society would greatly benefit from such variety and multiformity. American Jewish communities also markedly benefited from the new trend and American Jewish culture, in its numerous denominational forms, experienced a new renaissance. The Holocaust was accorded special place and status as an event around which Jews could unite, irrespective of the lifestyle and belief system each community followed.

The new awareness of the benefits of plurality did not stop at ethnic groups; other minorities also demanded equal rights. Such groups included people with disabilities whom the able-bodied world had long relegated to the sidelines, and, of course, homosexuals, who for centuries had suffered religious, social, and legal persecution. Both Christianity and Judaism viewed homosexual practice as an "abomination" (Lev. 18:22), while society saw homosexuality as "deviance" or "perversion." In the legal systems of many states it was a serious crime. Throughout many centuries, homosexuals were forced to keep their sexual identity a secret; if their secret was discovered, many faced punishments ranging from death to imprisonment. The trial and incarceration of English author Oscar Wilde in 1895 is a particularly well-known example. Today, homosexuality is recognized by law in many states; nevertheless, this particular struggle for equality is far from over, especially as regards homosexuality's legitimacy in the eyes of public opinion and the current lack of legal recognition of single-sex families and of the marital and spousal rights accorded to heterosexual couples.

A steadily intensifying demand for pluralism and equal rights has been generated by women since the resumption, as the twentieth century began, of the women's liberation movement in a world dominated by men. For so long, women have constituted a very special sub-population. Numerically, they are in fact in the majority, but socially and legally they bear the status of a minority and underclass, a status, according to most of the world's religions, decreed absolute by God Himself. In every generation some women have fought for recognition as full if different human beings, but the forces of male hegemony and religion persuaded the vast majority to resign themselves to "heaven's decree." It was the legitimacy won by humanism that stimulated women to fight for their rights, first and foremost, for the right to vote and to stand for office. In 1900 this right was unknown and inconceivable to most men, and it took half the century before the suffragette movement[18] had carried women's suffrage across most of the world. Women then rose to the highest positions in government and other central institutions—presidents, prime ministers, and chief justices. In the 1950s the movement regathered its cohorts and again set out to campaign under the banner of "feminism"; this time it set its sights on equality of pay and opportunity in the workplace. Once again important victories were achieved: in many states, particularly in the industrial world, legislation was passed requiring employers to provide equality of workplace pay and opportunities and amendments were made to the laws governing educational and family status. For the most part and however slowly, public opinion has adjusted to this redivision of power. New methods of birth control and the resultant ability to regulate family planning gave women greater sexual freedom, which, until that innovation, had been reserved for men only.

By the late twentieth century, the successful battle for women's rights had led the way to a sea-change in public attitudes. The place and rights owed to several groups of "the other" in society's key institutions had been fought out in the public arena, and the campaign was even carried into international organizations. Literature, theater, cinema, the plastic arts and television all gave vivid expression to the new trends under the collective label of "post-modernism." The interests and struggles of minority sub-cultures, former "outsiders" and "misfits" of various kinds, provided artists with a range and diversity of material. Increasingly, women write novels or make films about issues relevant to women; homosexuals create art works and entertainment centering on the issues or lives of homosexuals; both subjects, among others, have entered mainstream fiction. Now, more people than ever before are able to see them represented in art and entertainment and, just as importantly, are able to access the issues than concern groups other than their own.

By the late twentieth century, the "Rights of Man" included the equality of value of every individual and equality of rights for every individual. Discrimination by ethno-racial-geographical origin, gender, religion, age, sexual identity, and worldview has all been outlawed in most, but not all, countries. The rights of women and children and of specified minorities have been written into many national and international laws. Social pluralism and equality of rights for all population groups have won acknowledgement as core values governing relations between both the citizen and the state, and the state and other states. Together with the victory of freedom and human rights recounted in the previous section, the achievements of pluralism, still being consolidated in the face of determined resistance from religious fundamentalists and other conservatives, deserve also to be recognized as an outcome of secular humanism.

Tolerance and Toleration

It is impossible to conceive of egalitarian social pluralism without tolerance and toleration, that is, without the full acceptance of the other and the eccentric within a pluralist social system and culture. "Tolerance" refers more to a personal capacity to tolerate and "toleration" to institutional policy and practice. Toleration, as we know it, was the forced outcome of the wars of religion between Catholicism and Protestantism in sixteenth-century Europe, bloodbaths that, in the absence of decisive military superiority, compelled Catholic and Protestant rulers to accept the existence of the other, while each ruler maintained the right to choose the religion for his state. Over time, the concept spread to take in all religions, and many even considered it to include freedom of conscience. Later still, the demand for toleration came to stand for opposition to the unity of religion and state, under which the state acted as the secular strong arm of a single organized religion, while the pulpit preached respect for centralized government. In the Middle Ages this symbiosis was a common model of governance and in certain places it remains alive and well to this day. Not until the seventeenth century did it come under widespread philosophical attack, after the English philosopher John Locke recommended religious toleration as the best means for propagating ideas and opinions: he noted that in this way they might or might not find acceptance according to the degree of truth in them and not by dint of institutional coercion. Toleration and the serious issues it brought into question occupied philosophers for centuries. Spinoza raised the issue of to what extent toleration should be granted to the enemies of toleration. Hegel saw toleration as an expression of the dialectical thinking that emphasizes the ever-changing and ever-developing nature of phenomena. Lessing elevated toleration to a cardinal element of rational thought, as did many others. Broadly speaking, the concept of toleration is currently taken to cover the natural rights to freedom of opinion and to be different without having to pay for it by persecution, pressure, and discrimination. Historically speaking, this is new ground. Toleration first entered our societies as a show of benevolence by a ruler toward non-conforming individuals and groups or toward certain of their activities. It was by no means a natural right; rather, it depended entirely on the ruler's goodwill and if it did not serve his interests, it was likely to be denied. It was, in fact, dependent upon the whim or wishes of a paternalistic system and as such was far removed from modern-day egalitarian pluralism and incompatible with democracy as we understand it.

An element of paternalism is also evident in a more recent model of toleration, in which humans are deemed entitled, perhaps even free, to err and live in their error at their own responsibility. This is the "toleration" of one, who confident in his possession of the single and absolute truth, out of his largeness of heart and anxiety to avoid extremism is prepared to show tolerance for the followers of "false" ideas. The three monotheisms, for example, each zealous for its own truth and dismissive of any other belief system, are capable under certain social circumstances of adjusting to this degree of condescension. There are political ideologies, too, that in the name of democracy are prepared to adopt the same tolerant stance. But an egalitarian pluralism would be ill-advised to build its foundations on this sort of toleration, the ultimate aspiration of which is religious, ideological or political uniformity. This paternalistic tolerance may or may not waive the use of force. It is no coincidence that in many languages, the verb "to suffer" is a synonym for "to tolerate." Genuine toleration, by contrast, is willing to accept the other—with all that other's differences and strangeness—as intrinsically of equal value to anyone else. It will likewise make room for opinions that diverge from the majority consensus and for lifestyles that disregard the accepted norm. All are legitimate and deserving of respect and understanding as long as they do not violate the law and the right of others to their own peculiarities. No goodwill is required for this type of toleration: it is the natural right of every individual and group to be accorded respect and recognition. The quality of toleration can be tested in specific circumstances, when it may get into difficulties. To bear with opinions and behavior that are part of the norm is no challenge: it is when one's gorge rises and one's instincts scream that true tolerance shows itself—or fails to do so. In the famous words attributed to Voltaire: "I disagree with everything you have said, but I shall defend with my life your right to say it." Another quality that is necessary in a pluralist and tolerant society is the willingness to open oneself to uncertainty. To assume that any opinion differing from mine deserves attention and respect is in essence to allow that it may contain a measure of justice and truth. I can be profoundly sure of the truth and justice of my own way and yet still remain open-minded enough to constantly re-examine my own position. Tolerance also demands the courage to admit a mistake. A great deal of honesty is needed to admit the truth of a rival opinion and to alter one's own accordingly, as the poet Yehuda Amichai puts it: From the place where we are right flowers will never grow, it is tread and hard like a backyard, but doubts and love make the world loose like a mole, like plough.

Another question that arises is the one that puzzled Spinoza and is currently the subject of much debate in Western society, since the events of 9/11 in particular. Should one show tolerance towards intolerance and towards those who are intolerant of others? Such intolerance includes, for example, demands to curtail freedom of conscience and speech; xenophobic nationalist propaganda; incitement against minorities, the weak, or minority groups. One definition of democracy holds that it must not restrict any expression of opinion that is not translated into actual violations of democratic practice, or that does not incite such violations. A dissenting definition argues that tolerance ends when tolerance ends, that is, anyone not prepared to show tolerance for other people and other opinions forfeits the right to tolerance towards himself and his opinions.[18]

HUMANIST CULTURE

The classical culture of Greece and Rome was markedly homocentric. Its thought, literature, painting, sculpture and architecture all evince a high regard for man, for his mind and body, for his beauty and physical strength, a regard that is nonetheless tempered by a vivid awareness of his limitations. Humans are frequently depicted in dealings with the gods, the contrast pointing up their slight physique and feeble powers but, at the same time, the grandeur of spirit that gives them the boldness to confront these mighty beings. In the realm of the intellect, Greeks and Romans pursued penetrating and far-ranging philosophical enquiry and produced superb poetry and drama in their efforts to develop and establish human reason but at the same time they never neglected or belittled physical culture. The Greek city states proudly competed against each other in the Olympic Games. Christianity, especially in medieval times, when the Church was at the zenith of its power and authority, took a very different view. It never tired of rehearsing man's nothingness, his dependence on God's mercy, and the worthlessness of the physical body. Man's true essence, thundered the priest, resided in his immortal soul, which in turn resided in the lap of God, once the body was dead and rotten. Although artists took their lead from Church doctrine, the might and immensity of medieval cathedrals, the power of their murals, carvings and relief, and the radiant beauty of their stained-glass windows—all evidence of the extraordinary summits attained by medieval artistic endeavor—demonstrate the grandeur of the human spirit as much as they celebrate the glory of Mother Church. As feudalism declined, the hegemony of the Church weakened, particularly in Italy, which had remained closest to classical civilization and culture. A new wind set in, a secular wind, bringing back the humanism of the classical age. It was called the Renaissance, the rebirth.[19]

Renaissance Culture

Taking root in Italy in the fourteenth and fifteenth centuries, this rejuvenated, yet centuries-old vision of man and humanity spread quickly to the rest of Europe. The doctrinally dictated Christian denigration of man was pushed aside in favor of a reinterpretation of the ideas of classical Greece and Rome. Renaissance people took pride in their homocentric outlook, in the value they placed on the life of the individual, the grandeur of the human spirit, and the power of human reason. Their vision found magnificent expression in philosophy, painting, sculpture, architecture, fiction, and poetry, in one of the greatest flowerings of art and thought to which the human spirit has ever risen. Architecture proclaimed the noble aspirations of the human mind, not its vacuity in relation to God. Painters and sculptors depicted the human body with love and pride, displaying its grace and strength. Interweaving the mythological tales of the Old and New Testaments with those of classical Greece and Rome, they rendered their revered heroes and heroines in human dimensions. They revived the classical tradition of representing the gods (now the one God) in the image and likeness of man. Poetry and stories were composed in a language the people could understand, in vernacular Italian instead of the Latin favored by the medieval church, and dealt with secular life, from the daily rounds of the author's contemporaries to mocking exposures of ministers of government and church, exposing

their deep-rooted venality, greed, and readiness to exploit their positions. The genius of the Italian Renaissance's shining stars—Dante,
Boccaccio, Brunelleschi, Da Vinci, Michaelangelo, and hundreds
more—has transcended every century since, including our own.

In the natural sciences the Renaissance also took enormous strides
forward, in the process defying the hitherto-unchallenged authority of
the Church and its intractable dogma. Disdaining the need for truth to
be sanctified, they conducted their own observations and research, from
which they began to compose a new understanding of the structure of
the universe. Basing its doctrine on the Holy Writ and other religious
traditions, the Church had decreed that the Earth was at the center of
the universe, that the Sun and other known heavenly bodies revolved
around the Earth, but Copernicus, Galileo, and other astronomers observed that the opposite was the case and said so. Many scientists paid
with their freedom or their lives for assailing the ecclesiastical preroga-
tive of knowledge, as well as for daring to turn a new page in scientific
exploration. To their pioneering bravery we owe the foundations of our
modern science.

In this progress of ideas, Italian Jewry played an active part, not in
the plastic arts to which they contributed little, but in literature, philosophy, and science. Immanuel of Rome, one of the greatest of Hebrew
poets, lived in the fourteeenth century, a contemporary of Dante and
deeply influenced by him. He applied forms from Italian verse to secular Hebrew poetry and even composed in Italian. He may even have
influenced contemporary Italian culture, as the twentieth-century poet,
Sha'ul Chernikhovsky, claims:

> [Immanuel] is one of our greatest poets and certainly the greatest to come
> from Italian Jewry. . . . He is also the only poet of ours that we know of from
> the Renaissance period, from its very early days indeed—his poetry is full of
> the influence of one of the greatest poets of all time [Dante], an influence
> he absorbed directly. If he himself was not one of the instigators of the Re-
> naissance, he may have been one of a circle of Jews who certainly were
> among the creators of that cultural ferment, Jews whose notable and out-
> standing work came to light only after Immanuel's death. Burckhardt says
> that "The literary activity of Italian Jews was intense and widely known and
> of considerable influence on other Italians, not an influence to be dismissed
> lightly."[20]

Immanuel's poetry fuses two traditions: the Hebrew poetry of Spanish
Jewry and Italian Renaissance poetry. As Hebrew poets had done for
generations, he used a wide variety of forms, including sacred verse,

poems of glory to God, dirges, and prayers, but his work is also suffused with the spirit of the Renaissance, with frivolity, love of life, and delight in sensual joys. He wrote drinking songs, love poems, humorous poems, even daring to poke gentle fun at religion and sacred matters. One of his sonnets, *Eden and Tophet* (*perhaps modeled on a contemporary French tale, Oxanne et Nicolette*) pokes fun at sacred cows, mockingly abdicating the promise of an idealized next world in favor of the love of beautiful women:

> Having thought the matter over deeply,
> Eden would be horrible and *Tophet* preferable
> For *Tophet* has honeycomb dripping with nectar
> And every pretty girl shining with lust.
>
> What good is an Eden with no loving women in it,
> Only ugly ones uglier than sin,
> And old lichen-covered hags—
> What a misery-making company!
>
> What good are you to me Eden if you collect
> Only the misshapen and the disgusting?
> Having given the matter thought—none!
>
> No, *Tophet,* you're the place for grace and beauty
> Where every girl looks her best
> Each one more desirable than the next.

As Chernikhovsky says of this sonnet: "It is enough for Immanuel to be surrounded by ugly women 'uglier than sin' to turn Eden into a *Tophet* for him, and vice versa; all the torments of *Tophet* are as nothing if the place has pretty girls in it."[21] The Renaissance stimulated Italian Jews to cultivate the art of writing and, only a short time after the invention of printing, to establish printing houses capable of producing a handsome page of printed Hebrew. The community was distinguished by physicians of high repute and by important scholars in medicine and astronomy. There were poets and authors, too, as well as composers of music, singers, and instrumentalists, stage actors, and other theater people. This period witnessed an outburst of thriving humanist art and scholarship that laid the foundations for the *Haskalah,* the Jewish movement of Enlightenment, three centuries later and was one of its chief sources of inspiration and encouragement.

When, towards the end of the sixteenth century, the religious counter-reaction set in, Renaissance culture and Italian humanism with it, went into decline but not before it had laid down a tradition and inheritance that had penetrated deeply to every part of Europe and would not be easily eradicated. No less than a cultural revolution had been achieved, primarily in the blow it inflicted upon the absolute authority of church and organized religion, and in its insistence that man rather than God was "the proper study of mankind." The values of secularism had been exalted; affirmation of life, tolerance and toleration, the autonomy of the individual, and the beginnings of human rights. The pluralism intrinsic to human life had been acknowledged and the mindset of objective rationalist criticism recognized as vital to the progress of science. Art and literature had imbued Europeans with a new secular, human-centered spirit that a few centuries later gave us what we call the "modern period." The critical mindset, so characteristic of humanism, rose to prominence again in seventeenth-century Western Europe, in the philosophical inquiries of Francis Bacon in England and of Rene Descartes in France. Both declared the supremacy of reason and experiment as the sole route to the understanding of reality. To rely on the Holy Writ of a mystic faith was no longer acceptable. The ethics and the theory of international relations set out by the pantheist Spinoza made the same point. The breakthroughs made by these and other thinkers created the platform upon which modern science and modern thinking would develop, would have been quite unimaginable without the precedent and legacy of Italian humanism. In the seventeenth century, the seeds that Renaissance art had sown and the examples it had set sprouted with renewed vigor in an outpouring of painting, poetry and drama. In France, England, and the Netherlands, the prodigies of this reflowering, Molière, Shakespeare, Rembrandt, and so many more, reached new peaks of achievement seldom paralleled in human history.

The Enlightenment

In Western and Central Europe during the eighteenth century, humanist ideas blossomed again in the movement that came to be called the Enlightenment. Following in the footsteps of English and French thinkers of the previous century, the visionaries of the Enlightenment demanded liberal democracy, equalization of civil rights, the protection of the individual against arbitrary force of power, and the withdrawal of church and state authorities from their intrusion into and control of citizens' personal affairs. The relationship between the citizen and the state, as conceived for instance by Jean-Jacques Rousseau and other

French scholars, was that of a "social contract." Montesquieu formulated a set of principles for enlightened government that became the foundation of ninteeenth-century political theory and of the democratic governments that were first established then; this set of principles remained influential throughout the twentieth century and into the twenty-first century. Voltaire in France and Lessing, Kant, and Herder in Germany were among the famous thinkers who spoke out in praise of toleration and rationalism and were convinced that the implementation of these ideas would bring greater happiness to all elements of society. In redefining the human being's place in the world, they added another pillar to the edifice of modern homocentric thinking.

Perhaps the apogee of eighteenth-century Enlightenment's sociopolitical thought came in the last quarter of the century, first with the American's Declaration of Independence from England, then with the constitution they drew up for their society after their victory, and some years later, with the French revolutionaries' Declaration of the Rights of Man and the Citizen. These three documents were all based upon the precepts and principles of humanism. In the arts, the impact of the Enlightenment found its most movingly expression in the work of its poets—Schiller, Goethe and others—and in several composers of genius, among whom Bach and Mozart are the best-known. Bach, in particular, embodies the true spirit of Renaissance humanism, and his work makes frequent use of religious themes to express human realities.

Among the Jews of Central and Eastern Europe, the Enlightenment's ideas were met with vibrant response. Jewish thinkers, of whom the best known is Moses Mendelssohn, took an active role in developing and spreading the new concepts, and when these were translated into sociopolitical practice by the Emancipation, which in Central and Western Europe gave Jews civil rights equal to those of Christians for the first time since Christianity became an established religion, Moses Mendelssohn initiated and developed the *Haskalah,* the Jewish Enlightenment that was a direct response to the new concepts. Within its much narrower sphere, the *Haskalah* was no less revolutionary than the Enlightenment, for it revolutionized the way Jews saw themselves, the structure of their communities, their thinking, way of life and education, and every other component of Jewish life in Central and Eastern Europe. A second effect was to trigger a huge surge of interest in Jewish studies and flood of Jewish creativity in the arts and other fields. One of the channels into which this creativity poured was the expansion and rejuvenation of the Hebrew language.

Liberalism and Socialism

In sociopolitical terms, the whole of the nineteenth century is over-
shadowed by the great humanist revolutions of the late eighteenth century, the American and the French. A second transforming force was
the concomitant advances in science, technology, and industrialization.
The huge national and social movements aroused by these forces gave
humanist ideologies such a momentum that within a hundred years, the
social face of Europe and the world beyond it had altered beyond recognition.

When an English biologist, Charles Darwin, put forward the theory
of evolution, which held that forms in which the human species and
other life had developed on our planet were the end results of a very
slow process extending back billions of years, it was nothing less than a
slap in the face of the three great monotheisms. Was it not written down
in black on white, in the holiest of texts, that approximately six thousand
years ago, God created the world, together with every single species of
animal and plant in it, in just six days, and that nothing had altered
since? Like Copernicus and Galileo before him, Darwin's theories shattered the ancient foundations' of organized religion. His discoveries
brought the notion that religion is the source of authoritative knowledge
to its knees. Though Darwinism has itself evolved a great deal since it
was first propounded, the essentials that make it impossible for Christianity, Islam, and Judaism to swallow remain undisputed by the secular
world. To this day, the mullahs, rabbis, and bishops label it atheism and
a profanation of the Holy Name.

Revolutionary theory made its impact upon the social and political
spheres in the form of two new systems of thought: liberalism—the belief system underpinning capitalist democracy—and socialism, the representative of the struggle for social justice.[22] Having witnessed the
flagrant injustices perpetrated by capitalism and experienced the inhumane and deepening inequalities between rich and poor, socialism
aspired to dismantle society's class structure and put an end to exploitation and poverty.

Liberalism is the child of eighteenth-century political philosophy and,
by the nineteenth, its theory influenced the thinking of Western Europe. Its core stipulations were the freedom of the citizen and the necessity of protecting him against arbitrary government power. All men
are equal, it proclaimed, especially in relation to the law and state services. The government must act rationally and impartially, it must guarantee its citizens' personal safety and legislate just laws enshrining their

liberties and their right to lead the lives they wish, and to do so according to their own understanding and free of coercion, as long as they do not impinge on the similar rights of others. Liberalism believed in the inevitability of progress, the constant advancement of the achievements of freedom, equality, and material welfare until they would be extended to every person. It fought, for equality between all peoples and races, against the exploitation of peoples and individuals and against the slavery that was then institutionalized by many states. As for religion, liberalism held that every faith should be accorded equal status within the state. Since religion is a matter for the citizen's private conscience, every religious community should be entitled to maintain its institutions and practice its rites without state interference or intervention. Religious toleration was a cardinal principle of liberal thinking.

By the later decades of the century the main liberal freedoms were those of employment and free trade. However, the main benefits of these two freedoms were being harvested by the owners of capital, the middle and upper classes. The principle of the "liberty of the individual" left each person, even the poorest, free to fend for himself. This principle was taken to the point of even denouncing the concept of state-provided welfare, a system designed to support the weak in times of calamity or distress. While liberalism held sway and the socioeconomic structure of capitalism remained unmodified, social inequality grew ever more entrenched until the colossi of business faced a laboring population who possessed nothing, could hope for nothing, and were sunk in a shameful poverty.

In the 1830s, disappointment with the social injustice of capitalism, for all the liberal freedoms it preached, had generated the idea of socialism, the vision of a society free of the exploitation of man by man and without the huge divisions created by accumulated wealth. Socialism was direct heir to the ideas of the Enlightenment. When Robert Owen, Henry de Saint-Simon, and Charles Fourier expound its vision, it was taken for an utopia,[23] a secular response to the religious utopia that the priests prophesied would follow God's redemption of humankind. From the mid-1850s on, socialism was associated with the name of Karl Marx, the philosopher, historian, and economist who constructed the system that was later named after him. Close study of the historical trends in the development of economy and society and a thorough analysis of the structure of contemporary capitalism had convinced Marx that societal revolution was inevitable and that it would bring an egalitarian, classless society in its wake. While the exploited workers themselves would implement the revolution, they would need the leadership of intellectuals who had seen the destination towards which history was moving. After Marx, other thinkers proposed the possibility that socialism might be accomplished through democratic channels, without recourse to revolutionary violence.

The socialist idea spread rapidly, for workers' associations and political parties saw in it a crusading ideology that they could incorporate in their battle for improved conditions. Throughout the latter decades of the nineteenth and the first half of the twentieth century, the socialist struggle for improvement of workers' conditions achieved successive victories. One industrialized state after another yielded to the demand for reform of wages and conditions. Legislation was amended, new laws granting and protecting workers' rights were passed, and the institutions of a welfare state became the norm in much of Western Europe.

An extreme wing of the socialist movement, led by the Russian revolutionary Vladimir Lenin, argued that the exploiting classes would never willingly cede their power; hence, it saw no choice other than to install a "dictatorship of the proletariat" to force through the desired reforms. Lenin thought that once the fundamental societal transformation was accomplished, the dictatorship would give way to a free classless society, able to create the resources to meet the whole population's needs without recourse to exploitation. In 1917, his party, the Communists, seized power in Russia and converted its empire into a federation of "autonomous" socialist republics, the Soviet Union.[24] The regime it set in place was totalitarian and all individual freedoms and human rights were suppressed. But the promised reform of workers' working conditions and welfare was indeed made a practical reality.

In the years following the Second World War, Communist regimes took control of several states in Europe, Asia, and South America. The Soviet Union's magnificent part in the defeat of Nazism had given it a halo of glory all over the world. In Asia and in Africa, people living under colonial regimes, and in South America, peoples suffering under corrupt capitalist-military dictatorships, the Communist ideology became very popular, and the Soviet Union was considered as a supporting power in the struggle against the oppressive regimes. By the end of the 1980s, seventy years of repressing freedom, human rights and individual initiative had brought the Soviet Union itself to a point of collapse and dismemberment. This has not stopped the genuine humanism that animates socialism from continuing to carry the hopes of millions around the world for a better, just society. Indeed, social democratic parties have recently been elected to power in some European states, indicating the continued desire for socialist reform.

Those two great offshoots of humanism, liberalism and socialism, both of which set civil and economic freedom as their chief goals, have failed to build anywhere that free, equal and just society that would realize the ideal of liberty for all. Nevertheless, the struggle for those goals has improved the conditions of life for people all over the world to an undeniable degree, in some cases beyond recognition. With all its severe shortcomings and crisis points, the conditions of life for most people in today's world are surely a vast improvement on conditions a hundred or two hundred years ago.

Existentialism and Psychoanalysis

Another great secular humanist idea that greatly influenced the twentieth century was existentialism. We have already mentioned Søren Kierkegaard, who argued the impossibility of our ever understanding the relationship between man and God, and also Kierkegaard's heirs, who made the absence of God a presupposition of their thinking. For the leaders of the existentialist school, in particular the French philosopher-writers Jean-Paul Sartre and Albert Camus, it was a given that man's creation had neither reason nor purpose. "Projected" into the world, man had no choice but to accept responsibility for his own acts and, furthermore, to accept the fact that he must die and perhaps utterly vanish from the world. Sartre and Camus recognized and explored the way in which the non-existence of God and the possibility of his own non-existence fill man with an existential anxiety that he tries to conquer by forming relationships with others, but such relationships are impossible or, at the very least, extremely problematic, and so it comes about that modern humans find themselves alienated from themselves and from each other, strangers in their own world. In order to cope with this strangeness and alienation, they must find a value-system that will give meaning and worth to existence, because the one proffered by organized religion—given the non-existence of its God— has been exploded once and for all. Yet we need values, for without them we are defenseless against the absurdity, illogicality and meaninglessness of an existence that has been given to us unaccompanied by predetermined values or any explanation for our presence. Existentialism shoulders us, and us alone, with the responsibility for forming our own values and finding reason for our own lives.

Other humanist branches of thought that have left their deep impression on twentieth-century culture are the various schools of psychology and psychotherapy, all of them the offspring of the work and discoveries of Joseph Breuer and Sigmund Freud in the late nineteenth and early twentieth centuries. In response to people looking for an explanation of their problems and of the nature of individual existence, these schools, each in its own way, give the same answer: study yourself. At bottom, all the psychologies regard experience and experiences as a key determinant of individual and social behavior and attribute many of the difficulties of individual life to the refusal to acknowledge some of these experiences and work through them. Some mental processes, say psychologists, may be unconscious but are nonetheless decisive for the way we behave and the life choices we make. Different schools regard different factors as most critical. Freud thought that human mind was animated by sexual energies, which he named collectively "the libido." Alfred Adler stressed the centrality of interpersonal relations within social structures, particularly that of the family. Common to all schools was the tenet that humans themselves, either knowingly and purposefully or unknowingly and unconsciously, determine the nature and quality of their existence.

An outstanding exception to the prevalent humanism of psychology, were the theories of Carl Jung, who found mystic and irrational elements in human mentality. He talked about a "collective unconscious," which he held to have its source in humankind's acquired experience of history as a whole and to be passed down, by inheritance, to each individual. Subsumed in the human mind, said Jung, were collective memories that give rise to cultural structures he called "archetypes." One locus for these encoded collective memories is the complex mythologies that so many disparate cultures have created.

All the ideologies and schools of thought discussed in this section—liberalism and socialism of the late nineteenth century, that saw humans as first and foremost social beings; existentialism, which sees humans continually struggling for meaning to their lives; and psychology, which takes as seminal the struggle with and within the self, laid down the lines of thinking that the twentieth century proceeded to develop. All place humans at the center of the world's scheme of things; all are confident that, with their courage and personal resources, humans have the capacity to face up to any challenge the world might throw at them.

The Jews of the late nineteenth and early twentieth centuries responded eagerly to these great movements in thought and politics. Jewish nationalist and socialist organizations sprang up under the influence of European nationalisms and socialism, as we shall see later. Other Jews played roles, even leadership roles, in the wider, non-sectarian movements. Karl Marx, the father of socialism, was a Jew by birth;

Moses Hess, Ferdinand Lassalle, Eduard Bernstein, and others were among the leading thinkers of social democracy. The creator-discoverer of psychoanalysis, Sigmund Freud, was a Jew, as was one of the greatest physicists of the modern period, Albert Einstein, who revolutionized physics and cosmology and whose work forms the basis of so many crucial later achievements, up to the present moment. The thought and work of all these thinkers were affected to a greater or lesser degree by their Jewishness.

Modern Culture

The great social and national struggles of the nineteenth century and its new ideologies struck a deep chord in the arts of the time. Realistic trends in literature, music, and the plastic arts strove to represent the sufferings and terrible living conditions of ordinary people. At the same time, Romantics declaimed the cultural uniqueness of each people celebrating their national myths and legends. In every sphere and genre, art rose to peaks of achievement, contributing to the magnificence of humanist culture. New forms, subject matters, and genres were developed by a range of innovators across the whole field of artistic endeavor. In literature, Tolstoy, Dostoevsky, Balzac, and Flaubert; in the theater, Chekhov and Ibsen; in poetry, Heine, Rilke, Byron, Keats, and Shelley; in music, Beethoven, Brahms, Berlioz, and Wagner; in painting, Renoir, Cézanne, Van Gogh, and Gauguin, to mention only a few.

By the close of the century, a new cultural movement had begun to take shape, later to be called "modernism." This is a blanket term used to cover a great number of trends, styles and schools, all of which made their mark in the late nineteenth and the first half of the twentieth centuries. The movements' uniting characteristic was a revulsion against the realism that demanded that reality, especially social reality, be depicted objectively and in all-inclusive detail. "Modernism" retorted that such a demand was impossible to achieve since every artist inevitably perceives reality from a partial and subjective point of view. The point of art was not *what* it depicted, but *how*. Modernism began in the conception that art is an esthetic entity, expressing only itself, "art for art's sake" was a famous catchphrase.

The movement known as modernism began in the 1870s in painting. The Impressionists, prominent among them Renoir, Manet, Degas, Toulouse-Lautrec, began rendering natural and household scenes in a very subjective manner, painting what they saw just as they saw it at the moment, and not as it was supposed to be "in reality." On their heels came the Expressionists[26] and other modernist painters and schools, including Van Gogh, Cézanne, Gauguin, Munch, and others, who depicted their chosen subjects according to their own deeply subjective and idiosyncratic perception. As the twentieth century advanced, the direct surface relation between a painting and what it depicted altered greatly and various abstract painting styles appeared. One of the earliest of these was Cubism, which rendered its subjects in geometric shapes. Cézanne had said that "Everything is spheres, cubes and cones"; other artists such as Picasso, Kandinsky, Miró, and Klee developed different styles and forms with which to depict the world as they saw it. Surrealism broke even further from the world of reality and set out to depict the landscape of the mind, including the content of dreams. Dalí, Magritte, and Chagall are some of the best-known Surrealists.

The same determination to explore new territory is found in literature. Joyce, Proust, Genessin, Virginia Woolf, S. Yizhar, and others, plumbing the depths of consciousness, also explored the world from the viewpoint of a deeply subjective and idiosyncratic perception. Kafka, Beckett, Borges, Agnon, A. B. Yehoshua, and many others trod the path of the fantastical, of dream-logic and surreality. Music, theater, cinema, and other art forms were also caught up by these ideas.

Artists found more ideas and inspiration in the twentieth century's new sciences and philosophies. A deep awareness of psychology is apparent in their work, as is a consciousness of the social difficulties that ordinary people suffer. A third dominant theme is the struggle to find a meaning to existence, the struggle with solitariness, with the sense of being alienated from this world and a stranger in it, in other words, with the whole complex of existentialist ideas. Yet while the philosophy may be in essence pessimistic, the art stimulated by it depicts the courage humans display in withstanding their inevitable solitariness and alienation, and in finding resources to cope with existential anxiety and the fear of death.

One of twentieth-century culture's most remarkable claims to fame belongs to its architects. The challenge set them was to build housing for the masses on an unprecedented scale. Their successful response was to find dignified, but relatively inexpensive solutions, based on a profound understanding and awareness of the structure, the relationship of the building to the environment, the interaction of humans with the building, while maintaining high esthetic standards. Walter Gropius, Mies van der Rohe, Le Corbusier, Frank Lloyd Wright, Oscar Niemeyer and others rose to this formidable challenge in the true spirit of democracy.

While the daring and originality of modern art's explorations in form and subject, and the depth and complexity of the ideas animating it characterized one line of its development, a secondary but perhaps no less important line was the exploration into folk and popular art. This expanded the content, horizons and quality of mainstream art, bringing the diversity and energy of popular art back into the previously esoteric world of "proper" art. In this way, popular art was given its rightful place as an important expression of human creativity, of deep and high quality, without making it any the less popular or understandable. Here, too, art was energized and inspired by the growth of democracy, democratic values, and popular power. The whole development of jazz is case in point: it emerged from the realm of popular art and yet its artists became some of the greatest in the United States and elsewhere—from Jelly Roll Morton and Louis Armstrong through George Gershwin, Glenn Miller, and Benny Goodman to Ella Fitzgerald and Duke Ellington. As well as music, popular art's greatest successes came in painting, theater, and dance and, above all, in the arts of cinema and television. Later came pop art, best known by the painting of Roy Lichtenstein, Jasper Johns, Richard Rauschenberg, Andy Warhol, and others. The peaks to which nineteenth-century operetta was elevated are especially notable. Operetta was transformed into the twentieth century's musical, a framework that embraced almost every style of music—jazz, pop, mainstream, rock, and more—and within which scriptwriters and songwriters, directors, choreographers and stage designers, not to mention the performers, step by step constructed a magnificent and outstandingly popular art form.

One of the great mechanisms driving modern culture has been the extraordinary expansion of mass communications. Art forms that till the late nineteenth century had been the preserve of small elites became the subject and object of popular demand. Literature, poetry, drama, painting, and sculpture all found a new class of consumer, but most characteristic of all to the new twentieth century were the new arts made possible by scientific invention and technological advances. Photography, cinema, and television attracted audiences in the tens of millions. But just as significant was the fact that these new means of self-expression were easily available, enabling many to engage in artistic creativity. Millions made one art form or another their hobby with the result, too, that audiences became better informed and more discriminatory: the major new art forms attracted huge new audiences, who knew how to appreciate what they saw and heard.

In this expansion and refinement of modern and popular culture, many Jews played renowned and leading roles, especially those who risked working in the wider, non-Jewish society and became absorbed in their host nation's culture. They made their names in every sphere and genre of the arts and sciences, and in many cases achieved international fame. A relatively large number have won the highest formal accolade the world awards, the Nobel Prize. The civilization and culture of twentieth century would be much the poorer without the writings of Franz Kafka, Herman Baruch, Shmuel-Yoseph Agnon, Saul Bellow, Primo Levi, and many others; the music of Gustav Mahler, Arnold Schoenberg, George Gershwin and Leonard Bernstein; the paintings of Marc Chagall, Chaim Soutine and Amadeo Modigliani; the films of directors too numerous to mention (they range from Sergei Eisenstein to Woody Allen). Their work all shows the imprint of their Jewish background. Modernism worked in the opposite direction too, greatly influencing Jewish culture, invigorating the new Hebrew-speaking and Israeli culture, and the Jewish culture of the Diaspora. Important contributions to many spheres of Western culture have been made by a range of Israelis, authors such as S. Yizhar, David Shakhar, Yitzhak Orpaz, Avraham B. Yehoshua, Amos Oz; poets such as Yehuda Amichai, Natan Zach; and Israeli artists and scholars in a plethora of other fields have likewise played a part in the development of Western culture.

A Pluralist and Humanist Culture

The progress and successes of modern civilization rest on the achievements of humanism and humanists in all preceding generations. Twentieth-century modernism entrenched the qualities and values of nineteenth-century liberalism and democratic socialism, the openness to multiformity, the aspiration of raising the quality of life for as many people as possible, and above all, the penetrating critique of society, however much modern artists may profess that art expresses only itself. In conquering the West, modern thought and art gave it new cultural norms, causing totalitarianisms of both the right and the left to reject modernist art as "decadent." By nature, any totalitarianism, religious or secular, must demand uniformity, unanimity, and unchallenged assent to the regime's goals and policy. Modernist thinking nurtures pluralism, a critical eye, and a variety of form and content, values that only a humanist and secular democracy is apt to accept, support, and encourage.

In this chapter, I have traced a bare outline of the values and riches of secular humanism; I have done no more than skim its surface. It is a culture and scheme of values of vast dimensions, power and ramifications, embracing as it does every national culture and, for they are major contributors to human civilization, the values of every religion. The genius and greatness of Jewish culture and religion is part of this universe of secular humanism; within it, for Jews, Jewish culture naturally takes pride of place. Jewish culture embraces both the Jewish religion, with its roots stretching back to every generation of Jews, and to every land in which Jews have lived, and the culture of those Jews who have lived outside the bounds of rabbinic authority and who, because of this, could extend Judaism's and Jewry's horizons to every corner of the globe. Across the world, these non-rabbinic Jews continue to stimulate and expand Jewish culture.

3

Jewish Identity

CENTURIES PASSED AND JEWISH IDENTITY REMAINED A SETTLED, UN-
questioned thing, as obvious to the Jews themselves as to their neighbors. Under *halacha,* a Jew is defined as one born to a Jewish mother
or someone who had *halachically* converted, but in practice a Jew is
anyone accepted as a member of an acknowledged Jewish community
and who in turn accepts the authority of the religio-communal leadership on all issues pertaining to lifestyle and opinion. This religio-communal acceptance is understood to include acceptance into the corpus
of the Jewish people. Those who saw themselves as Jews and are seen
by others as Jews, were thus Jews: This is their religion and their people.
An identity as self-evident as this was possible only when there was a
unitary Judaism. And indeed, for centuries, Judaism was such a unity, a
strict and tightly bound religion comprising three entities: the God of
Israel, the Torah of Israel, and the people of Israel, that is, their faith,
their law, and their self-definition as a people. This unity was rigorously
maintained by one sole and acknowledged law-making authority.

True, there were severe problems with the concept and practice of
such a unitary notion. It was born in controversy and sustained through
considerable dissent. There were disparities of practice and interpretation between communities and across periods of time; from time to
time, two or even three law-making centers vied for authority. But none
of this made any impact on the tri-partite unity of faith, law and membership of a single people comprising all Jewish communities everywhere. Thus, as long as this unity could be sustained, there was no real
problem of Jewish identity. But once this unity had been broken and
each constituent achieved its own autonomy, Judaism became a multi-
faceted, pluralistic religion. Almost immediately, the issue of authenticity raised its head: Which Judaism is the true one and who is a true Jew?
What does it mean to be Jewish and what makes a man or woman a
Jew? In other words, the whole issue of Jewish identity became subject
to scrutiny. This last question, what makes a man or woman a Jew—is

by no means a simple one. We have touched upon it in earlier chapters, but here we shall examine its various aspects, carefully analyzing how this question has developed over time and the diverse ways in which it has been addressed. Finally, I shall offer my own answer to it.

NAMES AND APPELLATIONS BY WHICH THE JEWS HAVE BEEN KNOWN

We Jews are known by a variety of names and appellations, all originating in myth and many still in use today. But in fact designations such as "Semites," "Hebrews," "Israelis," and "Jews" are by no means synonymous: rather, each represents a facet of the way in which Jewish identity has been perceived.

Semites

"Semite" and "Semitic" both have their origin in "Shem," one of the three sons of Noah. As the book of Genesis tells it (Ch. 6–10), only Noah and his family survived the Flood, which is presented as God's way of eliminating the whole population that then inhabited the world so that He could start humanity all over again, The three sons of Noah— Shem, Ham, and Japheth, were the forefathers of the whole human race. According to Genesis, Shem fathered the peoples of Asia, to the extent to which it was then known: "[He was] the father of all the children of Eber" (Gen. 10:21). Japheth fathered the peoples of Europe, and Ham the peoples of Africa. The greater part of Shem's descendants were held to be the inhabitants of Aram-Naharayim (Mesopotamia), today's Iraq; biblical myth deemed the Canaanites inhabiting the Mediterranean coastlands to be descended from Ham, even though their ethnicity and language proclaimed them descendants of Eber and therefore Shem-ites (Semites). A later Jewish legend, *aggada,* exalts Shem and Eber as among the Jewish people's righteous forefathers, tzaddikim, for providing study houses to teach Torah and moral conduct (Gen. Rabba 62–63). Shem thus stands for the Jewish Torah, sometimes as opposed to Japheth, who represents the wisdom of the Greeks. But nowhere in the Jewish sources, early or late, do we find "Shem" used to designate the Jews as a whole. "Semitic" was the term selected by eighteenth-century linguists to designate the family of languages (Akkadian, Ugaritic, Aramaic, Hebrew, Arabic, Amharic, and others) spoken by the peoples of Western Asia, the biblical descendants of Shem.

It took nineteenth-century Europe's theory of the world's races to apply the term specifically to the Jews. This was the theory, elaborated upon with particular interest by the Germans, which held the Aryan race, the ancestral race of most European peoples, to be superior to all others and consequently held all non-Aryan races, including the Semites and particularly the Jews, to be the offspring of inferior racial stock. In its vicious application to the Jews in particular, the theory came to be known as anti-Semitism, using "Semite" as a synonym for "Jew." So Shem survives to this day as the forebear of a family of languages and as the object of racial contempt.

Hebrews

"Hebrew" is a transliteration, via Greek into English, of the biblical word *ivri*, which in turn is the adjective formed from the name Eber, who was a descendant of Shem and one of the forefathers of Abraham the Hebrew (Gen. 11:15–17). As the exploration of the roots of "Semite" shows, late Jewish tradition honors Shem and Eber as among the forefathers in righteousness of the Jewish people, but there are good grounds for preferring the explanation that *"ivri"* goes back not to the man, Eber, but to the preposition *ever,* meaning "across," "on the other side," and referring to peoples whose roots are on the other side of the River Euphrates and who at some time or other crossed over to the western side, especially to the lands bordering the Mediterranean Sea. We have evidence from the book of Joshua: "Thus said Yahweh, God of Israel: Your fathers dwelt on the other side of the river in old time . . . and I took your father Abraham from the other side of the river and led him throughout all the land of Canaan . . ." (Josh. 24:2–3). Indeed, Abraham is called "Abraham the Hebrew *(ha'ivri)*" (Gen. 14:13).

In most instances when it is mentioned in the Bible, "the Hebrew" or "the Hebrews" is a name that other peoples, especially the Egyptians and Philistines, use for the Israelites as well as the name that the Israelites apply to themselves in their dealings with these two peoples. In Genesis, Joseph tells the Egyptians that the land he comes from, Canaan, is "the land of the Hebrews" (40:15), while the Egyptians themselves call Joseph "a Hebrew," and "a Hebrew slave" (39:14,17) and "a Hebrew young man" (41:12). Exodus tells of Pharaoh's daughter's maidservant who finds the basket containing the baby Moses floating in the Nile and who identifies him as "one of the Hebrew children" and fetches "a nurse of the Hebrew women" for him (Exod. 2:6–7). Moses himself, before returning to his people, sees "an Egyptian smiting a Hebrew" (ibid., 11) and later "two men of the Hebrews strove together" (Ibid. 13). Later still, he appears before Pharaoh with the demand that he let his people go, a demand delivered in the name of "God of the Hebrews" (3:18; 5:3; 7:16; 9:1). In Samuel, we find the Philistines calling the Israelites "Hebrews": "The Philistines heard the noise of the shout, they said, 'What means the noise of this great shout in the camp of the Hebrews?'" (1 Sam. 4:6); "for the Philistines said, 'Lest the Hebrews make them swords or spears'" (13:19); "Then said the princes of the Philistine, 'What do these Hebrews here?'" (29:3), and so on. The prophet Jonah introduces himself to his fellow ship passengers as "I am an Hebrew and I fear Yahweh, the God of Heaven" (Jon. 1:9). When biblical law wants to distinguish the legal status of an Israelite and non-Israelite slave, "Hebrew slave" and "Canaanite slave" are the terms it uses (Exod. 21). This dichotomizing context is almost the only one in which the Bible uses "Hebrew" or "Hebrews" as a name for the Israelites, which leads one to suppose that this is what the Egyptians and Philistines, two non-Semitic neighbors, called them. At one time, some scholars suggested that the origin of *ivri* lies in the Egyptian "*habiru*," meaning slaves or inferiors, but the first notion is now generally accepted. Modern scholars agree that *ivri* designates the geographical origins and language of the peoples settled along the Mediterranean's eastern shore, Ammonites and Moabites, whom tradition credits with being descendants of Lot, Abraham's nephew; Edomites, descendants of Esau, Jacob's twin and grandson to Abraham; the peoples of Canaan, including the Israelites; and those of the territory to the north of the Israelites, Tyreans, and Sidonites, Hebrews by both extraction and according to their spoken and written vernacular.

Nor is *ivri* any more common in the Mishna and Talmud and it remains rare into far later periods. Even the Hebrew language was usually designated as "the holy tongue." Not before the nineteenth century CE was "Hebrews" adopted to designate all Jews. It was the idea and particular practice of *Haskalah*, Hebrew Enlightenment, scholars and authors who felt that "Jew" carried some negative connotations; indeed, in most European languages it had become more or less a term of abuse. For example, in Russian *zhid* (from *yehudi*) was an insult, whereas in polite speech the term for a Jew was *yevrei* (from *ivri*). In English, according to the *Oxford Dictionary,* a Jew is also "a person considered to be parsimonious or to drive a hard bargain."[1] The Jewish national liberation movement also preferred "Hebrews," feeling that it linked the Jewish people back to their ancient land of origin and their early history, whereas "Jew" bore the hallmark of exile. The name "Hebrews" also deliberately distinguished those Jews who had resettled in the ancient homeland from those in the Diaspora. Today, however, the appellation "Hebrew" is seldom used to describe the people, surviving mostly as the name for the language. To distinguish the citizens of the State of Israel from their Diaspora brethren the noun "Hebrews" has been supplanted by "Israelis."

Israelites and Israelis

Throughout recorded history, from the Bible and later sources down to our own day, the commonest name used to specify the Jews as a people is "Israel," the "Children of Israel," the "people of Israel," "Israelites," or the latter's modern equivalent, "Israelis." Our myth-makers tell us (Gen. 32:28) that Yisra-el was the name bestowed on Jacob, grandson of Abraham the Hebrew, by a mysterious figure of enormous strength with whom Jacob had wrestled an entire night. This figure, depicted in some versions of the story as an angel, gave Jacob this name "For you have striven [*sarita*] with God and with men and have prevailed." Jacob's twelve sons were the forefathers of the twelve tribes that constituted the people of Israel. Jacob's grandfather Abraham had other sons apart from Isaac, as well as grandsons, and they also fathered whole peoples: His firstborn son Ishmael, by his concubine Hagar, was to become the progenitor of all the Arabs. Then came his second son Isaac, by Abraham's wife Sarah, from whom the people of Israel trace their descent. Isaac had twins, Jacob and Esau; the latter is the forefather of the Edomite, but it was the sons of Jacob who together fathered the people called by Jacob's new "God-given" name, the people of Israel. We may see this new name, therefore, as indicative of a process of selection from among Abraham's descendants, ending finally in the choice of the sons of Jacob to be the people who would sanctify themselves to the worship of Yahweh and who would take the name of the last of their three great ancestors. Indeed, from this point on in Genesis, the text calls them *bnei yisrael,* variously translated as "the children of Israel," "the sons of Israel," or "the Israelites." Genesis goes on to recount how they went down into Egypt (42:5) and lists the names of "the children of Israel who came to Egypt, Jacob, and his sons" (46:8). From this moment in the story up until the last book of the Bible, and from that last book throughout all subsequent ages and changes the collective is usually called "the people of Israel" and henceforth, that became the appellation by which our people identified themselves.

The land upon which the people of Israel settled is usually referred to in the Bible as the "Land of Canaan"; only very rarely does it use the name the "Land of Israel" and then it is usually denoting the Kingdom of Israel or those parts of the land situated outside the frontiers of Judah. In the book of Ezekiel, for example, it says: "Judah and the Land of Israel, they were your merchants" (27:17). The first book of Samuel does use the phrase to mean the whole land: "No smith was to be found in all the land of Israel" (13:19), but the book of Kings, like the book of Ezekiel, uses the phrase only in the sense of the Kingdom of Israel, as does Chronicles on a number of occasions. It was not before the mishnaic and talmudic periods that "Land of Israel" came to signify the whole land, and that has remained its meaning down to our own time.

The use of the term "Torah of Israel" to mean the laws of the religion is also a relatively late designation. The Bible refers to the laws as the "Torah of Moses" or occasionally the "Torah of Yahweh." By contrast, the God of the Bible is regularly called the "God of Israel"; this usage first appears during Jacob's lifetime (Gen. 33:20) and henceforth becomes one of His most frequently used titles. In our own time, in 1948 "Israel" was the name officially adopted for the state that was founded on part of the Land of Israel. It was a gesture intended to honor the Jewish people's ancient name, but in actual practice it blurred its meaning and confused the issue, for now the name "Israel" had become the name of a state and of a citizenry, not of a people or a homeland. Suddenly, it was possible to talk of Israelis who were not Jews, such as the Arab Muslim and Christian citizens of Israel.

Jews

The Hebrew word *yehudim* is now translated "Jews" but its earliest meaning was "the people of the tribe of Judah" (*yehuda*), the one out of the twelve tribes that was named for Jacob's son, Judah. After the dissolution of the united kingdom during the reign of Solomon's son, Rehoboam, the southern kingdom, made up of the tribes of Judah and of Benjamin, was called Judah (*yehuda*) and its inhabitants, Judeans (*yehudim*). In the book of Esther, Mordechai is described as an *ish yehudi*, that is, "a man of Judah," although it is then specified that he was an *ish Yemini*, "a Benjaminite" (2:5). In 2 Kings 18:28 and again in Isaiah (34:12), the language spoken by the people of Judah is called Judean (*yehudit*). After the fall of the Kingdom of Israel and the exile of its inhabitants (some assimilated with the Judeans, others were swallowed up among other peoples), Judah and the Judeans remained the sole bearers of the Israelite identity and faith, so that Israel, in its widest sense, and Judah were now one. The term "yehudi," meaning a Judean, makes its first appearance in the Bible in Jeremiah, in his prophesy after the fall of the Kingdom of Israel, and in the books composed early in the Second Temple period, primarily in the books of Esther, Ezra, and Nehemiah.

In the Second Temple period, under the rule of the Persians and then the Greeks, through the period of renewed independence under the Hashmonean kings, and then later under Roman rule, the area of the Land of Israel settled by the Judeans was known as Judah. It is from this period on that we call ourselves, and are called by other peoples and religions, *yehudim*, Judeans, especially when the reference is to individuals and not to the whole people. The Israelite religion too is now known as the "Judean religion" (*hadat hayehudit*), especially by non-Jews. The people as a whole is still usually called the "people of Israel." The phrase, "the Jewish people" (*ha'am ha'yehudi*) is an eighteenth-century invention.

As we have seen, in most European languages "Jew" was an offensive denomination. In English, as in French, Russian, and other languages, "Jew" became synonymous with a usurer or unscrupulous merchant. Whereas the English language rehabilitated the word "Jew," Frenchmen wishing to show respect spoke of *Israelites* and Russians of *yevrei* (Hebrews). From the late eighteenth century, when Jews began to involve themselves in the affairs of their non-Jewish fellow citizens, many Jews in Central Europe in particular began to regard the name "Jew" as a millstone around their necks. A "Jew" was someone immured in centuries of exile, culturally backward, isolated from the civic affairs of the citizenry. Enlightened Jews preferred the image conveyed by "Israelites," "members of the Mosaic faith," or "Hebrews." It took the Holocaust of European Jewry in the midtwentieth century to restore honor and respect to the appellation "Jew." Then, much of what for a long time had been "Israelite" became "Jewish." For example, we now talk of the Jewish people not the Israelite people. "Israel" has become firmly attached to the State of Israel and to some extent reflects an attitude of self-dissociation from Diaspora Jewry.

A Unitary Judaism

As I have observed, the substance of the Judaism that took shape in the Second Temple period and was preserved intact, if in various forms, for the next two thousand years was embodied in the strict unity of three concepts: faith, law, and self-definition as a people, or in the accepted formula of many of religious Judaism's key texts, "The Holy One Blessed be He, His law, and the people of Israel are one" (Zohar, Portion *Akharei*, 73a); this is the unity between "the God of Israel, the Torah of Israel, and the people of Israel." The Jewish faith rests on the biblical myths and has evolved within that matrix; *halacha* has its basis in the biblical code of law, upon which it has in turn elaborated. The identity of Judaism and Jewry as a people also rests on biblical mythology, but in the absence of a territorial or autonomous political base, it would have been impossible were it not for the messianic idea within Judaism, an idea also conceived in the Second Temple period and based upon scattered allusions in the Bible.

Faith

During the centuries after its birth, the Jewish faith underwent numerous and profound changes.[2] The original pagan conception of Yahweh was that He was only one, although the mightiest, in a pantheon of gods; but towards the end of the First Temple period, and especially during the Babylonian exile and the Second Temple period, the teaching of the Yahwist prophets gained ascendancy and the belief took hold that only He ruled the universe, alone, omnipotent, and transcendent. This single transcendent God was nonetheless also "a living God," said His prophets, drawing on early texts and an ancient tradition, and thus they devised Judaism's first great contribution to world civilization and culture. For whereas under the pagan conceptualization, most gods were embodiments in human form and character of the forces of nature, Judaism elevated its god above and beyond the natural world. Moreover, Yahweh is conceived of as the creator of the universe and of everything in it, including the forces of nature, and so He has total control over them. Whereas many of the pagan gods were hostile to mankind and so required various kinds of appeasement, Yahweh is beneficent, allowing humans to take possession of the land and dominion over all other forms of life.

Linked to this idea of a God who gives humans the right to decide, control, and govern the world in which they live is Judaism's second contribution: the concept of freedom. Where other civilizations saw man subject to the decrees of gods and fate, Judaism saw him as a free creature and consequently responsible for his own fate and acts. Freedom of choice entails responsibility and, given the ability to tell good from evil, a power accorded to man in one of the earliest of the Judaic myths, the Garden of Eden story, it is his duty to choose the good. If he does so, God rewards him; if he does not, he brings punishment upon himself. This means that the relations between man and God, while based upon a system of punishment and reward, are also founded in a notion of morality.

Biblical mythology does not reveal why or with what purpose God creates the world and the human race, but the Old Testament makes reference to a special purpose, concealed from human understanding, and that God establishes a special people to realize that purpose and take on this divine mission. To father this people, He chooses Abram the Hebrew, whose name He changes to Abraham (Gen. 17:5). In due course, after a screening process lasting three generations, the descendants of Abraham form the chosen people, the people of Israel. They still have to pass through generations of slavery in Egypt so they could fully learn the meaning of freedom, individual and national. For four hundred years they serve and slave there until God brings them out of Egypt and, in that act, bestows upon them the freedom they need in order to undertake and accomplish the mission that God instructs Moses, the first of His prophets, to confer upon them.

In an ultimate revelation on Mount Sinai, God gives Moses His law and commandments, which then become the code by which Israel exists. Yahweh's Torah and *mitzvot* are the good that all Israel and every man of Israel must choose; if they choose the evil, they will be cast out. The reward for the people's faithfulness is the Land of Israel, blessed and prosperous; the penalty for disloyalty is to be exiled from that promised land. Individuals are rewarded for observing the *mitzvot* with prosperity, health, long life, children, and grandchildren; their punishment for not observing the commandments is hunger, pestilence, and death (see, for example, Deut. 28).

The idea of rewarding the good and punishing the evil presumes a personal providence, a God who knows what each person does, what they intend to do, and what their thoughts are. This notion of personal providence appears to negate the premise that each person has the freedom to choose and to act on that choice, for if God can anticipate one's actions, those actions must be preordained; if so, what freedom of choice remains? Many solutions in varying formulations have been offered to this problem. "It is all in God's hands, except for the fear of God itself," said R. Hanina (BT *Brachot* 33b). "All is anticipated but the choice is there" is R. Akiba's answer (Mishna *Avot* 3:19). In other words, God can anticipate each person's choice, but the choice is still to be made by the person, and the responsibility for that choice still belongs to that individual. God's prior knowledge means that He can anticipate the choices of His creations, so that He can guard and protect them, reward, and punish their acts appropriately.

Yahweh is conceived as a merciful God, long-suffering, patient, and ready to forgive the sinner who turns from evil. For this purpose, He sent prophets to warn and counsel society. Individuals and nation alike are cautioned about the evil that will befall them if they persist in sinning and are promised blessings in profusion if they follow the path of the good. In Judaism, prophecy is a God-sent mission; the prophet calls upon the people to keep faith and promises them, both as individuals and a people, rewards for doing so and penalties for not. In the admonishments and prophesies of these bearers of God's message, the people of Israel are forewarned of the destruction of the kingdom and of their own exile, but are consoled by the promise that, after years of wandering, they will return to Zion, where a king-messiah will reestablish the kingdom. "Messiah" (*mashiach*) is merely a synonym for "king": in Hebrew, it means "an anointed person," that is, a king.

One problem that troubled the sages of Judaism from the very beginning was the promise that the righteous would thrive and the wicked would suffer. Experience proved that this divine promise did not match reality: "Why does the way of the wicked prosper?" asks Jeremiah (12:1). "This is one thing . . . He destroys the perfect and the wicked . . . the earth is given into the hands of the wicked," claims Job (9:22, 24) as he examines the nature of divine justice. The answer he receives is the answer that has served believers down to this day: We cannot know the truths that are known only to God, since our capacity to understand is limited. R. Karelitz, the *Khazon Ish*, for example, takes recourse in this age-old explanation when he accounts for the "the terrible Holocaust that overwhelmed the people of Israel during the Second World War":

> No Jew may lose the pure faith that the Creator Blessed Be He always governs the world in justice and righteousness and I shall show you what I mean by an example from life: Someone who knows nothing of the tailor's craft who sees the tailor cutting and slicing the material in front of him would certainly think that the tailor is ruining and destroying the expensive cloth placed before him, but in actuality he is making from it a new garment, which will be worth far more than the cut-up cloth.[3]

Our sages furnish two other answers, one rational, the other mystical, to the question of providence's capriciousness. The rational answer is that

"Virtue is its own reward, sin its own punishment" (Mishna *Avot* 4:2);
the mystical one is that reward and punishment will be meted out "in
the next world." In line with the beliefs held by several pagan faiths,
late Judaism assumes that the world we live in, "this world," is not the
only one, that there exists another hidden world, "the next world."
Those who in their lives keep faith with the Torah, pass on to an eternal
life in that world, in a paradise known as the Garden of Eden. Within
this second world is a region called *Geyhinnom*,[4] or Hell, where the
wicked who have not kept faith dwell in eternal torment. In this scheme
of things, man is conceived as a dual being, comprising both a material
body and a soul, which was the totality of his consciousness. The body
is transitory and is destroyed by death, while the immortal soul survives,
leaving the body after death. It is the soul that wins its reward or suffers
its punishment in "the next world." From this mystical conception of a
dual being there emerged a second idea that the deserving of the souls
would at some future time return to life in this world. The two ideas,
clothed in vivid mythical depictions, fused together to create the great
vision of a messiah who at the end of Time would arrive and resurrect
the dead, granting them renewed life. During the Second Temple period, this messianic vision was denounced and resisted by large sections
of the people, most vociferously by the Sadducees who insisted that Judaism was an earthbound faith. After the destruction of the second
Temple the vision was received as an indisputable truth, and grew into
one of the articles of the faith.

Judaism's belief system thus contained many elements introduced at
relatively late stages in the people's history. Yahweh was transcendent,
existing beyond time and place, the world's omnipotent creator and
ruler, there was no other god. He had created humans and given them
the power and the freedom to choose between good and evil. He had
established the people of Israel and chosen it; He had given Israel His
law and commandments and it was their duty to live by these; He had
sent prophets to proclaim His word and will. He watched over all His
creations, knowing their acts and thoughts, rewarding those who adhered to His law and commandments, and punishing those who did not.
It was the prophets' task to warn the people of Yahweh's wrath but also
to console them with the promise of eventual reconciliation, when at
the End of Days, God would send a messiah to redeem His people and
the whole world, and the meritorious dead would be raised to a new
life.

Thus we can see that the essentials of the Judaic faith gradually
evolved and changed over thousands of years. The conception of divin-

ity underwent radical transformation from the pagan vision of a god of humanlike substantiality to the idea of a transcendent and abstract deity incorporeal and existing only in the conceptual and spiritual realm. Prophecy also underwent changes: thought at first to be the act of predicting the future, it was reconceived as a much more complex activity, as a conduit for the Word of God. Prophets are sent by Yahweh to maintain moral values and obedience to the Torah. The premise that the good will be rewarded, the bad punished, was challenged by the reality of actual experience, and was explained by a sophisticated reference to God's omnipotent plan, one beyond the ken of man. Belief in a next world and resurrection of the dead enters Judaism at a very late stage during the Second Temple period, and the messianic vision dates from this time too.

A millennium and more after the destruction of the Second Temple, centuries after the canonization of the Talmud, many articles of faith were still open to constant modification of interpretation and wording. The sages knew very well that the Judaic faith and law were constantly changing, and even endowed transition with holiness: "Bible, Mishna, halacha, Talmud, Toseftot, aggada, even what a senior student will say to his teacher, all this was told to Moses on Sinai" (Lev. Rabba 22:1). In conclusion, not only the Bible, but also the whole of the Oral Law, the tomes of *halacha* and their commentaries, the books of aggada, even the words as yet unsaid that will be said by some scholar of the future, everything was told to Moses on Mount Sinai. The sages were fully aware that the most recent developments in Judaism dated no farther back than the Second Temple period and, moreover, originated outside the Land of Israel. This fact was even put into midrashic dress, referring to the events of the revelation at Sinai:

> The Holy One Blessed Be He held the mountain over them like a basin and said to them: "If you accept the Torah, well and good; if you do not, where you stand is where you shall be buried." Rabbi Akha bar Yaakov said: Hence, the Torah can be denounced![5] Rabba says: Even so, the generation of the days of Ahasuerus did accept it, for it is written "The Jews ordained and took upon them" (Esther 9:27). They maintained what had been earlier undertaken. (BT *Shabbat* 88a)

In other words, in Sinai the Israelites received the Torah under duress and so refused to comply with it. Only in exile in Persia during the Second Temple period, when they received it a second time, did they take and keep it.

In the twelfth century CE Maimonides (R. Moses ben Maimon) drew up a firm and precise enumeration of the principles of Jewish faith as part of his commentary on the Mishna Tractate *Sanhedrin*. He found there to be thirteen such principles: God exists; He is the one and only God; He is without material form; He is eternal; no other may be worshipped; prophesy; The prophecy of Moses; the Torah was given by God; it is immutable; God has foreknowledge of everything; reward and punishment; a messiah will come; the dead will be resurrected. The Jews argued over Maimonides' formulation for centuries. Then in the fourteenth century Khasdai Crescas, in his *Or Adonai* (*The Lord's Light*) reduced the thirteen to six: God is all-knowing; divine providence; God is almighty; prophesy; free choice; the Torah is given for a purpose. Not long after, Joseph Albo composed his *Sefer Ha'ikarim* (*Book of Principles*), which cites only three articles of faith: God exists; He has revealed Himself; reward and punishment. Albo describes the remaining pillars of the faith as truths that do not necessitate faith and he holds other essentials as non-binding teachings; however, he does insist on the absoluteness of divine law. In the same century Isaac Abrabanel dismissed any distinction between cardinal articles of faith and non-cardinal articles. In our time, it is the Maimonidean formulation that has achieved general acceptance and that is found in most prayer books. It inspired the religious poem (*piyyut*) *Yigdal Elohim Chai* attributed to Daniel ben Yehuda of Rome, and sung in the synagogue service for Sabbath and the festivals:

> Exalted be the living God and praised,
> He exists, His existence unbounded by time.
> He is one—there is no unity like His oneness.
> Inscrutable and infinite is his oneness.
> He has no semblance of body nor is He corporeal;
> Nor has His holiness any comparison.
> He preceded every being that was created—
> The first, and nothing precedes His precedence.
> He is master of the universe: to every creature,
> He demonstrates His greatness and His sovereignty.
> He granted His flow of prophesy
> To His treasured splendid people.
> In Israel none like Moses ever arose again,
> A prophet who clearly perceived His vision.
> God gave His people a Torah of truth
> By means of His prophet, the most trusted of His household.
> God will never amend nor exchange His law
> For any other one, for all eternity.

He scrutinizes and knows our hidden most secrets;
    He perceives the outcome at the very inception.
He rewards man with kindness according to his deeds;
    He returns evil to the wicked according to his wickedness.
At the End of Days, He will send our messiah
    To redeem those longing for His final salvation.
In His abundant kindness He will raise the dead,
    Blessed be forever His glorious name.

The fundamentals of Judaism have been left as such, unelaborated, unspecified: to be interpreted and construed by each believer according to his or her own lights. Yahweh, for example, may be envisioned in this or that anthropomorphic form or as an abstract cosmic reality, the spirit of the universe, as long as one believes in one God, the Creator of Heaven and Earth. The coming of the messiah may be envisaged, as did the *amora* Shmuel, as an earthbound political event: "The only difference between this world and the days of the messiah is the enslavement of kingdoms" (BT *Brakhot* 34b), or one may follow the later mythological Kabbalist conception, where his coming signals the end of the material world and the return of all human souls to their divine source, as long as one believes in the coming itself and holds oneself in readiness for it. It is not a Jewish tradition to question an individual's faith. As long as one's fellow-Jews observe the Torah and *mitzvot* and live by *halacha,* their belief in the fundamental principles of the faith may be taken for granted. Thus, the fundamentals of the Jewish religion may be said to be found in *halacha.*

Halacha

Halacha is the collective name for the host of Jewish religious laws that are also called *mitzvot,* that is, divine commandments. This collection was built up over generations by the sages and other rabbis who interpreted the biblical code of law, as they ruled on questions the Bible and its elucidators had not resolved and on any matter open to doubt. That this vast edifice should be called *halacha,* meaning "walking" or "going," harks back to Jethro's words to Moses: "You shall teach them [the Israelites] ordinance and laws, and shall show them the way wherein they must walk" (Exod. 18:20). Thus *halacha* is a guide for how we are to walk through life. Observance of *halacha* and obedience to the commandments is the appointed obligation of every believing Jew. There is no need to know the reason why; in some instances no reason may be known; nevertheless, obedience is not dependent upon the believer's will or understanding. As the sages have said: "Let not anyone say, 'I am revolted by pork' or 'I do not want to wear garments made of two fabrics,'[6] but let them say 'I want, but what is my will when my Father in Heaven has decreed what I shall do'" (*Sifra* on the portion *Kedushim*).[7] The duty of obedience to every *mitzva* is laid down by the Scriptures, which is also the proof of each *mitzva*'s validity.

As we have seen, the foundation of *halacha* is the biblical codes of law, comprising 613 *mitzvot*, traditionally divided into 248 positive commandments that all Jews are exhorted to do, and 365 negative commandments that all Jews are prohibited from doing. The kernel of the code is the Ten Commandments that, according to the myth, were heard by the Children of Israel spoken by Yahweh Himself, and were engraved on two tablets of stone by His own hand, and were given to Moses on the summit of Mount Sinai for him to convey to the waiting Israelites. Through the generations, over the course of hundreds and thousands of years, the biblical code has been developed and elaborated by commentary and elucidation into a huge edifice. Since the biblical text itself is inviolate and immutable, it was elucidated by way of Midrash, a process that started in the earliest days of the Second Temple period. The earliest recorded instance of the beginning of this process is when we are told that "Ezra had prepared his heart to expound [*li-drosh*] the law of Yahweh, and to do it and to teach in Israel statutes and judgements" (Ezra 7:10).

The Mishna was compiled by *tannas*, who used an accepted set of rules to continue the work of the biblical Midrash. As Hillel formulated them, there were seven rules; according to R. Ishmael there were thirteen; others proposed different counts. They are known as "the rules for expounding the Torah" (*Sifra, Petikhta* 1; they are also to be found in the book of Prayer, "the *siddur*"), and are based on the rules of logic: for example, "Light and Heavy," *kal vekhomer*—that is, making an inference from a minor to a major premise; analogy, *gzera shaveh*—that is, drawing parallels between similar passages; induction and deduction, *klal veprat* and *prat veklal*—that is, generalizing from the particular and extrapolating a particular from a generalization; deducing a matter from its context or from its continuation, *davar halamed mi'inyano* and *dvar halamed mi'sofo*—that is, using textual comparison and other devices to deduce something logically that has not been made explicit. This "expounding of the Torah" can take either of two main directions, each proposed by a famous *tanna*. R. Ishmael said that "The Torah speaks in human language" (BT *Brakhot* 31b) and thus its words and sentences should be understood in their usual straightforward sense. This approach is called *pshatt* (from the same root as *pashut*, or "simple"). R. Akiba offers a very different approach, the approach of *derash*, from a root meaning "to ask," "to investigate." For him, the meaning of a biblical text can be tracked by any and every device imaginable. Legend has it that he would extract *halachic* rulings even from the ornamentation of tiny crowns that decorate the individual letters of a text, that his methods were so abstruse and so abstracted from the plain meaning of the sentence as to leave even Moses himself dumbfounded:

> Rabbi Yehuda said in the name of Rav: When it was time for Moses to ascend on high, he found the Holy One Blessed Be He sitting and attaching tiny crowns to the letters [of the Torah] and said to Him: Lord of the Universe, who prevents you [from giving Torah without this ornamentation]? [The Lord] answered: There will be a man in the future, in several generations time, Akiba ben Yosef by name, who will deduce mountains of *halachot* from each one of these crownlets. Moses said: Lord of the Universe, show him to me. [The Lord] replied: Turn around. [Moses] went and sat down at the end of the eighth row [the last row of benches in a study house] and could not grasp a word of what was being said. He was exhausted from his efforts when Rabbi Akiba came to speak of a certain case, his students asked him: Rabbi, where [do you draw this *halacha*] from? When he replied: They are *halakhot* given to Moses on Sinai, [Moses] was contented (BT *Minkhot* 29b).

It was thus R. Akiba who laid the foundations of talmudic *pilpul,* that method of casuistic, hair-splitting argument so tenuously linked to logic and to the plain sense of the text that is ostensibly being explained. It is, however, a method that allows free-ranging creativity, and in this way *halachic* innovation and the adjustment of old rules to new realities.

But the *pshatt* and *derash* methods of approaching the Torah were not the only techniques of access to the holy scriptures. Two highly mystical methods came into popular use, one drawing on allusions that the commentator claimed to find in the text and the other applying Kabbalist traditions; these are called respectively *remez*, an allusion, and *sod*, a secret. The four methods, known by the collective acronym of PaRDeS (*pshatt, remez, derash, sod*), were all employed by the *amoras* of the *Gemara* as they elucidated and expounded the Mishna for their own generations; and subsequently, every succeeding generation of *halachic* scholar-judges applied these same four methods. Century after century, Torah study—in essence, the study of *halacha* and its commentaries— remained the central, almost exclusive preoccupation of Jewish scholars, even when no new circumstance required it and no practical application was anticipated. Torah study became in itself one of the greatest of *mitz-vot*. We may say that in the conditions of *galut*, of exile without a fore-seeable end, Torah study replaced the Temple ritual at the center of Jewish life.

The right to make *halachic* rulings is given to *morei hora'ah*—instructors of the commandments—rabbis enjoying a recognized authority. They are the people's spiritual leaders, its legislators and its judges. Although at his *smikhut*, ordination, every rabbi earns the authority to make rulings, supreme *halachic* authority is in the hands of the national religious leadership. During the Second Temple period and for some time afterwards, this took the form of a council of seventy-one scholars called the Sanhedrin,[8] which constituted Jewry's supreme court. Its president held the title *nasi*, president, and was recognized as Jewry's senior *halachic* authority, until the fifth century CE. Then the mantle passed to the heads of the great academies in Babylonia, of which the three greatest were at Nehardea, Sura, and Pumbedita, and whose heads, from the seventh century on, were given the title *gaon*, learned or talented. With the decline of Babylonian power, the mantle of *halachic* authority was passed on again: in the tenth century, it passed to the centers of learning in North Africa and Spain, and also to *yeshivas* founded in the Central European towns of Mainz, Spier, and Worms. At this time Jewry had been divided into two parties, one living under Islam (later became known as the Sephardiim, from the Hebrew name for Spain) and the other under the Christian nations (later became known as the Ashkenaziim, from the Hebrew name for the German areas of Europe). In the thirteenth century, there was a great influx of Jews into Eastern Europe, in particular into Poland, and by the six-teenth century, the Polish *yeshivas* were acknowledged around the Jew-ish world as the major centers of Torah study. In the last 250 years no single center has been able to win the recognition of all Jewish commu-nities.

The great corpus of *halacha* is made up of four categories of legisla-tion. One sub-corpus regulates daily life, encompassing every act of a believing Jew's waking existence, day and night, from the moment he or she opens their eyes to the time they fall asleep, from the moment of birth to the moment they pass away. The second category regulates the cult and worship of Yahweh: one section of this category comprises the laws and procedures of the Jerusalem Temple ritual when it still stood while the remainder prescribes those for religious rites and worship after the Temple's destruction and in the Diaspora. The third category is civil law and torts, regulating the dealings between people. The fourth category is the criminal law, specifying the acts prohibited under this category and the penalties for violating these prohibitions. All the thousands of laws, *halachot,* in all four categories are recognized by Judaism as derived from and elaborating upon the Torah's 613 commandments; ostensibly, a religious Jew owes obedience only to these 613. Ancient custom may indeed call the whole accumulation of Jewish law "the 613 (*taryag*) *mitzvot,*" but in reality they are more numerous and complex by a very long mark. Yet another ancient custom acknowledges this, for it gives one Aramaic name to the scriptural commandments—*mitzvot mideoraita,* or *mitzvot* from the Torah—and another to those legislated by the sages of Mishna and Gemara—*mitzvot miderabanan, or mitzvot* of the sages. If a practical circumstance arises in which a commandment from the second corpus clashes with one from the first, the first always takes precedence. Furthermore, there is an order or precedence within the corpora ruling that a commandment set down by the *tannas,* the makers of the Mishna, takes priority over one set down by the *amoras,* who made the *Gemara.*

One of the ways in which the body of *halacha* increased is by the practice of erecting *sayagim.* A *sayag* is a fence ("to make a fence around Torah" [Mishna *Avot* 1.1]) and the governing idea is to issue a class of *halachot,* obedience to which makes it all but impossible, even by accident, to violate an original commandment. The original commandment is fenced in. For example, Exodus 23:19 states: "You shall not seeth a kid in his mother's milk," a negative commandment apparently aimed at pagan rituals practiced at the time by the Israelites' Canaanite neighbors. To eradicate the slightest shadow of doubt about compliance with this scriptural commandment, the sages categorically forbade Jews to eat any of form of meat or meat product with any form of milk or milk product. Even eating chicken with milk was forbidden, when it is quite impossible that a young chicken can be cooked "in its mother's milk." The point is to prevent transgressions that would occur if the human eye mistakes one thing for another, for instance, mistaking beef for chicken, which would thus result in eating the supposed "chicken" with milk. Another group of offenses "of mistaken appearances," *mar'it ayin,* form a class in themselves; these are offenses committed when no commandment is actually violated but it appears to be violated. An example is sitting at a table in a non-kosher restaurant, even if one eats nothing.

Two other forces that have contributed to the expansion of *halacha* are custom, *minhag,* and precedent, *ma'aseh.* A custom in this case is a practice that, without any basis in written law, nevertheless establishes itself as part of Jewish life and that is then made *halachically* binding. A famous example is the custom that now obliges Jewish men not to leave the house without covering their heads. As the sages have said, "Our forefathers' custom is our law" (*Tosefot Minkhot* 20:2). The force of precedent is that a previous ruling on a matter subject to doubt is accorded the status of a binding judgement. In these and other ways, a vast number of the current laws, amendments, prohibitions, and interdictions have built up and these regulate the actions of religious Jews every hour of every day. *Halacha* lays down what education their sons and daughters will be given, what the syllabus and content of that education will be, what a boy may and may not be taught, and what a girl may and may not be taught. The laws of *kashrut* determine the daily diet: for instance, a religious Jew may eat only what is expressly permitted—that is, it is forbidden even to eat foods not explicitly forbidden by *halacha* if they are not explicitly permitted either. Religious people are bound by a series of commandments regulating marital life. *Halacha* states at what times sexual relations may take place and in what manner. It also regulates who people may marry: a divorced woman may not marry a *cohen*, a Jew considered to be descended from Aaron the first High Priest; certain degrees of kinship may not intermarry, but the concept of incest is extended further to include all the offspring of prohibited marriages or of prohibited extramarital sexual relations, *momzers*, permitted to marry only each other. Within the marriage bed, relations are forbidden during the woman's menstrual period and for "seven clean days" afterwards to ensure that relations take place for the purpose of procreation only. Perceiving marital relations as a source of "uncleanness," *halacha* requires regular "cleansing" or "purification" by immersion in a ritual bath (*mikvah tahara*). Collectively, the rules governing marital relations are known as "the laws of family purity."

For a religious Jew each step and every matter is controlled by the relevant halachic rulings, but only rabbis and the judges in religious courts, *dayanim*, are required to possess comprehensive knowledge of the whole corpus; one of their functions is to provide the relevant ruling whenever an ordinary Jew inquires into it. Religious Jews learn much of their body of obligations from childhood on, from their education in school and home, and from the run of daily life, what prayers and blessings to say when, which rites and ceremonies go with what occasion, what must and what may not be done on Sabbaths and Holy Days, what food may be eaten, what clothes may be worn, and so on. Every doubt and question is taken to the rabbi, whose *halakhic* and judicial authority is absolute. If two religious Jews cannot settle a dispute, the rabbi will adjudicate. There is nothing in the life of a religious Jew for which *hala-cha* does not have an answer, and this includes his or her own religious identity.

The People of Israel

As is seen, throughout the centuries the Jews' religion and peoplehood were bound together in one package. To be a Jew by religion was to be a Jew by ethnic belonging. It was a oneness that went back to the very origins of Judaism, when the gods were gods of ethnic groups, tribes, and peoples and when their power stretched only up to the frontiers of the territory held by the group who claimed them as their own deity. Yahweh was the god of Israel and His power was confined to the Land of Israel. Dagon was the god of the Philistines and his power was confined to the land of the Philistines. Biblical mythology tells us that Yahweh selected Abram to father the people whose god He would be, promising that Abram and the people who would spring from his loins would inherit the land of Canaan: "I will give to you and to your seed after you the land that wherein you are a stranger, all the land of Canaan, for as an everlasting possession, and I will be their God" (Gen. 17:8). The promise given to Abram was repeated to Isaac (26:3) and again to Jacob (28:13). Thus, according to Jewish mythology, it was not the people who selected Yahweh to be their god, but Yahweh who selected the Israelites, who even created them in order to be His people. Since then, the Jewish people trace their ancestry to the mythological three patriarchs, Abraham, Isaac and Jacob, each chosen by Yahweh. This ancestry was more ideological than genetic. Israel intermixed with many other peoples and accepted into its group in various ways numerous outsiders from its host and neighbor nations, just as numerous Jews left Israel, Israel as a religion, and Israel as a people, and took up with other religions and peoples. This did not prevent the national myth of a common patriarchy from being carefully preserved and every newcomer to the Jewish people and religion being enrolled among the adoptive children of Abraham, Isaac, and Jacob.

As noted, the myth includes Yahweh's promise to the Israelites that the land of Canaan would remain the patrimony of the generations to come. Since at that early time Yahweh was a territorial deity with jurisdiction limited to Canaan, Israel could not devote itself to His worship without such a promise, and the promise was duly given on condition that the Israelites obeyed the Yahwist commandments: "You shall therefore keep all My statutes and all My judgements and do them; that the land whither I bring you to dwell therein spew you not out" (Lev. 20:22). The Israelites were regularly warned by the prophets that this fate was a real possibility: "And you have done worse than your fathers, for you walk every one after the imagination of his evil heart, that they may not harken to Me. Therefore I will cast you out of this land unto a land that you know not, neither you nor your fathers; and there shall you serve other gods, day and night; where I will not show you favor" (Jer. 16:12–13); that is, in their lands of exile they would be compelled to worship other gods. But the prophets' second promise was that once they had served out their punishment, God would bring them home, restore them to their homeland and the land of their fathers. In Jeremiah, for instance, this consolation follows upon the prophesy of divine wrath: "The days come, says Yahweh, that it shall no more be said, 'Yahweh lives that brought up the children of Israel out of the land of Egypt,' but 'Yahweh lives that brought up the children of Israel from the land of the north, and from all the lands whither He had driven them,' and I will bring them again into their land that I gave to their fathers" (14–15). Other prophets repeat this undertaking of an eventual redemption, so that throughout all the years of exile Jews persisted in seeing the Land of Israel as the land promised to their forefathers, from which they, the descendants, were banished for their sins and to which, come the promised redemption, they would return with songs and rejoicing. With this vision in their minds, the Jews throughout the many centuries following the destruction of the second Temple, seldom saw themselves as having an ethnic-national affiliation to the host nations and lands where they dwelt; rather, they saw themselves as exiles from their own territory and homeland, living in the Diaspora for a period of time that would eventually come to a triumphant end when they returned to their home, the land of Israel.

It was this cultural-mythic bond to a supposed common ancestry and ethnicity, to a national territory willed to them by their God, and His prophets' promise of a redemptive return to this land that enabled the Jews to define themselves as a single people. Scattered across continents, with no real common origin, without even recognizably common ethnic features, they considered themselves as a single people. That would not have been possible were it not for the vision of redemption offered by the promise of the people's national-political restoration. We call this vision and faith "messianic"[9] and it is this aspect that later developed into one of the keystones of Judaism and Jewry.

The Messianic Idea

In the name of God, His prophets promised that Israel would be redeemed. In certain instances, the same promised future of plenty, peace, and righteousness is promised to the whole world, as in Isaiah's famous depiction of the End of Days when "nation shall not lift up sword against nation; neither shall they learn war any more" (2:4) and "The wolf shall dwell with the lamb, and the leopard shall lie down with the kid" (11:6). Some passages speak of a messenger herald who will bring news of the deliverance: "How beautiful upon the mountains are the feet of him that brings good tidings, that publishes peace and salvation" (Isa. 52:7). One of these passages names the prophet Elijah as the herald: "I will send you Elijah the prophet before the coming of the great and dreadful day of Yahweh" (Mal. 4:5). But deliverance will not come from any messenger, only by the hand of the Lord Himself: "For I am Yahweh your God, the Holy One of Israel, your savior" (Isa. 43:3). A few passages depict redemption as the return of a righteous king to take up his reign in Jerusalem: "Your king is coming to you. He is just and having salvation, lowly and riding upon an ass, upon a colt and foal of an ass" (Zech. 9:9). This motif of a king in a state of poverty, riding on a donkey, grew into one of the central images of popular messianism. Some said that the king would be descended from the line of David, son of Jesse: "And there shall come forth a rod out of the stem of Jesse, and a branch shall grow out of his roots" (Isa. 11:1). Daniel calls the redeemer "the Messiah" (9:25–26)—the anointed one. With the passage of time, the motifs came together and the hopes of redemption were focused on "an anointed king" who will be descended from David, who will redeem his people and the whole world and and will reign in Jerusalem.

Originally, anointment signified that God had appointed the individual to fulfil the solemn function of king, prophet, or priest, and that appointment was consecrated by pouring holy oil (Hebrew, *mashakh*) on the head of the anointed one. Leviticus talks of "the anointed priest" (4:3, 5 et al). In several places, the book of Samuel gives Saul and David the title "Yahweh's anointed." God commands Elijah to "anoint Hazael to be King over Aram, and Jehu the son of Nimshi shall you anoint to be king over Israel, and Elisha the son of Shaphat of Abel-meholah shall you anoint to be prophet replacing you" (1 Kings 19:15–16). The Book of Isaiah even designates Cyrus of Persia as "Yahweh's anointed" (45:1). The book of Psalms uses the title "anointed one" many times to signify a king of the Davidic line and this title was in common usage throughout the Second Temple period. In this sense, it later fused with the yearning for deliverance and the figure of the great deliverer came to be identified as "an anointed one." To this day, he remains known as "the messiah."

The messianic idea took shape in the Second Temple period. The line of Hasmonean kings had alienated itself from popular sympathy; it was followed by the Herodian line, which was kept in power by Roman support; and then came the hostile rule of the Roman proconsuls themselves. By this time, the people longed for national/religious independence, an aspiration that became attached to the divine promise of messianic deliverance. The idea assumed a variety of forms. The prophetic vision of the End of Days foresaw an anointed king from the line of David. At first, he was envisioned as a human king who would lead his people to freedom through a political struggle. With time, however, he acquired mystical qualities, drawn from the visions or redemption suggested by the book of Daniel, which links the coming of the messiah to divinely commanded miracles and mythical wonders. Nationalist aspirations fused with the utopic vision of a just and marvelous new world that would arise after the End of Days, when Israel would be redeemed. According to Daniel's visions, this redemption would be preceded by a period of cataclysmic disturbance and terrible wars, and only those who survived that apocalyptic period would witness redemption.

During the period of the Second Temple, messianic expectations were rife, the nation seethed and there were frequent uprisings against Roman rule. Several prophets claimed to be the predicted messiah and messianic sects proliferated. The sect of Jews who believed that Jesus of Nazareth was indeed that long-awaited messiah grew eventually into the worldwide religion that we know as Christianity.[10] The Great Revolt of 66–70 CE, which ended in the destruction of Judea and Jerusalem and the burning of the Temple, was largely motivated by messianic ideas, which retained such a strong hold on the people's imagination that they were to become central to their struggle for survival after the destruction. In 132 CE, a second great revolt against Roman rule broke out in Judea. Its leader, Shimon Bar Kosiba, was designated the "Nasi" or president of Israel; R. Akiva, the greatest Mishna sage of his time, proclaimed him "the king anointed" and, drawing hope and inspiration from the verse "There shall come a star out of Jacob" (Num. 24:17), he called him Bar Kokhba (from *kokhav*, star).

The Bar Kokhba revolt lasted three years and ended in even worse disaster than the Great Revolt sixty years before. Hundreds of thousands of Jews died in battle or from hunger and disease and, with the rebellion crushed, the Romans massacred or sold into slavery tens of thousands more. The Romans also suffered severe casualties. Judea was left a wasteland, barely populated. The sages and other leaders began to realize that their vision of messianic deliverance carried with it a threat to Jewry's very survival, thus they proposed that the coming of the messiah was part of the unforeseeable future, and to help instill this new idea they emphasized and redoubled the scale of the upheavals that were predicted to precede the messiah's coming. Some of them said: "Let him come, but not in my lifetime" (BT *Sanhedrin* 98b). They posited impossible conditions for his coming, such as: "The son of David will not come until there comes an entirely innocent or an entirely guilty generation" (ibid., 98a); "The king anointed will not come until there have been created all the souls God ever thought to create" (Gen. Rabba 24). They issued a prohibition on taking any steps to bring the day of the coming of the messiah nearer: "Four oaths . . . God made Israel swear: not to rebel against kingdoms, not to precipitate the End of Days, not to reveal their mysteries to the nations of the world, and not to try to end their exile by force" (Song of Sol. Rabba 2:18).

The idea of redemption was not wholly suppressed, far from it. It became one of the central articles of the Jewish faith, but the expectation that the anointed king would arrive soon gave way to a focus on the daily round of routine activities, based upon the assumption that the messiah would arrive some day and that until then, our task was to live in a way that would merit his coming. The messianic vision was encapsulated in the anticipation, rather than the actualization, of this coming and this is precisely how Maimonides set out the relevant article of faith: "I believe with complete faith that the messiah will come, and though he may delay, nonetheless I shall expect his coming every day."

Over the succeeding generations, messianic faith developed along both of the disparate paths we have already noted, the rational and the mystical. The one affirmed that the coming would be by natural means, in the context of world history, and would bring about Israel's restoration as a political-territorial entity. Earlier in this chapter, I quoted the amora Shmuel's stand on the matter: "The only difference between this world and the days of the messiah is the enslavement of kingdoms" (BT *Brakhot* 34b). Maimonides agreed with him. However, the mystics followed a path that, over time, merged with the Kabbalah's mythic visions: The redemption would be a cosmic transcendental event involving supernatural forces. The messiah might be depicted in the texts as a flesh-and-blood king, but he also commanded superhuman powers that drew on divine sources. In later Kabbalist elaborations, the messianic idea was incorporated into the prophetic vision of the End of Days, while in the same period, the concept of a political restoration and redemption faded. The coming of the messiah and his subsequent reign is depicted as a supernatural event, when the world and humankind's material existence will come to an end, and the universe will return to its divine source and become one with it.

The sages might have proclaimed a strict ban on calculating when the End of Days should occur and taking any action designed to precipitate the messiah's coming, But periodically a Jew would appear and announce that his presence heralded the great time. Fervent cults grew up around several such would-be messiahs, but their passionate tumult always collapsed in shattered illusions or, worse, physical disaster. The most far-reaching and tumultuous of these movements was the commotion surrounding the cult of Shabbatai Zevi[11] in the mid-seventeenth century, which drove Jewish communities across Europe and the Near East into a frenzy of expectation. The intermittent emergence of these messianic cults, together with the recurrence of the commotion they caused, demonstrates just how deeply rooted and cherished were the Jews' yearnings for deliverance and how much hope was placed on the messiah. We see the same yearnings expressed in synagogue prayers, folk tales, and great poetry. In Solomon ibn Gvirol's "geula" for instance, he writes:

> Age succeeds age for us in poverty and vileness;
> We hope for light—to get scorn and abasement.
> Slaves rule over us, sunk in our exile;
> Deliver us, Lord, for the power is in You!
>> For Your name's sake, Lord, send us a sign to encourage,
>> Lord, How long until the end of these wonders?[12]

In contrast, Immanuel of Rome, in his *"Make Haste, Anointed of God,"* seeing the degradation and abjectness of the Jews around him, recoils at the depiction of a messiah "in poverty riding on a donkey" and would rather have him come at a later, better time, if at all:

> Awake Messiah of ours and deck yourself out,
> Come riding a galloping horse or in a harnessed carriage,
> For my bones are scattered, there is not one whole,
> But if, Lord, you think to come on a donkey, then go back to sleep
> That, revered Messiah, is my sincere advice;
> Seal the End and close down the vision.

Modern poets too have found material in the Jews' unrequited long-
ings for deliverance. Uri Zvi Greenberg writes in his "Besod Hamas-
hiah" *"Within the Mystery of Messiah"*:

From the first generation of all: the generation of kingdom-destruction-exile,
To the call for Messiah cries out, from then till now,
From the blood between the hewn bodies[13] in middle-Europe we called to
   him,
As did the dead of Israel from the bowels of the foreign earth, . . .
In fast-day *piyyutim*[14] and the Holy Day *hallel*,[15]
From the pipings of a *kheder*[16] boy expounding the law before his elders,
To the last gasped words of an old man on his deathbed.
And to this day the messiah has not come,
The messiah has not come.

Immanuel of Rome, Greenberg and the work of many other poets
and authors make it clear that for all the depth and passion of these
yearnings for redemption, fed equally by Yahweh's promise and by the
misery of a *galut* existence, Jews nonetheless felt severe doubts as to the
actuality of the messianic vision in their day-to-day reality. Ha'im Hazzaz wrote a short story, "Hadrasha" "The Sermon," which probes into
the vision's dual import:

It's a wonderful story, a work of genius, . . . not without some caricature, not
without a lacing of bitter Jewish humor and wit: To arrive riding on a
donkey! . . . and it's this story of all stories that decided the people's fate,
generation after generation, forever . . . but one thing is clear . . . crystal
clear, absolutely certain, that if it hadn't been for this story . . . sooner or
later we would have had to go back and at once to the Land of Israel or leave
the world altogether in some other way . . . They invented for themselves a
messiah in heaven, something still to happen in the future . . . and with it
they tied themselves hand and foot, loaded themselves down with chains,
signed their own death warrant, and then made sure to observe it and honor
it to the very last letter, to make sure that they could never, ever, ever be
delivered!

Whatever one considers to be the consequences of this anticipation of
messianic redemption, it was certainly the key to the Jews' ability to sustain their self-definition as a people and not merely as a population of
co-religionists, and it reinforced the bond between Jewish communities
scattered across the world. It also made them the object of non-Jews'
animosity, hatred, and persecution, which in turn reinforced Jewish co-

hesion and unity, evoked a sharper self-consciousness of themselves as Jews and strengthened the solidarity of Jews wherever they were.

Anti-Semitism

Although the term "anti-Semitism" was coined by Wilhelm Marr, a German anti-Jewish agitator, only in the modern era, we shall use it for all manifestations of anti-Jewish prejudice and hatred down the ages. This hatred was exacerbated by the Jewish habit of segregating themselves from their non-Jewish neighbors and living as an alien entity among their host nations. As Haman, the Persian king's vizier, tells him: "There is a certain people, scattered abroad and dispersed among the people in all the provinces of your kingdom, and their laws are diverse from all people; neither keep they the king's laws" (Esther 3:8). As outsiders, it was natural for them to be suspected of disloyalty, as the Bible quotes the pharaoh of Egypt: "Let us deal wisely with them, least they multiply; otherwise when there falls out any war, they join also to our enemies and fight against us" (Exod. 1:10).

In the Second Temple period, the main stimulant of anti-Semitism was the Jews' objection to pagan cults and to an extensive system of idolatry. Greco-Roman culture was polytheistic, and as such it was able to tolerate the diverse cults practiced by the various peoples who made up the Greek and Roman empires. Every people's gods were respected by every other. In every Greco-Roman city was a pantheon, a temple dedicated to all the gods, where no god was refused a place. Pagans could not understand why the Jews refused to bring their Yahweh into the pantheon so that He could be worshipped along with all the other gods of the Empire, as other peoples did, and why they refused to install the Emperor's cult in their Temple in Jerusalem. They were naturally offended to learn that in Jewish eyes, all their gods were abominations and that Yahweh would not accept their pagan "unclean" worship. Inevitably, Judaic monotheism came into conflict with the Imperial policy of merging all national cults into one Imperial divine cult. Jews compounded their refusal to pay homage to other gods and to receive homage to Yahweh from pagan worshippers by refusing to marry non-Jews, to live in their neighborhoods, and even to eat with them. The texts of this period are rife with anti-Jewish invective and violent clashes on the streets were common, especially in Alexandria where the Jewish community was large. After the Bar Kokhba revolt was crushed, Emperor Hadrian issued decrees calculated to decimate the great strength of the Jews throughout his empire: they were forbidden to study the Torah, to keep the Sabbath, or to circumcise their sons. Early Christians found a way around this obstacle by substituting baptism for circumcision, Sunday for Saturday, and so on. However, for the greater part of their duration, the Greek and Roman empires forbore from declaring an official anti-Jewish policy; there were times, indeed, when Jews were favored with special privileges, particularly in trade.

This changed in the fourth century CE when Christianity became the official Imperial religion. Anti-Semitism now took on new dimensions. Christianity, like Judaism, was a jealous faith, and "mother" religion, Judaism came in for particularly bitter antipathy, for its "daughter" now regarded itself as the true Judaism and expected the Jews to do likewise. Although many Jews complied and formed the nucleus of new Christian communities that sprang up all over the empire, the Pharisee rabbinical establishment refused to adopt the new faith, and large sections of the Jewish populations of Palestine, Babylonia, North Africa, and elsewhere followed the rabbinical line. They spurned the new religion out of hand, mainly because the early Christians rejected the rabbinical *halacha,* and accepted faith as the most important principal of their religion.

The victorious and rapid expansion of Christianity led the new Christians to the deduction that the Jews had brought God's hatred upon themselves by their sins and by their rejection of His messiah, Jesus, who was sent to atone for those very sins. However, they had to explain why the Jews as a people had not disappeared altogether—and the answer was not difficult for a virulently anti-Semitic mind-set to find: They concluded that the Jews remained in order to show the world the degradation to which their sins had brought them. It was their destiny to exist forever, abased and shameful, a living reminder to the faithful of the punishment for unredeemed sin. Hatred and persecution of Jews thus became institutionalized as an article of the Christian faith and also as official Imperial policy. Laws were passed designed to separate Jews from Christians: Jews were evicted from positions of influence, from the Imperial administration, and from the sources of economic power.

During the Middle Ages, in Christian and Muslim empires alike, Jewish space was further constricted—the crafts and professions they were allowed to practice, the areas in which they were allowed to live, the property they were allowed to own, even the clothes they were allowed to wear were increasingly confined and laid down by law. Periodically, the authorities would descend on Jewish communities to plunder the inhabitants and would then expel the Jews from their towns or from the entire country. The murders of Jews by rioting mobs were frequent, as were more formal executions by the "powers of justice." During the

Crusades of the twelfth century, whole communities were massacred, the Rhineland Jews suffering most of all. Horrific but enduring rumors of rites and conspiracies were concocted that were then attributed to the Jews, the most notorious being the blood libel, which alleged that Jews needed to mix the blood of a Christian child into their Passover matzos.

During the later Middle Ages, the European Jews' situation deteriorated even further. The post-Reformation Wars of Religion hit them very hard. The Catholic Church imposed even worse anti-Jewish legislation, further reducing the trades by which Jews could earn a living and obliging them to wear distinguishing clothes and live in separate closed and walled neighborhoods, which became known as *ghettos*.[17] Initially, the new branch of Christianity known as Protestantism thought that Jews would welcome and accept their brand of Christianity, but when it became clear that Jews would not relinquish their own faith, the Protestants endorsed the existing anti-Jewish laws. One of the aims of Church-inspired anti-Semitism at this time was to induce Jews to convert and indeed, many succumbed to the pressure upon them and did so. They were subsequently free of any form of discrimination or retaliation and were utterly assimilated into their host society. But Jew-hatred had practical uses too. Plunder was one; another was to furnish all governments with a means of diverting their people's attention from the level of poverty and the conditions in which they lived, and most particularly, from focusing on the real causes for that poverty and those conditions. For every disaster and calamity that occurred, there was a ready scapegoat: the Jews. In the Islamic world, anti-Semitism was much more moderate, and the treatment and status of the Jews no worse than that of other "infidels." They were heavily persecuted only in a few places and at specific periods, when a fanatic religious extremist came to power.

In the late eighteenth and early nineteenth centuries, the power of organized religion fell into decline and consequently the religious-based hatred toward Jews declined. After the citizens of European states such as France, Germany, Austria, and England had been granted civil rights, the Jews were emancipated, the discriminating legislation was repealed. In Eastern Europe, where the greater part of the Jewish people lived, rights were not granted at all, and the oppression of Jews continued. It was predominately because the Czarist rulers used anti-Semitism to absorb people's dissatisfaction and anger, and the Jews provided a useful means of deflecting that anger away from the regime, the real authors of its misery. To the peasants and workers, the Jews were depicted as money-grabbers and exploiters, grinding the faces of the poor into the dirt. The upper classes saw them as leaders of social revolution, anti-establishment agitators and the instigators of riots. In the mid-nineteenth century, a new racist theory called "anti-Semitism" swept Central Europe. According to this theory, the Jews, as Semites, were of a racial stock that was inferior to the "Aryan" stock to which most European peoples belonged. Worse, according to this new "anti-Semitism," the Semite racial stock was decadent and if it intermingled with Aryans, it would contaminate and adulterate their nobler civilization and culture. The Jewish nation was also alleged to be planning to take over economic and financial power across the industrial world. At the beginning of the twentieth century, a document was even "discovered" corroborating all these allegations; it is known as the *Protocols of the Elders of Zion*. Although it has long been exposed as a forgery, concocted by the Czarist police, its power is such that it continues to be believed to this day. The new theory of anti-Semitism incited a huge wave of anti-Jewish political parties and organizations all over Europe and this came to a head in the 1940s when six million Jews were exterminated by German and other Nazis, which had adopted and elaborated upon the existing theory. Modern anti-Semitism is a racist ideology, but like its predecessor, religious anti-Semitism, it is manipulated for sociopolitical ends, to deflect the blame for socioeconomic adversity from the national political leadership.

After the Second World War, racism, including anti-Semitism, was outlawed in most countries, and the United Nations adopted resolutions condemning racial incitement. This did not mean that prejudice against Jews vanished; it simply took on new forms. However, the scale of the phenomenon decreased greatly, as the slaughter of six million Jews had rendered anti-Semitism no longer respectable and racist opinions became unacceptable in civilized society. Down through the ages, anti-Semitism has taken a terrible toll on the Jews. Huge numbers have lost all they had, including their lives and the lives of their families, and thousand upon thousands abandoned their religion under the threat of loss of livelihood or of death. For those who remained resolute, anti-Semitism was rather a unifying factor, because it accentuated the differences between Jews and their "hosts." In the ghettos, for example, Jews lived under a form of self-government, *halacha* was the civil and criminal law for all dealings between one Jew and another. Essentially, anti-Semitism forced Jews to define who they were and to grasp the fundamentals of their Jewishness, just as the

Jew-haters had to know which personal and national characteristics they could use to stigmatize the Jews. In many cases, it was the surrounding non-Jewish, even anti-Semitic, society that defined Jewish identity for many Jews. In Sartre's words, "A Jew is someone whom other people regard as a Jew."[18]

4
Moving Toward Jewish Pluralism

THE EVOLUTION OF JEWRY AND JUDAISM DURING THE PERIOD OF THE
Second Temple (515 BCE–70 CE) was characterized by dispute, division, and particularly by political and religious separatism. One major
faction was that of the Pharisees, whose authority was accepted by the
majority of the people. Their chief leaders are held up today as the great
sages of the *Mishna,* the minds and personalities who were responsible
for setting the character of normative Judaism for hundreds of years to
come. There was constant rivalry and controversy between the Pharisees and another major faction, the Sadducees who were backed by the
elite, the major landowners, the priesthood, and the royal Hasmonean
court. The conflict between the Pharisees and the Sadducees[1] was long
standing and extensive, ranging from matters pertaining to the central
articles of the faith and to the forms of rites and rituals, to issues relating
to the pattern and practice of daily life. A third faction, the Essenes,[2]
were smaller than the other groups, but they had a strong spiritual influence: they led a frugal life in isolated, communal settlements where
they developed an extraordinarily austere doctrine of their own. Then
there were the Zealots, the instigators and leaders of the Great Revolt
in 67 CE against Roman rule over Judea. Josephus makes the following
observations about these four "denominations" of the Judaism of his
time:

> The Pharisees are known as very learned men who know how to expound
> the law. . . . They say that everything depends on providence and God, and
> only whether to do good or bad deeds is in the hands of man. . . . The Saddu-
> cees deny divine providence and say that God is far removed from the deeds
> of men. . . . The teaching of the Essenes leaves all in God's hands. They
> believe in the immortality of the soul and that the reward of the righteous is
> worth striving for, . . . they hold their property in common . . . The fourth
> sect [the Zealots] agrees with the Pharisees, except that they have an invinci-
> ble love of freedom and are convinced that God is their leader and sover-
> eign.[3]

The destruction of the Second Temple in Jerusalem and the loss of independent statehood tore the ground from under the Sadducean view of the world and their sect faded out. As for the Essenes, most historians speculate that they became assimilated into the ranks of the new Christian religion. The Zealots rose in revolt against Rome and died under Roman swords. Only the Pharisees and their doctrine survived, and from this point in history, they become the sole voice of normative Judaism, that now demanded, and fiercely enforced, absolute allegiance to a unified faith. As long as the three components of Jewish identity—faith, *halacha,* and peoplehood—remained indivisible, and as long as Jewry's scattered communities deferred to one acknowledged center of *halachic* authority, Jewish unity lasted. It remained intact for fifteen hundred years, during which all attempts at reverting to other forms or factions of Judaism were suppressed by excommunication and banishment. Sects that were too strong to be suppressed were forced out of mainstream Jewry. Christianity, having started as a tiny marginal sect within the body of Judaism, grew into a worldwide religion of vastly greater power and numbers than its "parent," whom it turned upon and reviled. The Karaites denied the authority of the *Mishna* and *Talmud* (the Oral Law), accepting only the authority of the twenty-four books of the Bible, and by doing so they excluded themselves from the rabbinic authority. For a time they flourished and even surpassed rabbinic Jewry in numbers, but their membership slowly dwindled to the few thousands who follow this version of Judaism today. Thus to all intents and purposes, rabbinic Jewry became the only form of recognized Judaism and it alone laid sole claim to the heritage of historical Judaism. From time to time, the mainstream *halachic* authority was shared among different centers.

In the tenth century an autonomous center in the Rhine Valley asserted its own rulings, not depending upon the traditional seat of judgment at Sura in Babylonia, and this was the genesis of the division between Ashkenazi Jews, those living in the Christian world, and Sephardi Jews, those living in the Islamic world. The division has held firm to the present day, but it has always remained a division, rather than a divorce. Sephardim have accepted the pronouncements of the foremost Ashkenazi sages, such as Rashi, while Ashkenazis have reciprocated in their respect for the greatest Sephardi exegetes, Maimonides, being the most prominent example. The wording of certain prayers, the order of the synagogue service, and daily customs might diverge; disputes have certainly arisen over matters of *halacha* and doctrine, and sometimes such disagreements have become embittered; but across the whole Jewish world the fundamental trinity of faith, *halacha* and nationhood remained unified.

In the seventeenth century a movement toward secularization began in Sephardi communities in Western Europe, in particular in the Netherlands, a foretaste of the great convulsion that would disrupt Eastern European Jewry two hundred years later. The seventeenth-century Sephardim, however, were not abandoning their religion or its values, but were merely transferring certain religious symbols and values from *halachic* to secular contexts, at a time when they were moving away from a traditionally *halachic*-defined lifestyle. Nor were they discarding their inner Jewish identity, their outward Jewish appearance, or their communal affiliations. Although the new trend did weaken the hold of the "traditionalist spirit" on Sephardi Jewry as compared with their Ashkenazi counterparts—a difference still palpable today—these first steps toward secularism remained confined to Sephardim in Western Europe, so that we cannot yet talk of a pluralism acknowledged across the Jewish world with regard to either numbers or to influence.[4] The next major blow to Jewish unity occurred in the eighteenth century when the advent of Hasidism and the implacable opposition to it from traditionally minded Jews created a bitter rift in Eastern European Jewry. While this crisis did not destroy the tripartite unity of Jewish identity, it did further reduce the already limited reach of *halachic* authority.

THE CRISIS OF *HASIDISM*

Hasidism[5] emerged in the eighteenth century at a time of great social tension and unrest for Jewish communities of Poland and Lithuania. The internal and external authority of the leaderships of the Jewish communities had been severely weakened by the massacres of Jews in Eastern Europe in 1648–49, as well as by the collapse of the popular messianic hysteria aroused by the claims of Shabbatai Zevi to be the Messiah shortly afterwards, and by the continuing disturbances provoked by offshoot Sabbatean messianic sects and movements.[6] Resentment began to rise about the wide gap that existed between the rabbis with their wealthy backers and the masses in their poverty. Social conflict between the people and the leadership was now an open issue, which incorporated a mystical dimension too, as it was motivated by the same yearnings and dreams that had fired the Sabbatean outbreak. Partly out of frustration at the collapse of that fantastic dream but also as an expression of bitter social criticism, many Jews took delving into the secrets and mysteries of Kabbalah.

Mysticism, inspired by Kabbalist teachings and ideas, is at the very heart of the *Hasidic* movement. Its founder and spiritual father is considered to be R. Yisrael ben Eliezer, known as the *Ba'al Shem Tov*, "Bearer of a good name", usually shortened to "the *Besht*." As far as is known, he was born into a simple family and first made his living as a teacher for hire, *melamed*, and as a synagogue beadle. Later, his reputation as a healer and miracleworker, as a writer of charms and whisperer of spells (*'Baal Shem'*) spread among the simple folk. Disciples collected around him, forming the first community of Hasids and preaching and proclaiming in the *Besht's* name a body of Hasidic teaching. After his death, thousands of new followers were attracted to his teachings; they in turn founded many new communities, each led by his first disciples and their disciples, and each local rabbi known as *rebbe* (Yiddish pronunciation of rabbi) or the *tzaddik*. In the early days the communal leadership passed down from the *rebbe* to his most outstanding student, but with time, it became hereditary, passing from father to son or son-in-law. Dynasties and sub-sects formed, most of them headed by descendants of the *Besht* himself or of his earliest disciples.

From the teachings of these disciples, it is clear that the *Besht* made no substantial alterations to *halacha* or to the articles of faith. His innovation was to demand of his followers a most intense *kavannah* ("mystical intention," "direction of inner purpose") in their observance of every commandment, but most especially in prayer, that must never be routine. Impassioned prayer was at the very heart of divine worship, even surpassing Torah study in importance. It was the chief path to communion with the highest *sefirot*, emanations, of the Godhead. The commandments were not merely to be obeyed but to be fulfilled with joy and exaltation, with singing and dancing. Even the effects of liquor were regarded positively, if the exaltation that was aroused was used to celebrate God's commandments. Thus, although Hasidism borrowed much from *Kabbalah*, it rejected the asceticism that Kabbalists believed to be the most fitting path to communion with the Creator. Kabbalists submitted themselves to prolonged self-isolation as a means of getting nearer to God, and they even considered such seclusion as an end in itself, but *Hasidim* saw it only as a means of sanctifying the self for spiritual leadership. The revered Kabbalist, fasting for days alone with texts, only he could understand and withstand, was replaced by the *tzaddik*—the leader, mentor and inspiration of a community of devoted followers. This was the *Besht's* remarkable innovation to the practice of Judaism.

According to the *Hasidic* view of the world, the *tzaddik* is "an ever-lasting foundation" (Prov. 10:25); the world exists by virtue of him and for his sake. He has the power to direct the *shefa* (plenty) that God sends down from Heaven to earth, and even to influence the divine government of the world. His righteousness is expressed in his leadership of his community. Indeed, this mentorship is his chief mission. He stands between man and God, to reconcile the one to the other, on the one hand, in mystical *dvekut* (adherence, communion) with God, and on the other, in "cohering" with mankind. He bears responsibility for the community of his believers, and so it is his duty to descend from the exalted plane of his existence in order to raise up his people. He may appear to all intents a simple man of the people, walking among ordinary folk, concerned with their everyday affairs, but in truth he is "a hidden *tzaddik*," conversing in unbroken communion with higher worlds. Ordinary Jews are capable of rising to a higher level but only when they fulfill commandments under the *tzaddik*'s direction and, in so doing, raise the "sparks of holiness" imprisoned in the *klipot* (shells) of the material world to their rightful place in the higher worlds, within the universal seeking for *tikkun* (correction).[7] Without this mediation, ordinary people would search in vain for the path to God. It is bearing this role in mind that we can appreciate the supreme importance and supernatural status that Hasidic society ascribes to the *tzaddikim*. They are so venerated that to recount legends and tales about their lives, deeds, and sayings is held to be one of the highest levels of divine worship, in some instances higher even than Torah study.

Hasidism, then, gave the ordinary Jew a sense of his own importance, as against the overbearing ascendance of the community's notables and the elite status accorded to full-time Torah students. Instead of the self-mortification and unceasing Torah study for which only the few are fitted, Hasidism's terms of admission were the worship of God in *kavannah* and joy, which is possible for everyone to do. Ordinary people flocked to the new movement and found compensation for their poverty and social inferiority. The movement expanded rapidly, spreading particularly quickly into the villages and small towns where ordinary working Jews lived. The dividing line between Hasidic communities and those who rejected their innovations, the *Hasidim* called them *mitnagdim* (objectors, opponents), grew sharper and more bitter. *Hasidism* moved over to the new Sephardi version of the prayer service, devised by Rabbi Isaac Luria of Tzfat and differing somewhat from the Ashkenazi version, which had been in use for generations throughout Poland and Germany. They introduced their own method of cattle slaughter, based on Kabbalist rules, which meant that *Hasid* and *mitnaged* could not even eat meat together.

In Europe at this time, the supreme *halachic* authority was wielded by the *Gaon* Rabbi Eliyahu of Vilna, one of the greatest Jewish minds of all time, *"Hagra."* *Hasidim's* belittling of Torah study and Torah students incensed him. He regarded its leaders as no better than vulgar ignoramuses and its cult of the *tzaddik* as pure and simple idolatry. Consequently, he ordered that Hasidism be repudiated and the Hasidic hounded, if necessary out of Jewish society entirely. Although this furious battle did not in the end result in Hasidism's expulsion from normative Jewish society and despite the fact that the excommunication against them was never implemented, it did create parallel and mutually dismissive centers of *halachic* authority. After the death of the *Besht*, the situation became even more complex by the fragmentation of Hasidism itself. Each *rebbe's* community or court became, to some extent, a law unto itself and bitter rivalries developed, even to the point of one community delegitimizing others by, for instance, banning intermarriage with another community.

In the literature of the period, especially in the writings of *Haskalah* Jews who fought Hasidism with all the resources they could summon, there are many fascinating descriptions of the strife and disputes between *Hasidim* and *mitnagdim* and between one *Hasidic* court and another. Later literature also has many examples; a famous and intriguing one features in S. Y. Agnon's story, "Tehila," where a girl's engagement is broken off as soon as the prospective groom's Hasidic tendencies are discovered:

> One Sabbath, four weeks before the day fixed for the wedding, Shraga failed to come over to our house. During the afternoon service Father enquired and was told that he had gone on a journey. Now this journey was to one of the leaders of the *Hasidim* and Shraga had been taken by his father to receive a direct blessing on the occasion of his first putting on prayer shawl and phylacteries.[8] When my father learned this his soul nearly parted from his body; for he had not known till then that Shraga's father was of the Sect. He had kept his beliefs secret for in those days the *Hasidim* were despised and persecuted and Father was at the head of the persecutors; so that he looked on members of the Sect as if, God forbid, they had ceased to belong to our people.[9]

Hasidism flourished in Eastern Europe because it met the real social need of ordinary Jews who were caught between the depredations imposed upon them by the civilian authorities and the strictures placed

upon them by their local communal leaders. Without changing the social structure of Jewish communities, without improving their economic
conditions, Hasidism gave the poor and uneducated a sense of self-re-
spect by according them a value never before allowed. Over time, however, the cliques ruling the many *rebbes'* courts became corrupt. A wide
gap opened up between the *tzaddik* and his "courtiers," who made a
luxurious lifestyle for themselves from the contributions of his followers,
and the poor believers, who remained as poor as they had ever been.

One sect within Hasidism has made itself particularly well-known
among Jews generally, and this is *Chabad,* the consonants of its name
being the initials of **Chokhma, Bina** and **Da'at** (wisdom, insight, and
knowledge). *Chabad* was founded at the end of the eighteenth century
by R. Shneur Zalman of Lyady, whose aim was to bridge the divide between Hasidic ways and the traditional Jews of Lithuania and Northern
Russia, who could not accept the disparagement of the role of Torah
study. Chabad Hasidism made a point, therefore, of giving a higher
place to the intellectual and theoretical over the emotional in its own
understanding of Judaism, emphasizing the importance of study, re-
flection, reasoning and understanding while insisting that these had to
be invigorated with the energies of *dvekut, kavannah* and fervor, which
were the very soul of Hasidism. Today, Chabad is controlled by the
Schneersohn family, descendants of the Lubavitch dynasty of rabbis.
Lately, its followers have been swept into a messianism, proclaiming
their last *rebbe,* Menachem Mendel Schneersohn, who died in 1996, to
be no less than the Messiah, and as such, not really dead at all but soon
to reappear and reveal himself in his true stature.

Despite the profound modifications to belief and *halacha* that Hasidism has made, it has not disrupted the unity of Judaism, although it has
resulted in the dispersal of religious authority between a scattering of
mutually hostile individuals and councils. None of Judaism's many sects
and denominations has succeeded in expelling a rival from the worldwide community of Jews. Though the *mitnagdim* may regard Hasidism
as heresy and idolatry, they have failed to have them labeled as "non-
Jews," and vice versa. Attempts at mutual delegitimization have lasted
to this very day, making the imposition of a strong central pan-Jewish
halachic authority impossible. In the 19th century, moreover, it opened
the way for a new movement to enter the arena and gather force and
followers. This was the *Haskalah,* the Jewish Enlightenment, which proposed solving the difficulties within which Judaism and Jewry had
trapped themselves by discarding rabbinic authority entirely. The rabbis
fought back as fiercely as they could, but they no longer commanded

the power to prevent *Haskalah* teachings from extending their influence across the Jewish world.

THE CRISIS OF EMANCIPATION: THE *HASKALAH*

The emancipation of Central and Western European Jews consisted of their release from the barriers that had prevented them from participating freely in society and their eventual admission to full civil rights. This process, which began towards the end of the eighteenth century and was completed towards the mid-nineteenth century, constituted the most important development, and perhaps caused the deepest crisis in the history of Jewry since the destruction of the Second Temple eighteen hundred years before. Emancipation changed the way in which European Jews lived their daily lives, from the cradle to the grave. It also ended the historical trinity of Jewish identity by, in one move, causing the component of national identity to become separated from the two religious components, faith and *halacha*. The force that propelled this historic breach was generated by the *Haskalah*, the Jewish Enlightenment, which was itself a direct consequence of emancipation.[10]

The newly emancipated Jews began to move into non-Jewish society, to learn its ways, and to adopt its concerns, goals and vision. The Jewish Enlightenment that would eventually generate a Jewish national reawakening was in fact an offshoot of the general European Enlightenment, that upsurge of humanist thinking and intellectual exploration, which began with the Italian Renaissance, gathered momentum from English rationalism, and declared that Man, not some supernatural divinity, was the mainspring of our world, and that Man's rational mind was capable of penetrating the truths of the universe, of natural phenomena and of human society. Proceeding from humanism's foundation that all men are of equal value by virtue of their very humanity, Enlightenment thinkers arrived at the question of civil rights for Jews. In educated circles the traditional and centuries-old hostility toward Jews began to shift. This began a long and gradual political process that was to become known as the emancipation, which reached its culmination first in the Edict of Tolerance issued by Emperor Joseph II of Austria in 1782, then in the proclamation of full civil rights for the Jews of Western and Central Europe in the aftermath of the French Revolution, and continued up to the middle of the nineteenth century.

Some trace the *Haskalah* to Italian roots, others to French influences, but as a movement it first signaled its potential in late-eighteenth-cen-

tury Berlin, centered around the figure and the thinking of the philosopher Moses Ben Menachem Mendelssohn. Mendelssohn was deeply
concerned with matters pertaining to the essential nature of the Jewish
religion. He believed in the concept of divine revelation and of the giving of Torah at Mt. Sinai, but he could not accept that its purpose was
to lay down generalized religious truths; these, he held, human logic
could infer for itself. In Mendelssohn's view, Torah was given to us as a
legal foundation upon which the Jewish people could base their life and
society, so that Jewry could act as paradigm to the world. The heart of
Judaism was not the distinction between truth and falsehood but between good and evil, and the destiny of the Jews was to carry Jewish
morality—the morality of the prophets—to all the peoples of the world.
Certainly, it was the duty of every Jew in every generation to fulfill the
mitzvot, but in the domain of faith and opinion Judaism had left broad
areas open to inquiry and disagreement, so that *mitzva* observance was
entirely compatible with tolerance and freedom of thought. Mendelssohn also endorsed the separation of religion and state on the grounds
that only the state possesses the authority to impose its laws upon individuals. As religion possesses no such powers of coercion, its truths
could only impose themselves by persuasion. His approach to Judaism
denied the authority of the Jewish communal leadership to control the
behavior of its people, while it summoned them to take their place in
the host states' wider political system. It was within this religious philosophy that the *Haskalah* found its intellectual mainspring.

Mendelssohn's disciples applied his founding principles to everyday
life. In implementing his call to Jews to move into the wider society,
they demanded changes in Jewish education: crucially, they held it necessary to put general schooling before Jewish studies and to invest much
more in training members of the Jewish community for the trades and
professions. The stereotype of the "parasitic Jew" had to be broken by
Jews gaining access to productive, useful lines of work. Modifications
to religion and religious practice were a second demand; whatever was
required to enable Jews to fulfill the obligations of their citizenship was
of paramount importance. They coined the slogan "be a Jew at home; a
human being out of home," that is, the *mitzvot* were to be fulfilled in
the privacy of the home, while in public Jews were to behave like everyone else. Mendelssohnians even openly and explicitly retitled themselves as "Germans of the Mosaic faith."

It was a self-definition that explicitly set the national component in
Jewish identity apart from its religious component. For the first time in
Jewish history in exile, a demarcation was made between a Jew's religion

and his national affiliation. But such a division could not be fully realized without dealing with the messianic concept which lay at the root of the Jews' self-definition as a people and which clearly did not sit well with the *maskilims'*[11] self-definition as full citizens of their non-Jewish states. They were indeed challenged often and in many ways as to what they would do when the messiah came: would they stand by their German or French citizenship or prefer their Judaic nationhood and follow the messiah to the Promised Land? While the *maskilim* generally insisted that they would remain Europeans, they did not abandon the messianic idea; instead, they recast it as an abstract concept, a metaphor, a symbol of the worldwide religious unity of Jewish religious communities.

Another innovation that we owe to the *maskilim* of Central Europe is the inauguration of modern scientific research into the "sources of Judaism," which they called *die Wissenschaft des Judentums* ("the Science of Judaism"). Essays were written about Jewish religious practice and its origins; Jewish concepts, *mitzvot,* and customs were given historical reinterpretations; research was renewed into the core elements of the Hebrew language; and the foundations were laid for the scientific study of Jewish history. Heinrich Graetz's great opus *History of the Jews* was a landmark, the first ever comprehensive historical study of the evolution of the Jewish people from its emergence up to the modern period.

The Hebrew language assumed a status and role of special importance. It was to be restored to its original "purity" and its grammar thoroughly reanalyzed. Yiddish, the current spoken vernacular among Jews, was dismissed by *maskilim* as a "jargon," a mongrel concoction of disparate elements lacking even a grammar of its own. Even the Hebrew then in use in certain specialized contexts (synagogue sermons, *halachic* rulings and exegetics, and some business correspondence) they disowned as an adulterated, hybrid concoction. They held that for the authentic tongue, one had to go back to the Bible, and especially to the Prophets. In Berlin, with Mendelssohn's active involvement, a new Hebrew-language monthly, *HaMe'assef (The Collector),* was founded in order to bring Jewish enlightenment to the Jews. The modern age of Hebrew literature had begun.

The Jewish Enlightenment was propelled by a central concept, that each member of the Jewish faith belonged to the people who inhabited the country in which they lived; in this respect, Jews were no different from Catholics or Protestants or any other group of believers. To make a reality of this new way of being Jewish, to become "one of the people," they would clearly need to remodel their way of life and religious practice sufficiently to enable them take their place in the national economy and culture. They had to learn to speak the national language, to adopt a "normal" lifestyle, at least, outside home, to move into more "productive" occupations. As for a Jewish language, the only genuine candidate was biblical Hebrew.

Of course, none of this was welcomed by conservative Jews and their rabbinic leaders. They immediately declared war on these dangerous new ideas; if they had been able, the rabbis would have proclaimed an edict of total ostracism against *maskilim* and *Haskalah*, even to the point of excommunication from the body of Jewry. In such a cause the rabbis would even have joined hands with the abhorred *Hasidim*, but a fragmented leadership and the rapid spread of *Haskalah* ideas and practice gave them no time to organize. They laid all *Haskalah* books and journals, which they declared mouthpieces of heresy and atheism, under the severest ban, but this was not enough to inhibit the Jews' assimilation of *Haskalah* ways and *Haskalah* thinking. Pluralism had come to Judaism and it had come to stay.

THE *HASKALAH* IN EASTERN EUROPE

When, in the early nineteenth century, the *Haskalah* reached the territory of the Russian Empire, where the great majority of the world's Jews lived, it was no longer the same movement that it had been in Central Europe nor would it have the same effect. For the Jews living under Tsarist rule, emancipation was nothing but a dream, no civil rights of any kind were ever granted, neither to Jews nor to other people. Furthermore, Russia's Jews did not live among or interact with other Russians, nor with any other people of the Empire; in fact, they had never done so. Russia's Jews were confined to the Pale, a wide belt of land along the Empire's border with Central Europe, allocated by the Czarist regime for Jewish small towns, (*shtetls*), and there, by and large, they lived segregated from the non-Jews in the region, not even speaking the local languages.

The *maskilim* in Russia blamed the absence of a European education and way of life among the Jews not only for impeding emancipation, but for many of the factors that led to Jews' inferior status. They even held that the Jews' self-segregation and "Jewish" way of life was the reason for local anti-Semitism. They thought the implementation of the program of the *Haskalah* would cure all ills. A European education, learning to talk the local language, and participating in the local lifestyle would give Jews access to all the good things that the country had to offer and would guarantee them a happy welcome among their neighbors. So ran the theory, but, in practice, to which people were the Jews to attach their new identity? The Belorussians or the Poles, the Lithuanians, or the Ukrainians? Certainly not the Russians themselves, since Jews were not allowed to live in the territory of Russia proper. Even in the Pale they were forbidden to enter the cities and the large towns, so that their "neighbors" and "fellow Russians" were mostly ignorant peasants, who had even less general education and civil rights than the Jews did.

The *maskilim* of Eastern Europe were forced to recognize that Jewish life in the Russian Empire was a national existence, but they gave it a new meaning. They accepted that Jews were indeed one people, but held that they were just one of the many peoples making up the Russian Empire, no different to the Poles, Lithuanians, or Ukrainians. The nationhood of the Jews was thus not repudiated, as it had been in Central and Western Europe, but it took a very different form to that of the traditional notion of Jewish nationhood, which had been based on the ancient messianic idea of a people sentenced to exile, waiting for the messiah to come and deliver them back to their promised land. The Russian *Haskalah* leaders called upon Russia's Jews to regard themselves as one of the peoples of Russia and to see Europe as their homeland; thus declared Yehuda Leib Gordon (*Yalag*), the greatest of the Haskalah poets and one of its leading spokesmen. Here is his programmatic Hakiza Ami "Awake, My People!" [1863]:

> Those lands where now we are born and live
> Are valued as provinces of Europe!
> Europe, smallest of all the Earth's portions,
> But in science and scholarship all surpassing.
>
> Shall this land of Eden not open you its arms,
> Shall its sons not call you "Our brother"?
> How long are you to remain a mere sojourner amongst them,
> Why keep you always this cold distance?
>
> They'll lift the burden of suffering from your shoulders
> And the yoke from off your neck,
> They'll wipe hatred and false thinking from their hearts,
> To stretch out their hand and make peace for us all.
>
> Raise your heads high, stand straight,
> Turn to them eyes of love.

Give your hearts to knowledge and science,
Be a people of education and in their tongue converse.

Let all men of learning among you study the sciences,
All artisans and craftsmen every craft and trade.
The valorous shall go for soldiers
And the farmers purchase field and plough.

To the State's treasury bring the fruit of your labor
And from its wealth take your due share and gift.
From home, a man of the people be; at home, a Jew,
A brother to your fellow-citizen and your king's servant . . .

The poem was written in 1863 when Czar Alexander II's small ventures along the road of reform had sparked visions of a liberalized Russia. Gordon rehearses all the fond hopes of Russian *maskilim* at this time, how Russianized Jews, talking fluent Russian, participating in the nation's culture and economy, practicing productive professions, serving in the army, paying their taxes, would put an end to centuries of Jewish existence as the miserable objects of mindless persecution.

One of the weapons that the *maskilim* fashioned to spread their message and fight for their ideas was a Hebrew-language press, which, with its rich and diverse content, was able to recruit the writers of the new Hebrew literature to its cause. *Haskalah* publishing enterprises offered a platform to new poets and authors, some of whom were highly gifted; they included poets such as Micha Yosef Lebensohn and Yehuda Leib Gordon, and novelists and short story writers such as Abraham Mapu and Peretz Smolenskin. They sang the praises of the *Haskalah* while depicting with cruel sarcasm the fate of the ignorant *shtetl* Jews, held under the thumb of obscurantist rabbis and self-regarding notables. At the same time, they opened a window to European culture by translating masterworks of Russian, French, German and English literature into biblical Hebrew and introducing into Hebrew literature genres never before treated in Hebrew. In 1853, for example, Abraham Mapu wrote the first Hebrew-language novel, *Ahavat Tzion* (*Love of Zion*), which created a great stir at the time and remained revered for many generations.

The issue of the Jews' continued existence as a people does not appear in Gordon's early poetry. His later work, [1881] *Binareinu Ubizkeneynu Nelekh* (*As One*), for instance, offers the prospect of the Jewish people maintaining its integrity as one of the many people living under Russian Imperial rule:

One people we have been and one we shall remain
For hewn are we all from that one single vein;
Together we have shared both joy and pain
In the two thousand years of our scattering.
From nation to nation and land to land
Young and old, we went as one. . . .

"A people there is"—whisper the informers—
"Whose religion is not ours, who our kingdom's faith transgress."
You lie in your teeth! Openly we have ever lived,
As Jews keeping God's Torah,
But when the king's commandment is proclaimed,
Young and old, we go as one.

One people we are for one God we have
And hewn are we all from that one single vein;
One Torah too, its tongue ever with us,
Those golden chains bind us together:
Bound together by that three-strand cable
Young and old, we go as one. . . .

By our God we shall hold, his faith never leave,
Nor our lips e'er forget His holy Tongue,
Evil we have seen, but the good we shall also see
In this land we have lived in so long;
If it is God's will that we continue to wander,
Then, young and old, we shall go as one.

"The king" here is the Czar of Russia, not the Messiah King; and when
the poet promises that "the good we shall also see / In this land we have
lived in so long," he means Russia not the Land of Israel. He conceives
of Jewish identity as resting on a golden trinity—the God of Israel,
Torah, and the sacred Hebrew tongue. That the Jews are a people is
taken as a simple fact, for they come from the one stock and are moving
perhaps towards a shared destiny. None of this, however, subtracts one
jot from Gordon's loyalty to his country, the Russian Empire, and to his
king, the Czar of the Russians.

Gordon wrote *As One* when the *Haskalah's* failure to solve Russian
Jewry's problems could no longer be denied, when he realized both that
the Jews were not going to be welcomed as equals by the people of the
land, and that the Czar had no intention of improving their conditions,
as had seemed to be the case twenty years earlier. Even in the face of
accusations not dissimilar to those leveled against the Jews in the tale

recorded in the book of Esther, Gordon nurses the hope that the *Haska-lah* vision can yet be brought to pass by reiterating Jewry's loyalty to king and country. He now also began to consider the possibility that the mindless hatred might well force the Jews out of Russia. In his poem, "Ahoti Ruhama" (My Sister Ruhama)[12] written in 1882 after a series of pogroms in the Ukraine (pograms that were called "storms in the south," in order to bypass the Czarist censorship), he openly canvasses this possibility, even resurrecting the hope of messianic redemption in some future time:

> It was not I who abandoned my country,
> I still dreamed of good times,
> But to bear with your shame I could not find the strength,
> Come, let us go, Ruhama my sister!
>
> Come, let us go—alas, to dwell in safety
> In a loving mother's home I cannot give you;
> We have no mother and no home of hers to dwell in—
> We shall take ourselves to another guesthouse,
> Till our Father takes pity on us, there
> We shall sit and wait, Ruhama sister mine.

The "guesthouse" is America, with Gordon acknowledging that even there the Jews will not be full citizens. We shall remain temporary guests in whatever country we happen to find ourselves in "till our Father take pity on us"—till the coming of the Messiah.

MOVING TOWARD JEWISH SECULARISM

There are those who argue that the *Haskalah* collapsed into total failure. The peoples of Europe refused to accept Jews as equals and compatriots. Hebrew language and culture remained a minority taste—the younger generation preferred to speak Russian or German, and the turn of the century was accompanied by a tide of assimilation. The riots and pogroms of the time against Jews in Russia and the Ukraine only seemed to hammer more nails into the *Haskalah*'s coffin. Even its staunchest spokesmen admitted the failure; Gordon's "Lemi ani amel?" ("Who Am I Toiling For?") expresses their dejection:

> My brother *maskilim* studied the sciences,
> With an inadequate glue they stuck to their people's language,

Mocking their old mother at her distaff still:
'Abandon a language whose time has come and gone,
'Leave its literature no flavoring can make readable;
'Leave it for we shall each now talk our country's tongue!' . . .

And our children? The generation coming after us?
From their youth they will act toward us like strangers,
My heart agonizes for them—
They are pushing forward, year by year,
Who will know to call a halt? Where will they arrive?
Perhaps to a place—from where there is no way back . . .

In truth, the *Haskalah* movement deserves credit for much more than inaugurating a new Hebrew literature and establishing a sound scientific foundation for research into Judaism and Jewry. The *Haskalah* was responsible for transforming the way in which Europe's Jews lived. When Jews assimilated into non-Jewish society, they were realizing part of the *Haskalah*'s vision of a new Jewish life. Although many discarded every trace of their Jewishness and others converted to another religion, thus being lost to Jewry entirely, still others sought only to assimilate, not to be totally absorbed. Unwilling to convert, these Jews found ways to preserve those parts of their Jewish identity that they considered significant, in ways that enabled them to live comfortably with both their Jewishness and the culture into which they sought to assimilate. They still composed novels, poems, and essays on Jewish themes, expressing Jewish concerns and Jewish life, but rather than writing these in Hebrew or Yiddish, they chose to use the language of their countries, first German or Russian and later also French or English. Thoroughly integrated into their local economy, often commanding leading positions in manufacturing, commerce, and the professions, they still regarded themselves as and called themselves Jews. Today they form a large and vital component of the Jewish population outside Israel. The great majority of them are secular, the Judaism in their lives is a cultural tradition, a deep feeling of shared destiny, and a sense of mutual responsibility among and for Jews, wherever they may be living.

Reform Judaism is another *Haskalah* creation. It reshaped the religion and its practice in exactly the ways in which the *Haskalah* had proposed. It retained the centrality of the special role and mission that believers considered had been entrusted to Judaism and Jews—namely, to carry the teaching and ethics of the prophets to the nations of the world—and it introduced sufficient adjustments to religious practice to

enable Jews to be an active and central component of non-Jewish society, indispensable if they were to carry through their mission. Reform
Judaism today is numerically world Jewry's largest religious denomination.

The *Haskalah,* then, changed Jewish society profoundly, both in appearance and substance; this was the most radical change to have taken
place since the recasting of Jewish life at the close of the Second Temple
period, almost two thousand years earlier. The *Haskalah* made the Jewish world a pluralist one and brought Jewish secularism into that world.
Nor did the collapse of the Eastern European *Haskalah* as a cultural
movement put an end to its effectiveness; its ideas were used in diverse
ways and applied by many, some of whom were its sworn antagonists.
The idea of a Jewish national entity forming part of a multinational empire was taken up by the Autonomists, a Jewish nationalist movement,
whose spokesman was the outstanding historian, Simon Dubnov. They
in turn passed this idea on to Jewish socialists, whose organizations also
raised the demand for an autonomous national Jewish entity within a
multinational framework and who resisted every pressure to relinquish
their Jewish identity. Two other key *Haskalah* ideas, "productivization"
and the revival of Hebrew as the Jewish people's authentic language of
speech and writing were also adopted by the Jewish nationalists. They
agreed emphatically that Jews ought to be employed in useful and productive trades, most especially in agriculture and other constructive
manual occupations, and that Hebrew should be once again the vernacular. Both the Jewish nationalist and socialist movements owe an enormous ideological debt to the *Haskalah,* beyond the fact that it was the
Haskalah that made possible their existence in the first place.

However, nationalism and socialism refused to take from the *Haskalah* its conception of Jewish identity. For *maskilim,* particularly those in
Western Europe, Jewish identity was above all a religious identity and
thus they were quite ready to relinquish their Jewish nationhood altogether; but for the emerging Jewish nationalist movements, national
identity was, of course, the very heart of the matter, while religion was
peripheral. So it came about that, with Jewish socialists refusing to
stomach religion at any price, and with the main nationalist movement,
the Zionists, being essentially and extensively secular, the two religious
components of Jewish identity, faith and halacha steadily lost support
and influence and for the first time in the history of the Jewish people,
secularism set its foot on the stage. Today it is far more that just a bit
player: it currently vies for the leading role in Jewry's future.

Jewish Socialism

From socialism's earliest days Jews were at the forefront, both in matters of doctrine and in leadership. Behind them the ranks were filled with ordinary working Jews, far in excess of their numbers in the general population. Socialism stirred the Jewish imagination. It promised a general redemption, which they trusted would include the Jews. Some even saw socialism as bringing to pass the vision of the prophets, a sort of secular coming of the messiah, so they adopted the socialist ideology out of deep affiliation with Jewish tradition. Demographically too, it transpired that manual workers and craftsmen made up a much larger stratum of Jewish society than anyone had thought and, moreover, they toiled under a double repression and exploitation—first as workers and again as Jews. Many Jewish workers were persuaded by this to set up or join their own local Jewish trade unions, known as "Funds." In 1897, within the framework of Russian Social Democracy, the General Alliance of Jewish Workers of Lithuania, Poland, and Russia was inaugurated, better known by its abbreviated Yiddish name, der Bund (the Alliance). Expanding rapidly, the Bund soon became one of the largest organizations in Eastern European Jewry, combining scattered individual unions into one powerful body, substantial enough to conduct strikes and campaigns on a broad scale. Its popularity grew even more when in the anti-Semitic disturbances of 1903–7 it organized Jews into self-defense units. Not long after that, it was also at work among Jewish immigrants in England and the United States and in the new lands of immigration in South America, where it set up welfare agencies for the immigrants, in addition to fighting for better working conditions.

The first socialist tracts and educational materials for Jews now began to be written using the Hebrew language. One of the earliest Jewish activist in Russia was Aharon Shmuel Liberman, known as the Father of Jewish Socialism. Forced to flee from Russia, he continued his activities in London, where as early as 1877 he had already founded the first Jewish socialist newspaper in Hebrew, HaEmet (The Truth). Soon afterwards, when it became clear that very few Jewish workers or craftsmen could read Hebrew, a Yiddish journal appeared, called der Poylischer Yidl (The Polish Jew), which was the first of Yiddish newspapers and periodicals in the United Kingdom, the United States, Mexico, Argentina, and other countries to which Jews had immigrated. Even Russia had its underground Yiddish-language socialist literature.

So strong and active was the Bund that not only was it a partner in the founding of the Russian Social Democratic Party in 1898, it was even thought appropriate to hold the party's founding congress in Minsk, inside the Pale. Within the new party, the *Bund* retained its independence on all issues pertaining to Jewish questions. One of its proposals was for the party to demand that Russia be restructured as a federation of nations, in which each national entity would retain its autonomy at the national level; one of these entities would be a Jewish one. In this, as we noted before, the *Bund* embraced the *Haskalah* concept that the Jewish people are one of the peoples of the Russian Empire. After several years, the concept won the acceptance, if with considerable reservations, of the party's Bolshevik wing and when, a few years after that, the Bolsheviks established the Soviet Union, the Soviet Communist party included a Jewish Section (the *Yevsektsia*). In the form of the Union of Soviet Republics, the Communists finally brought to reality the *Bund*'s idea of a "federation of nations," dividing the Empire into a federation of national autonomous entities. There is even a Jewish autonomous republic within the Russian Federation, in the region of Birobidjan, in the far east, but very few Jews live there.

Like other socialist organizations the *Bund* would have no truck with religion or religious institutions: they considered these to be merely one more device manipulated by the rich to exploit the working poor. Similarly, it dismissed the Jewish nationalist movement as a whole, and Zionism in particular, as elitist and as a tool of the Jewish bourgeoisie. It held that these movements only distracted the repressed workers from their real conditions and from the real struggle, namely, the class struggle, which promised the only true solution to their adversity. The *Bund* also repudiated the Zionist-nationalist idea that Hebrew was the Jews' only authentic language. The *Bund*'s target population, the Jewish working masses, spoke and read Yiddish, not Hebrew, and consequently the *Bund* poured its resources into the development of Yiddish. However, this anti-religious, anti-Hebrew stance went hand in hand with a vigorous and enthusiastic defense of Jewish popular culture and traditions. *Bundists* proudly identified themselves as full and unadulterated Jews. Their achievements include a magnificent Yiddish-language culture, which expanded and flowered at a remarkable rate, so that by the end of the nineteenth century, it had reached outstanding dimensions. At the end of the nineteenth century and the first half of the twentieth century, Yiddish culture developed into a full-fledged cultural genre, finding expression in diverse spheres of art, from prose fiction and poetry, to music, painting, and drama, and even a Yiddish-language film industry. This outburst of productivity and creativity was explicitly and openly secular, but it was no less Jewish for all that. Jewish tradition and culture provided the essential inspiration and sources. Artists sang and told of the conditions of the Jewish poor; while they demanded change, they also depicted the poverty-stricken Jewish shtetl with affection or even with sharp humor, but never, as *Haskalah* writers had done, portraying it as a grotesque environment. Here, for instance, is how Isaac Leibosh Peretz, considered one of the greatest of writers in Yiddish and Hebrew, describes the suffering and poverty of the Jews of his time:

> I open the door. A room without beds or furniture. Straw mattresses on the floor. In the middle—an upturned barrel, with four small wild-haired children around it; on the barrel a large yellow earthenware bowl, full of soured milk . . . the children taking from the milk with one hand and gnawing at crusts of bread in their left. In one corner a white-faced woman; tears running down her cheeks into the potatoes she is peeling . . . while the man is sprawled on a mattress in another corner . . . I ask him what his work is.— I'm a tailor.—And the reason you want to emigrate?—Hunger . . . pure and simple! A hunger written plain on his forehead and on his wife's and glittering from the eyes of the children, seated around the soured milk.—No work? He shrugs: Isn't it obvious . . .—And where will you go?—To London . . . I was there once, and I made a living . . .—And why didn't you take your family with then?—I couldn't; I didn't go there to stay. . . . It's all clouds and fog there . . . I only had to close my eyes to see my home-town, my home-land, just like a day dream, the river, the forest . . .—True, I put in, the countryside around here is very beautiful . . .—O sure, very beautiful!— repeating my words mockingly—Fresh air, only half-price . . . three years now we've been living on it . . . Now I'm leaving with the wife and kids, and good riddance to the lot of it.—You won't miss the forest?— The forest?— His laugh is bitter and scornful.—The day before yesterday my wife went to pick berries in the forest, got found by the keepers and whipped. . . .—What about the river? I persisted.—O yeh, the river . . . one of my kids drowned in it . . . ("The Emigrant")

Here Peretz depicts not only the abject poverty but also the ambivalent feelings of poor Jews toward the country in which they live, the pain of leaving places that they regard as home and a country they feel to be their homeland. In the work of our greatest Yiddish poets, poverty and hunger are also important themes, and their treatment of these issues were often shaped by their socialism. Here, for instance, are a few lines from Yitzik Manger's "Di Balade fun Weisen Broit" Ballad to White Bread:

> Their faces are white, their arms have all held a dead child—
> Thirteen mothers herald to hunger the mighty.

Over their heads the night hangs out a round moon,
Round and shiny as a loaf of white bread.

The women stand; to the high heavens,
to the white bread they strech out their hands, . . .

Come down, bread of heaven, come down, deliver us!
The hunger kneads our children's bones! . . .

In the doorways the mothers stand and stare,
Want in their faces and death in their eyes.

And their lips tremble a whispered *Kaddish*
For that gleaming white bread—and the child now dead.[13]

All the Yiddish authors and poets of this period display a deep allegiance and affinity to the sources of Judaism, whether they be ancient, such as the Bible, midrash and aggada, or more contemporary, such as the Hasidic tales of their own time. Y. L. Peretz and Sholem Asch, two of the Yiddish greatest story tellers, reworked Hasidic tales to reveal their own perspective of Jewish experience. Yitzik Manger retold biblical stories that he relocated in the *shtetls* of Eastern Europe. All of them employed these sources despite their own anti-religiousness; yet it would seem that this very secularism enabled them to recognize the rich layers available in Jewish religious culture, layers which they could harness in new ways to create art that would speak powerfully to their society. While retaining a deep respect for the majesty of the sources, and always acknowledging their cultural authority, the artists' secularism gave them the license to treat their materials with liberty.

Bundists were active in the resistance and ghetto uprisings as well as in the Jewish communal organizations that tried to provide assistance during the Nazi era, but together with most of the rest of European Jewry the *Bund* was destroyed by the Holocaust. The heroism of *Bundists* in the face of the horrors of that time are hauntingly expressed, recorded in the work of several Yiddish-language poems, such as S. Kaczerginski's famous "Ponar," and H. Glick's "Song of the Jewish Partisans." Here are a few lines from Kadia Molodowsky's "Yidn" ("Jews,") composed "in memory of the writers who fell in Warsaw together with the rest of the Jews":

> Writer's pen in hand, he sits. Desk, sheet of paper,
> The unfinished line laid on the page.
> Then Death knocks but does not move on, . . .

"I'm waiting for you.
And the Jews are waiting for both of us
Out there,"—says Death, whispering—
"I've come to go with you and them."
The pen dips and writes its last verse, up to the full stop:
"I am a Jew. Death is waiting for me.
Out there are waiting for me other Jews.
Today, see, hand in hand with Death we come
To say to our enemy and oppressor
That the victory is ours." . . .

After the war no vestige of the *Bund* was left. A few minor branches maintain a limited existence in the United States, Mexico, Argentina, and in Israel, issuing periodicals in Yiddish, English, and Spanish, and maintaining a few schools in which Yiddish is the language of teaching.

As a worldwide Jewish movement, Jewish socialism has vanished. Even the *Yevsektsia*, the Soviet Communist Party's Jewish section, is no more and the Jewish autonomous republic of Birobidjan is almost empty of Jews; certainly, its Jewish character, if it ever had any, is fast disappearing. There remains, however, the historical and incontrovertible fact that Jewish socialism revolutionized Jewry. The socialist movements demonstrated over a period of almost one hundred years that a confident and proud Jewish identity is perfectly feasible without it needing to be subject to either a religious faith or a *halacha*-regulated lifestyle. By rooting self-definition in Jewish nationhood and making creative use of Jewish cultural tradition, the Jewish socialist and nationalist movements established an authentic alternative framework for a secular Jewish life.

Jewish Nationalism: Zionism

Although most of its leaders were intellectuals, Jewish socialism attracted most of its followers from the ranks of Jewish manual laborers and craftsmen. Among the intelligentsia and the middle class, the movement that was most popular was the Jewish national movement, Zionism. Like socialism, Zionism followed the *Haskalah* concept of regarding the Jews as a people like any other engaged in productive, constructive work within society. It parted company with socialism by promoting Hebrew as the Jews' vernacular and primary language, and with the *Haskalah* in that it considered that the sole possibility of the Jews ever becoming "a people like any other" was if they were to estab-

lish and settle in an autonomous territory, preferably in the Land of Israel (Erets Israel).

Jewish nationalism diverged from the *Haskalah* when, during the
1870s, several *maskilim*, among them David Gordon and Peretz Smolenskin, who were disillusioned with the results of emancipation, suggested the alternative of Jewish settlement in the Land of Israel. The
idea did not gather serious support until 1882 when, after a new outbreak of pogroms in Russia, Leo Pinsker, a Russian doctor and writer,
published a pamphlet in Berlin entitled "Auto-Emancipation." Pinsker
had once been a leading light of the *Haskalah*, preaching Jewish integration into Russian culture, society, and economic life. Now he was
openly recanting, arguing that the only way to end anti-Semitism was
for Jews to return to being a people like all others, inhabiting their own
national territory; and that the best choice of territory was the Land of
Israel. His pamphlet struck a chord. Several Jewish national associations
quickly rose to pursue these goals by calling upon young Russian Jews
to leave for their ancient homeland. These associations joined to form
the *Khovevei Tzion* (Lovers of Zion) movement, and the first group to
actually attempt the new objective emerged from among its members.
They called themselves BILU, an acronym constructed from the words
in Isaiah 2:5, *"bet Yaakov lekhu venelekha"* (house of Jacob, let us walk
[in the light of the Lord]).

An early adherent of *Khovevei Tzion* was Asher Ginzburg, an essayist
and polemicist well known under his pen name of Ahad Ha'am (one of
the people). While he had no faith that settlement in the Land of Israel
could solve "the problem of the Jews," he did think that a national spiritual center might be set up there which, by attracting the energies of
Jewry's best minds, might possibly influence Diaspora Jews towards a
greater sense of Jewish nationhood and solve the "problem of Judaism"
that way. At first, the new Zionism found very few recruits in Central
and Western Europe but that changed dramatically when in 1896 a
pamphlet entitled "The Jewish State" appeared. It was composed by an
Austrian author and journalist, Theodore Herzl, and it argued that since
the Jewish "problem" was a national problem its solution would also
need to be national; that is, it required the establishment of a Jewish
state. A wave of nationalist enthusiasm swept through European Jewry.
Only a year later, in 1897, Herzl was able to organize the first Zionist
Congress, in Basel, Switzerland, which collectively declared that "Zionism aspires to create a refuge for the Jewish people in the Land of Israel, guaranteed by international law." The Zionist movement steadily
expanded, until its goal was finally achieved in the founding of the State

of Israel. Zionism had established a Jewish identity of a new kind, one without precedent in the history of Jewry.

Of course, this drive toward national restoration placed the element of nationhood highest out of all the constituents of Jewish identity. Although Herzl regarded the "religion of our forefathers" as a factor uniting Jews throughout the world, he presented the heart of the Jewish question as the issue of Jewish nationality, and therefore of Jewish identity too. While he did not discount religion, he did issue a categorical and unambiguous declaration, stating that the character of the new Jewish state was to be secular: "We shall bring to nought all maneuvers by our men of religion to establish a theocracy . . . Everyone shall be free in his faith or his lack of it." Ahad Ha'am went even further. His essay, "Subjection Within Freedom," stated that Jewish identity was a problem only for the Jews of Western Europe because they had traded their national identity for civil rights and made an empty shell of their Jewishness, leaving it a mere "theoretical concept." For the Jews of Eastern Europe, he claimed, the problem did not exist, since they had never been accorded any civil rights and thus they preserved their national Jewish identity. It was the circumstances of the Western European Jews that he labeled "subjection within freedom," a state of affairs he was not prepared to countenance even in exchange for all the civil rights in the world. For Ahad Ha'am, his Jewish identity was not a question at all. He stood confidently upon his nationality as a Jew, a platform that he maintained had no need of reinforcement whatsoever from *halachic* observance; as long as one keeps his Jewish nationality safe, there is no need to keep a strict conventional Jewish lifestyle; even the articles of the faith could be questioned. Likewise, Zeev Jabotinsky, a scholar and writer who led the nationalist movement's right wing, considered that nothing was of greater importance to Jewry than the issue of the Jews' nationhood. From his perspective, religion was by no means the source of national identity; it was merely one facet of the nation's existence and self-awareness. The real source of Jewish identity resided in what he termed Jewry's "racial make-up."

The Jewish nationalist movement defined itself as secular: in the trinity of Jewish identity, it held the nationalist element paramount. While the *maskilim* had felt compelled to reshape Jewish religiousness by removing its nationalist component, similarly Zionism reshaped the Jewish sense of nationhood, but by removing faith and *halacha*. The idea of messianic redemption, the mainstay of Jewish nationhood for time out of mind, was in effect thrust aside in favor of a secular and political messianism, a concept that operated on a totally different plane. The Zionists also matched the *Haskalah* in inventing a new name for themselves: while the *maskilim* had renamed Judaism "the Mosaic faith," the Zionists called themselves not Jews but "Hebrews" (*Ivrim*). Jews in exile remain Jews, but Jews re-energized by the pioneering vision of a new Jewish state were Hebrews. This old-new name dominated the institutions of Jewish Palestine between the world wars: the Jews who settled there were "the Hebrew *yeshuv*" (population), Tel Aviv was "the first Hebrew town," and its high school was called the Herzliya Hebrew Gymnasium; other notable instances include The Hebrew University, the General Federation of Hebrew Workers, and the Hebrew Writers' Association. A new slogan was coined: "Hebrew, Speak Hebrew!" This pride in their new name was supported by a complete ideology, of which the contemporary "Canaanite" school of literature, founded by Yonatan Ratosh, was the most extreme voice.[14] This rejection of the traditional Jewish identities for the new Hebrew is also to be found in the writings of Micha Yosef Berditchevsky, Sha'ul Chernikhovsky, Zalman Shne'ur and others. Only after the Holocaust, and when Israeli society was facing an identity challenge from its Arab citizens, did "Jew" return as an acceptable self-appellation.

As the *Haskalah* and the Jewish socialist movements had done before them, so Jewish nationalism also found a strong voice in the rich Hebrew literature of its time, known as the literature of *Hathiya*, or revival. In common with Jewish socialism and socialist authors, the new nationalism and its literary voices also show evidence of a profound loyalty and affection for their cultural heritage, making lavish use of its sources and themes, even while applying new meanings to them. The design of the Zionist movement's flag, later to become the national flag of Israel, was based on the traditional prayer shawl. Zionist authors borrowed symbols and terms from the Bible and Jewish history and projected them onto new nation-building realities to endorse their new vision. For instance, the new settlement of the Land of Israel was linked to the settlement of Canaan by the twelve tribes as narrated in the book of Joshua. For Sha'ul Chernikhovsky these were the true roots of his Jewishness, and these roots were so secure, so substantial, that he had no need of the religious and *Galut* ingredients of Judaism. He articulates this in his poem, "This is My Song:"

> What blood are you, teeming within me, blood of an ancient age,
> The blood of lords of ancient days, from the farthest reach of the sun's light?
> The secret voice of that first generation, of new-minted men, of mighty men,
> The voice of the blood of men who wrestle with their God and scorn enemy swords.

And what blood are you, seething in my veins?
The blood of those who died reciting the Name of the One?
Of my God I have despaired, and walk His ways no more;
Wettened wool over the heart, as the presence of its God drains away,
Has no terrors for one who knows to fight with sword and shield. . . .

What blood are you, seething in my veins? Blood of the wilderness
generation? Yes!
My blood is the blood of the conquerors of Canaan, gushing without pause.
That clarion song calls to me again, melody of blood and fire:
Assault the hill, trample the plain, take all that you see—it is your
inheritance!

With his faith lost and despairing of God, the narrator rejects the notion
of choosing a martyr's death to glorify His Name. He feels no sympathy
even for the ten famous sages who, after the collapse of the Bar Kokhba
Revolt, were burnt at the stake by the Romans as an example to other
Jews. The Talmud tells us (BT *Avoda Zara* 18a) that pads of wet wool
were placed on the chest of one of these sages, R. Hanina Ben-Tera-
dion, when he was burnt by the stake, to ensure that his death would be
slow and painful. Chernikhovsky instead identifies with the "heroic"
first generation of Jews, the generation born in the wilderness and conquered Canaan.

The idea of a secular messiah appears quite often in the Hebrew literature between the world wars. This messiah comes in the shape of the
"pioneers," the first of the new settlers of Israel, or in the shape of Jews
or Hebrews working their own land, ploughing and sowing, quarrying
rock, laying roads, or busy with other constructive tasks. Uri Tzvi Greenberg's "Beoznei Yeled Asaper" *"As I Would Tell a Child"* is a good example:

He didn't come, the messiah . . . As an eagle soaring over blood-filled
chasms.
Day and night I heard the beat of his wings.
He arrived at Jaffa Harbor in the shape of a man with a knapsack: wretchedly
poor, bearing vision and sword—
And I saw him again later, a ploughman working his field under the blazing
sun
And a stoneworker hammering at the rock of Jerusalem.

The manual labor and construction work required to build the new state
are even depicted in terms of prayer and sacred rite and, under the influence of Aharon David Gordon who extolled manual labor as the force

that could redeem the Jew and Jewry, some even talked of a "religion of labor." Avraham Shlonsky's poem, "Labor," uses the objects of Jewish religious ritual, the prayer shawl, and the phylacteries[15] and their straps to evoke the new shape that the land was acquiring at the hands of the pioneers, even going so far as to call the workers tilling the fields and laying the roads "creators," to whom the fine new town they are helping to construct offers its prayers:

> Dress me, my good Jewish mother, in my best striped robe,
> It is time for the morning prayer, so take me to the place of my labor.
> My land wraps its shoulders in light like a prayer shawl,
> Houses stand out like phylacteries
> And like their straps, the roads we have labored to lay wind down and
> around.

> To its creator the fine new town recites the morning prayer
> And among the creators Abraham your son,
> Poet and road-maker in Israel.

This borrowing of terms and concepts from religious tradition in no way betokens a Zionist religiousness; rather, it is evidence of an ineradicable connection to the culture created by and belonging to every generation of Jews. Even when the Hebrew writings expressly challenged traditional Judaism, as when it countered ancient "Jewish" practice with the new "Hebrew" culture, or when it treated pre-Israelite Canaanite idol worship as an important source of our own national culture,[16] there was no intention to foul or spurn the deep wells of Jewish culture, but rather to broaden the culture's sources beyond the limit permitted by the rabbis.

So, although Zionism and its literature, the "literature of the revival," were secular in both essence and substance, their foundations were rooted in the deepest strata of Jewish culture, cogent evidence of the new nationalism's profound connection to the ancient sources of Jewish history. As was true also of the Yiddish socialist writers, the Zionists' secularism, far from blinding them to traditional Judaic sources, afforded them a unique perspective on these sources. This generated a broader and more diverse appreciation of them than the traditionally restricted focus permitted religious readers. Secularism thus enabled a breadth of vision that nourished the literature of the revival, as well as the Hebrew and Israeli literature that followed in its tracks, to create a magnificent and justly famous body of work, one that spans a meta-historical bridge between the present of Jewish culture and all of its past, back to its very origins, and may perhaps also form a bridge between present and future cultures. The literature of the revival includes some of the greatest names in modern Hebrew writing: Bialik and Chernikhovsky in poetry, Berditchevsky, Brenner, and Genessin in narrative prose, and many others.

Religious Zionism

Fierce opposition to the idea of national restoration in the "Promised Land" came from the ultra-Orthodox, for it was their belief that Israel's redemption would come only at the will and hand of God. To take political action to such an end was to rebel against God's will and risk the terrible punishment that might ensue; God had visited upon the Jews a period of exile and thus it was forbidden and presumptuous for them to try to end their exile by force.[17] Indeed, fifty years later, some ultra-Orthodox scholars would interpret the Holocaust of European Jewry as divine punishment for Zionism's rebellious refusal to accept God's will. But in 1912, in an attempt to fight both Zionism and Reform Judaism, the Ultra-Orthodox established their own political movement, *Agudat Yisrael*, which to this very day in the State of Israel, proclaims its antipathy to Zionism and even, in part, to the very existence of the State. They disown the State's symbols and festivals (the flag and Independence Day, for example) and disparage all secular Jews by labeling them "Zionists."

In total contrast to the stand taken by the ultra-Orthodox rabbinate at this time, R. Isaac Jacob Reines of Vilna, a member both of *Khovevey Tzion* and of the Zionist Federation, founded and was the first president of Mizrakhi, a movement defining itself as "religious Zionism." Mizrakhi's slogan was "The Land of Israel for the People of Israel according to the Torah of Israel." For its authority in religious Judaism, it harked back to the work of two nineteenth-century rabbi-heralds of the Zionist program, R. Tzvi Hirsch Kalischer and R. Yehuda Solomon Khai Alkalai. As these two scholars read the sources, the conventional premise that the messiah's coming had to be passively awaited was incorrect. His coming was due to take place in two stages, the first by natural means and the second by supernatural means; and the second could not take place until the first had prepared the way. According to this reading, it was entirely appropriate that the Jews on earth should take an active part in bringing about the first stage. Blessed by this authority, the religious could claim to hear "the footsteps of the messiah" in the clarion call of Zionism.

The teaching of R. Avraham Yitzhak Hacohen Kook, Chief Rabbi to the Jews of Palestine in the 1930s, extended this interpretation of Zionism. Since the resettlement of Israel by Jews was but one stage on the road to messianic redemption of the whole world, the new settlers' secularism could be tolerated. Many were persuaded by this apparent broad-mindedness that R. Kook was a "pluralist," but this was by no means so. To his opinion, the settlers' secularism was to be simply a passing phase. As the redemption gathered strength, the Zionist builders of the Land would return to Judaism with rejoicing hearts and, in perfect faith, take up the yoke of Torah and the commandments. For R. Kook, secularism in no way stood as an alternative truth on a level with that of his own; as a transient deviation, it could be borne for as long as it assisted the process of redemption.

For several decades, while Rav Kook's policy held sway, religious Zionism worked together with the Labor Movement and its secular settlement arm. Religious Zionism even established its own settlement movement, but Israel's stunning victory in the Six Days' War changed everything. For the central and major section of the religious Zionist movement the victory meant only one thing—that a critical further stage in the process of redemption had taken place. The messianic idea, always at the heart of religious Zionism, rose to prominence, and pushed the movement to the extreme right wing of Israeli politics. From the start, many in the movement had never accepted the notion that Zionism could have a messianic role, and that included its founder, R. Reines. For them Judaism and Zionism existed on two separate planes. Zionism was a politico-historical phenomenon, whose entire and sole reason for existing was to save Jews in danger of extinction and to provide a solution to the needs of those who wanted to live in a politically autonomous Jewish entity. Such a program had nothing in common with faith in a God-sent and messiah-led redemption. Therefore, the secular character of Zionism was accepted without any doubts. The moderates in today's religious Zionism hold this view.

Socialist Zionism

The idea of combining Zionism with socialism—that is, of building a new Jewish national society in the Land of Israel on socialist principles—was proposed at the same time as the Zionist concept first arose. In 1862, one of the nineteenth century's greatest socialist thinkers, Moses Hess, published his *Rome and Jerusalem,* in which he described exactly such a combination. Then in 1898, Nakhman Sirkin brought out his paper, *The Jewish Question and the Jewish Socialist State,* proposing that the new state be built in accordance with "constructive socialism." "Jewish settlement in the homeland and all its major institutions," said Sirkin, "should be constructed on cooperative principles, not on the principles of free competition."

From 1900 onwards, a number of organizations were founded to implement this theory. In 1906 the Jewish Social Democratic Workers Party, *Poalei Tzion* (Workers of Zion), was established, headed by the philosopher, Dov Ber Borochov, who founded his movement's ideology on Marxist tenets. According to this view, the Jews' struggle for national liberation was part of the proletariat's class struggle, which would also win the Jewish proletariat its freedom. He called for the Jewish people to become "productive" and for the "territorial concentration" of the Jewish masses in the Land of Israel. Another party, founded in Palestine at the same time, was *Hapoel Hatza'ir* (The Young Worker), inspired by the teachings of A. D. Gordon, who urged Jews to take up manual labor, especially agricultural labor. He held such labor to be the supreme living value by which the individual, the Jewish people and the whole world might redeem itself. Berl Katzenelson, a political philosopher and *Hapoel Hatza'ir*'s pre-eminent leader, followed Sirkin in speaking of realizing the Zionist ideal by following the path of Constructive Socialism. As the phrase "socialist Zionism" implies, while the various trends in the movement all emphasized the national element in Jewish life and identity, they also stressed Jewry's class structure and the gap between rich and poor. They dismissed the Jewish religion out of hand, considering it an instrument of the rich for oppressing the poor. All the strands and organizations in socialist Zionism were avowedly and entirely secular.

It was socialist Zionism whose organizations, ideals, leadership, drive, and workers built the institutions and structure of Jewish Palestine. The socialist Zionists built the Labor Movement and their leaders directed the agencies that organized and controlled settlement and immigration; they set up self-defense forces; established economic enterprises and social services, youth movements, the education and health care systems, and cultural institutions. The structure they built was the structure upon which the State of Israel arose in 1948, the year it was officially established. The Labor Movement also undertook a second national enterprise—the creation of a new Jewish secular culture to reflect and represent the new Jewish life that was under construction. Yet, as we have seen, this secular culture rests, in essence, on the heritage from every generation of Jewry, back to antiquity. For example, the new settlers, particularly in the kibbutzim, made efforts to create new content and ceremonials for the calendar of ancient and traditional festivals by associating them both with the new experience of working the land and with the experience of the early Israelites. At the same time, they took care to preserve the centuries-old traditions associated with the festivals that had evolved in the Jews' lands of exile.

5

Judaism and Jewry Today

UNITARY JUDAISM NO LONGER EXISTS, NEITHER IN ISRAEL NOR ELSE-
where in the Jewish world. The parting of the ways between the Jewish
religion and the Jews' sense of nationhood, a separation first set in motion in the late eighteenth century, when European Jews were granted
civil rights, has proved irreversible. As we have seen, new branches of
Jewry later emerged, some of which defined their Jewish identity exclusively in terms of religious belief and practice, and disowned affiliation
to any Jewish national entity; others of which considered their Jewish
identity to be based upon the concept of nationhood, seeing the Jewish
religion as a secondary, inherited allegiance, an optional loyalty. Between these two poles, there were various intermediate positions: Some,
while not completely dismissing a definition of Judaism and Jewry based
upon nationhood, would accept it only with certain reservations, resulting in a concept that differed significantly from the traditional version
of Jewish nationhood. Other intermediate positions adjusted and
amended the conventional definition of that concept of Judaism and
Jewry that was based primarily upon religion. Only a small minority of
Jews, most of whom belonged to various Orthodox groups, clung and
still clings to its particular interpretation of the historical unity of faith,
halacha and messiah-centered nationhood. For many Jews Jewish identity has contracted into a parcel of ethnic bonds and loyalties, memories
and customs, which are manifested most importantly in communal ties
and the open self-definition as a Jew. The essence of Jewry and Judaism
today no longer resides in that unity of three core elements, as it had
done for so long, but rather in their disunity—in that parting of the ways
between the Jews' sense of religion and of nationhood. Today Jewish
identity wears many faces and has assumed many forms. That old unity
is now unlikely to ever be retrieved because Jewry no longer needs it
and because it is no longer the sole, or even the dominant, definition of
Jewish identity. Even the Orthodox now manifest a discord of world-

views and lifestyles and decline to submit to any single *halachic* authority.

THE GROUPINGS OF CONTEMPORARY RELIGIOUS JEWRY

The Orthodox

The Orthodox branch of Jewry came into being in the late eighteenth century and then developed in several directions during the nineteenth century. "Orthodox," implying exaggerated religious piety, was in fact a nickname borrowed by Reform Jews from the Christian Orthodox Church and applied mockingly to those other Jews who rejected all change or innovation in Judaism and in the ways of life derived from it. Jewish Orthodoxy was in fact a reaction to the *Haskalah* and Reform Judaism. Appalled by the directions in which they saw Judaism being taken, these Jews reacted by declaring the three-thousand-year evolution of Jewish belief, law, lifestyle, and custom was to be frozen, petrified forever and fixed as it stood at that point in time, namely, the closing years of the eighteenth century. R. Moshe Sofer, better known as *Hatam Sofer*, one of Orthodoxy's most forceful leaders in the early nineteenth century and an angry opponent of emancipation, Enlightenment, and reform, encapsulated this petrifaction in one dictum: "Innovation is forbidden by the Torah" (*Responsa of Hatam Sofer*, 1:28).

The Orthodox regard themselves, and would have others regard them, as the sole heirs to the three millennia of Judaism, for as they see it, nothing has changed in Judaism since the revelation at Sinai, everything that may appear to have been a change was in fact also handed down to Moses on that single formative occasion. They quote Ecclesiastes 1:9–10: "The thing that has been, it is that which shall be, and that which is done, is that which shall be done; and there is no new thing under the sun. If there any thing whereof it may be said, see, this is new, It has been already of old time, which was before us." In their opinion, all other Jewish sects, and particularly the secular, have deserted the beliefs and lifestyles that characterized Judaism from the beginning of its history and in doing so, have severed their bond to the authentic Sinai-inaugurated tradition. According to the Orthodox view, as it was in Eastern Europe in the late eighteenth century, so it was in the beginning, and not only regarding *halacha* and lifestyle. Their patterns of social life, manners and customs, the education system, the status of women, even dress and diet had to remain fixed as they stood, sanctified as the signs and emblems of "right-thinking" Jews. They simply closed their eyes to the plain fact that all these customs and practices were merely the end points of complex, centuries-long evolutions, which also bore the obvious imprint of their non-Jewish environment. They isolated themselves utterly from other schools and denominations of Judaism: the severest possible ban was placed on any teaching or practice that was not their own. Given that Orthodox doctrine says that anyone born to a Jewish mother is Jewish, non-Orthodox Jews had to be acknowledged as Jews, but were nevertheless seen as "wrongdoers" or "delinquent Jews" or, the mildest label possible, "*tinok she-nishba*," that is, abducted innocent "children" who had been unwittingly led astray. Yet Orthodoxy is in fact very far from being monolithic. Its many subdivisions vary widely and their mutual antipathy is notorious. We have already discussed the gulf between *Hasidim* and *mitnagdim*, and there is just as much enmity between the devoted followers of different Hasidic *rebbe-tzaddiks*. The Orthodox of Eastern European descent keep up marked differences of practice from those of Western European descent, and both of these differ from the Orthodox practices of Sepharadi, Iraqi, Yemeni, and other "Oriental" communities. Agnon weaves a telling picture of the divergence of the prayer services conducted by the various Orthodox congregations in Jaffa during the first decade of the twentieth century:

> At that time Jaffa was settled by *Perushim* and *Hasidim*. Although the one prayed an Ashkenazi order of service and the other a Sephardi order, the one service was not the Ashkenazi one . . . and the other was not the Sephardi service prayed in our little *kloyz*[2] using the service of the Polish, Moldavian and Ukrainian *Hasidim* . . . while the Jaffa *Hasidim* used the service of the revered Lyady rabbi.[3] In our old *Beit-Midrash* the prayer service was the one the people there had from their fathers, and their fathers from their fathers, all the way back to the time of the very first exiles to arrive in Ashkenaz, whereas the Jaffa Ashkenazis prayed a service prescribed by the great Vilna Gaon. . . . There were also two other Jewish communities in Jaffa, a Sephardi one and a Yemenite one, divided among several synagogues and differing prayer services. (*"And Not to Stumble"*)

Each one of these congregations not only scorned the idea of innovation in their own religious practice but also disparaged the Jewishness of every non-Orthodox community.

Today, the Orthodox, although constituting a 12 percent minority of Jewry worldwide, are found in almost every country where there are any

Jews at all. Their numbers are slightly greater in the United States, Israel, and Western Europe.[4] Of the approximately one million Orthodox Jews living outside Israel, two-thirds define themselves as "moderate Orthodox." Although they live a *halacha*-regulated community life, the formal Jewish education they give their children is usually limited to an extra morning's "Sunday school," on top of their full-time general education. They do not object to their children studying, and themselves teaching, in secular schools, colleges, and universities. They are stalwarts of the wider economy and society, although some may be thinking of immigrating to Israel for religious reasons. About 350,000 define themselves as *Haredim*, ultra-Orthodox, most of these belonging either to one of the *Hasidic* sects clustered around its *rebbe*, or to *mitnagdim* congregations who follow the "Lithuanian" synagogue service. For the entire distinctions that differentiate one ultra-Orthodox community from another, compared to other Jews they have much in common. They all live in very close, tightly disciplined communities, inhabiting exclusive neighborhoods, setting themselves apart by their dress and lifestyle, they take no part in the community life of other Jews, and even less in the life of non-Jews.

Orthodoxy's largest concentration is in Israel, and this population too, like all other national Orthodox populations, is a small minority of the total population, and divided within itself into divergent trends and mutually hostile communities. It has an extremist wing, made up of a number of ultra-Orthodox communities, *rebbe*-devoted Hasidim, "Lithuanian" *mitnagdim*, and various communities of Sephardic ultra-Orthodox, mainly of North African extraction, and organized around either a charismatic rabbi-spiritual leader or a communal father figure. Some of the Sephardic ultra-Orthodox have almost abandoned their own traditions and adopted Ashkenazi customs and practice. Like the ultra-Orthodox elsewhere, the Israeli branch lives in segregated communities and single-community neighborhoods, predominantly in the cities of Jerusalem and B'nai Brak. By dress and lifestyle, they set themselves firmly apart from all other Israelis.

Orthodoxy is also represented in Israel by those who define themselves as "*Datiyim*," observant Jews. They observe the *mitzvoth* and *halacha* but they dress and live as neighbors to other Israelis, they are part of the general society and economy and, to an extent, participate in the general cultural life. Externally, other Israelis recognize them by the *kipah* (skullcap) that they wear on their heads. Together, all Israel's Orthodox citizens, including all degrees of Orthodoxy, are reliably estimated at some 700,000, or 15 percent of the total population. Then there is the political dimension. All Orthodox denominations are also organized in political parties: There are three ultra-Orthodox ones— *Agudat Yisrael* (mainly Hasidim), *Degel Hatorah* (the Lithuanians) and *Shas* (Sephardis)—and one for the *Datiyim*, the National Religious Party, which is the Israeli version of the *Mizrakhi* religious Zionist movement.

The ultra-Orthodox, both the *Hasidim* and their *mitnagdim* opponents, in Israel and elsewhere, reject Zionism and the State of Israel to different degrees. Before the establishment of the state, their rejection was much more vehement than it is now and their political party, *Agudat Yisrael*, was vehemently anti-Zionist. Once the state was established and operative, some of them took their place in its political institutions but went no further. They still loudly reject the Zionist idea, upon which the state was profoundly based, they refuse to celebrate state holidays, they will not fly its flag, and they will not enroll in its defense forces (with the agreement of the state their young men are exempt from compulsory conscription). Their representation in the national economy is also far below their proportion in the total population because so many of their men-folk engage in full-time Torah study while receiving financial support from the state and from their fellow-believers abroad. A small ultra-Orthodox sub-sect, *Neturei Karta* (Aramaic for "the City Guards"), all living in Jerusalem's *Mea She'arim* neighborhood, do not even recognize the state's existence and refuse any involvement with any facet of its life. In contrast, the majority of the *"Datiyim,"* those represented by the National Religious Party, acknowledge Zionism as a messianic movement, and the state as the first step along the road to realization of the messianic idea, what they call "the first shoots of our redemption." A politically moderate minority of them regards Zionism as a politico-historical movement unconnected to the messianic idea; this minority has founded the *Meimad* Party (an acronym of, in Hebrew, "The Jewish state is a democratic state") and the two movements known as *Oz Leshalom* ("Strength for Peace") and *Netivot Shalom* ("Paths of Peace").

Reform Judaism

The dawn of the movement for the reform of Judaism coincided with the start of the nineteenth century. Although the name "Reform" might carry echoes of the Reformation of Catholicism instigated by Martin Luther in the sixteenth century, its direct inspiration and the bulk of its content came from the Central European *Haskalah*. Jews were being summoned by the *maskilim* to take their place in the life and culture of their German fellow citizens and to make reforms in the religion, in its practice and in the way they lived, that would bring them into line with the new post-Emancipation era. The first strides along this road were taken by Israel Jacobson, a German Jewish financier, who built "progressive" schools and synagogues in a number of towns. In 1810, he built a house of prayer to practice the principles he had been preaching and called it a "temple" rather than a "synagogue."[5] In his temple, and in those that followed his example, men and women sat side by side and followed a shorter prayer service. To the accompaniment of an organ, prayers were said in both German and Hebrew, and the rabbi gave his sermon in German only. In 1808, Jacobson convened a congress of Jewish leaders to debate proposals for religious reforms. One proposal was to introduce a coming-of-age ceremony at sixteen years of age, instead of the traditional *bar mitzvah* at thirteen. In 1818, a new temple in Hamburg followed a reformed *siddur* (order of prayer). In the 1840s, several congresses were held in Germany to decide on a direction for the new movement and to draw up a reformed prayer book for it. A range of strategies were proposed: Samuel Holdheim argued for radical reform, Zecharia Frankel for a moderate line. It was Abraham Geiger and others, taking the golden mean, whose views prevailed. These views were embodied in the principles of reform that were then adopted and in the reformed prayer book.

Yet for all the intense thought and material resources invested, the movement for Reform did not prove very attractive to German Jews and fared no better among the French and English Jewish communities. It was in the United States that it found its home. As early as the 1820s and throughout the 1830s American communities were going over to the new version, while the 1840s saw a veritable boom. In 1873 the Union of American Hebrew Congregations was established under the direction of R. Isaac Mayer Wise and this was followed in 1875 by the establishment of Hebrew Union College, a rabbinic seminary. In 1889 came the Central Conference of American Rabbis. If R. Wise was the movement's acknowledged leader, R. David Einhorn's more extreme views made him the ideologue with the most influence. Today, Reform Judaism encompasses a large section of American Jewry and has strong branches in South America, South Africa, Australia, Israel, and elsewhere. It is world Jewry's largest religious denomination.

In 1896, the Union Prayer Book, based on earlier prayer books devised and edited by Wise and Einhorn, won the acceptance of all the Reform communities. It was built upon the traditional Ashkenazi prayer service but changed large sections of the Hebrew text to recitation in English and excised all prayers and *piyyutim* promising messianic redemption and a return to Zion. Reform's leadership refused to countenance concepts such as miraculous redemption and restoration to the Promised Land. Modern Jews, they argued, regarded themselves as permanent residents of the countries in which they lived, not as temporary sojourners in exile. In place of messianism, they established the equally ancient vision of the Jews as a "Chosen People," chosen to serve as a "light to the nations," particularly in the moral realm, a historic mission that a mass return to the Land of Israel would vitiate entirely. They drew a firm distinction between the Torah, the Written Law given to Moses on Mount Sinai, and *halacha*, the Oral Law, devised and revised by the nation's sages over subsequent generations, and equally revisable in our day in the light of new circumstances, whatever the Orthodox might claim as to both Laws having been dictated by God at Sinai. Within the Written Law, Wise and Einhorn drew a further distinction between the eternal laws decreed by divine authority and the rules required by the circumstances of a particular time and, as such, amendable by a later generation living under new circumstances. Einhorn, in particular, propagated a philosophy of "continuous Divine revelation," which he held was as ever-present in our own time as it was in biblical times, a revelation that guides the amendments we make to our belief and *halacha*. Reform also emphasized the centrality in Judaism of the morality of its major prophets and the precedence this morality takes over matters of rite and ceremony. Some of its leaders were prepared to say that certain customs and *halachot* had outlived their time, such as the practice of covering the head or putting on phylacteries, some rules of *kashrut* and some of the rules designed to preserve the sanctity of the Sabbath. Reform's emphasis on the centrality of ethics led it into campaigns for social justice within the United States and elsewhere. As early as 1917, the movement passed a formal resolution in support of equal rights for women. Within Reform itself, women are eligible for all positions, administrative and religious alike, rabbi and cantor not excepted. In recent years, the movement's rabbis have sanctioned the marriage of Jews with non-Jews, recognized the right of homosexuals to hold religious posts in Reform communities, and even permitted same-sex marriages. Reform's abandonment of messianism in favor of Jewry's mission as a "light to the nations" led it also to repudiate Zionism, a standpoint it voiced loud and clear when the delegates convened the First Zionist Congress in Basel in 1897. With time, its anti-Zionism lost credit and by 1948, when the new State of Israel was established, Reform's leaders, rabbis Stephen Wise and Abba Hillel Silver, were able to declare the movement's unqualified support and sympathy for both Zionism and the new state, even as they insisted that Jews and Jewry still faced many difficulties that would require other solutions. Hebrew Union College built a campus in Jerusalem and in recent years, several Reform communities have established themselves in Israel under the name of the Movement for Progressive Judaism (*Yahadut Mitkademet*).

Conservative Judaism

Half a century of Reform in Germany provoked the Orthodox rabbis Samson Rafael Hirsch and Azriel Hildesheimer to respond with neo-Orthodoxy, an attempt to modernize and mitigate traditional Orthodoxy without going as far as Reform had done or threatened to do. Neo-Orthodoxy's slogan was "Torah with seemliness" (*Torah im derekh eretz*—following Rabban Gamliel, Mishna *Avot* 2:2). While not actually changing any Orthodox *halachot,* the two rabbis gave sanction to modifications in lifestyle such as wearing modern clothes, learning and speaking the local language—the rabbi gave his weekly sermon in the vernacular too—and certain amendments to the synagogue prayer service. The principal innovation was to introduce general secular studies into Orthodox schools. Neo-Orthodoxy backed up this breakthrough by playing down the nationalist element in Jewish identity in favor of strengthening Jews' affiliation to the German state and by encouraging them to participate in non-Jewish cultural and social life. It also took pluralism in Judaism a distinct step forward by withdrawing from the wider Orthodox community and establishing its own instruments of *halachic* authority. In many ways neo-Orthodoxy followed the lead of the German *Haskalah.* Today the essentials of its approach to Judaism are accepted by numerous congregations that define themselves as Orthodox.

Conservative Judaism entered the arena early in the twentieth century in the United States. Its conceptual universe was influenced by neo-Orthodoxy and by other movements searching for a golden mean between Orthodoxy and Reform, in particular from the standpoint of R. Zecharia Frankel, who sought to moderate Reform, so as to preserve tradition and maintain Judaism's bond to the ideas of a people of Israel and a land of Israel, and to the Hebrew language. The Conservatives sought a modernized format compatible with the spirit of the new age. The movement's ideological and organizational foundations were the work of Solomon Schechter, a scholar who had immigrated to the U.S.

in 1902 and joined the Jewish Theological Seminary of America in New York, which he proceeded to transform into Conservatism's main rabbinic training school, soon to be replicated in Los Angeles, Buenos Aires, and Jerusalem. In 1913 he founded the United Synagogue of America to unite the whole movement under one organization and, with this measure he in effect, set Conservatism on the road forward.

Schechter's conceptualization of Judaism was not so much theological as historical. He replaced God as the focus of a religious Jew's concern with the concept of the Jewish people. Emphasizing how Jewish thought and *halacha* were incessantly evolving throughout Jewish history, he pointed out how tradition had preserved a profound continuity between one generation and the next in the context of the people's historical development. In other words, Judaism was a dynamic system and operated within a life context; it was transferable from generation to generation and each generation could adapt it to its particular needs. Jewish thought and *halacha* down the ages were more than a tradition; they were the way in which Jews understood the worship of God. Schechter's perception of the bond uniting Judaism and the Jewish people was a purely religious one, not necessarily a nationalist one. It is this integrated system of ideas—a traditional Judaism maintaining itself within the Jewish people and tied to the Land of Israel, yet dynamic and ever-evolving—that has essentially supplied the motor of Conservative Judaism's intellectual development.

As a movement, Conservatism preferred not to formulate and publish a platform of detailed concepts and doctrine. Consequently, its principal ideas developed in several directions and by mid-century had been accorded different formulations by different leaders. Not until 1988 did the movement bring out a formal statement of its central ideas and tenets, under the title *Truth and Belief*, but even this document did no more than lay down broadly agreed limits, leaving ample room for dispute and divergences of opinion. The consensual Conservative position is that Jewish identity, by tradition bound up with the people of Israel and the land of Israel, is defined by the Jewish religion. *Halacha* obligates believers, but may be modified by a council of senior rabbis in the light of changing realities, as long as *halachic* tradition is respected. Within these wide limits, disagreement and controversy are—in the best tradition of Judaism and Jewry—the welcome signs of a system of thought that is alive and evolving. The Conservative prayer service is built on the traditional one but large parts are translated into vernacular languages and it contains several significant changes. The negative language of three of the daily morning blessings has been made positive:

"Blessed be He for not making me a gentile" has been replaced by "Thank you, *Adonai* our God, source of blessing, for making me a Jewish person"; "Blessed be He for not making me a slave" has been replaced by "Thank you . . . for granting me freedom"; and "Blessed be He for not making me a woman" has been replaced by, "Thank you . . . for creating me in Your image." Prayers for rebuilding of the Temple and re-institution of the practice of sacrifice have been removed altogether and all other mentions of the Temple and sacrifice have been put into the past tense.[6]

Over the years, the Conservative movement has transformed beyond all recognition the rights of Jewish women and their place and status in the religious community. From the earliest years of the twentieth century, men and women have sat together during the synagogue service, and in 1922, the first bat mitzvah was celebrated. In 1954, the decision was taken to allow women to make the weekly Sabbath reading from the Torah and recite the associated blessings. The wording of the traditional marriage contract, the *ketubah,* read out and signed before the marriage ceremony, was revised to grant women equal status in marriage and divorce—a great leap forward from *halachic* matrimonial law. Since 1973 women have been counted in the *minyan,* the quorum needed before public prayer can begin, in contrast to the Orthodox *minyan,* in which women are not counted. From 1984 on, women have been admitted to programs for the rabbinate, both as trainees and lecturers, as well as to all synagogue positions and functions. A substantial number of Conservative synagogues are now led by women ordained as rabbis. In other Conservative synagogues, women lead the daily synagogue prayer services and serve as cantors. Many women regularly wear a skullcap and even the fringed garment, *tzitzit,* and in the synagogue, some wear a prayer shawl, *talit*—a duty that in traditional *halacha* is reserved for men only. This transformation of women's status in the community and home was a step too far for some, and several groups quit the movement to set up their own organization, the Union for Traditional Conservative Judaism. For another group the change did not go far enough, they set up the Reconstructionist movement. Today Conservative Jewry numbers about one and a half million persons around the world. Lately, and for the first time, it has sprouted shoots in Israel too, where it goes by the name of the Movement for Tradition, *Hatnua Hamasortit.*

The Reconstructionists

The Reconstructionist movement for the renewal of Judaism was founded in the United States in 1922 when the philosopher and senior

Conservative rabbi, Mordechai Menachem Kaplan, set up the Society for the Advancement of Judaism. The Society aspired to "reconstruct" and "renew" Judaism by fusing the values of Judaism and Western democracy with the achievements of the social sciences. The Federation of Reconstructionist Congregations was founded by Kaplan in 1955. Since the early 1980s Reconstrutionist Jewry has been steadily expanding in numbers, mainly thanks to the energetic efforts of their Rabbinical College, founded in 1968 and significantly expanded in 1981. Although the movement is not large, comprising about eighty thousand members, Kaplan's outlook and teaching have had great influence within Jewish intellectual circles, especially in the United States and lately also in Israel.

For the Reconstructionists, Judaism is the ever-evolving religious civilization of the Jewish people. Its traditional beliefs, practices and life-style have always had to be adapted to the needs of the contemporary world. The traditional premise of an unalterable Torah, handed down in its entirety from God to Moses on Mt. Sinai, is rejected. Judaism is, and has always been, in a process of adjusting to the socio-cultural conditions, that each generation of Jews has encountered. Although the Jewish tradition that has come down to us embodies the most profound insights into and reflections on the meaning of human life, although it has been elaborated over generations and tested by time, for all that, it is not a finished product. Each new generation, and ours is no exception, must sustain the process of development by attuning the principles of Judaism to the conditions of its own time. The one fixed element in this process, the one element that never changes is the Jewish people on its journey through history, a matrix that is transmuted in Jewish community life down the ages. Reconstructionists put a very high value on the community as the pre-eminent vehicle for a Jewish way of life. A Reconstructionist community integrates individual and setting, with the individual translating the community's will and choices into the content of his or her own life. All community decisions are taken collectively, not by a rabbi or a single leader, but after thorough study and discussion involving every community member. From this perception of Judaism as Jewry's evolving civilization and culture arose a special regard for the Hebrew language, particularly as the language of prayer, and for retaining Jewish ceremonial ritual in its traditional form. From its inception, Reconstructionism was a committed supporter of Zionism, on the grounds that Jews in Israel could maintain a full Jewish life in a fully Jewish cultural environment, but this in no way detracted from its insistence that Jewish communal life in the Diaspora had to be energetically sustained.

Reconstructionism repudiates the idea of a supernatural interventionist God who meddles in human affairs, or for revelation by preternatural means. God is a continuity of experience, not a "personality," whatsoever. Our relationship with God is the accumulation of our experience of Him and of our dealings with Him down the ages: it is not a top-down command structure, not a bond dictated by "the word of God." The same pertains to *halacha* and the Torah's commandments: They are not directives to be obeyed because they are God-given, but rather because they are the cumulative voice of individuals' and the people's experience, reflecting the historical context of the origin of each commandment and *halacha*. Accordingly, all *halachot* are open to alteration at all times as values evolve and change, although such alterations must be made with caution and adhere closely to the moral code. Nor is the Jewish people the "Chosen People," no more so than any people who choose to walk in the ways of God.

Reconstructionist Jews celebrate Judaism's traditional ceremonies and study Jewry's sacred texts, because these are the vehicles that carry the values, the sanctified insights, and the worldviews of the generations of Jews who have come before us. Their prayer book, *Kol Haneshama, The Soul's Voice*, composed in 1989, combines a firm commitment to the traditional text with numerous amendments in line with modern ethics and democratic values, such as feminism. The Reconstructionists were the first Jewish denomination to give men and women equal status in religious practice and in the life of the religious community. As early as 1922, Mordechai Kaplan, then still with the Conservatives, held a bat mitzvah for his daughter. By the 1940s, women were participating in all religious ceremonies; in 1968 they were ordained as rabbis and in 1978 the equality of men and women was instituted in all matters of divorce. The Reconstructionist prayer book uses non-gender-specific forms of speech for addressing and categorizing God. Israel has no Reconstructionist congregation as such, although the *Mevakshei Derekh*, ('Searchers for the Way') congregation in Jerusalem regards itself as following Kaplan's teaching fairly closely.

Jewry's non-Orthodox denominations encompass about half of all Diaspora Jews[7] and together constitute a strong force for pluralism in Jewry, because they do not claim exclusivity and recognize the right of other denominations and worldviews to exist. Even secular Judaism is not disqualified.

The 'Tradition Maintainers'

There are many Jews, especially in Israel, who know definitely that they are not religious, but who will not label themselves as secular either. When asked, they say they are "traditional" *massorti,* or that they "keep up tradition," *shomrei massoret.* No "maintaining tradition" movement has been founded, there is no "maintaining tradition" ideology, just a widespread phenomenon of individuals and families who select from the body of Jewish tradition those customs that they choose to symbolically maintain. The selection has a great deal of randomness and arbitrariness to it, certainly no theoretical ideology; it is rather a matter of the taste of each individual and family. Some will observe certain rules of *kashrut,* such as not eating bacon or pork, but will not bother with the separation of milk and meat products or using only kosher-slaughtered meat. Others will keep up *kashrut* in the home, often so that observant parents or other relatives can eat with them, but are perfectly happy to eat non-kosher food outside. Some do not eat bread and other leavened food for the days of Passover; they may fast on the Day of Atonement or light candles on the Sabbath, perhaps even reciting the blessings over wine and food, *kidush.* Others make a point of nailing a *mezuzah* to one side of their front door but overlook the fact that it is supposed to contain a small kosher scroll of biblical passages. Maintainers of tradition generally circumcise their sons and celebrate their bar mitzvah at age thirteen (for girls, a bat mitzvah at age twelve); many choose to be married by a rabbi in a religious ceremony and, for Israelis, this is not only because under Israeli law there is no easy alternative; thousands attend synagogue on the great annual festivals, some even attend every Sabbath. The traditions of wearing *tzitzit* or laying phylacteries every day are less commonly observed; few of the men wear a skullcap and even fewer women keep their hair covered. On Sabbath they take the car out, watch football, or go to the cinema, often after going to synagogue in the morning. They certainly do not observe the three daily prayer services and usually not the Sabbath prayers either. They generally send their children to non-religious schools, although they welcome a certain amount of Jewish studies in the curriculum, enough to enrich their children's Jewish self-awareness, but not enough to seduce them into "returning to the faith."

The great majority of the maintainers tradition cannot be called religious because their day-to-day life rejects the demand of religion that it define our whole existence. Their way of life is essentially secular. It may include token religious practice but the source of this practice is an individual decision, not a religious faith or belief system. Some say they believe in God, but usually it is an abstract belief in some master reality, lacking any grounding in religious doctrine or faith, and far from a commitment to a *halachic* way of life. The observance of this or that practice does not derive from belief in God but from other sources, from a wish to preserve tradition, from respect for one's parents' lifestyle, or from a desire to demonstrate Jewishness in some public manner. In observing the customs they have chosen to observe, they certainly do not see themselves as obeying commandments, so that they cannot be categorized as *mitzva-* and Torah-observant. A better category would be "fringe seculars" or "reluctant seculars." Clearly, they are far closer to secularism than religion.

To balance the picture, some maintainers of tradition best fit a category of "reluctant believers." Although loyal to a lifestyle grounded in faith and *halacha*, nonetheless, and asking leave from no authority, they allow themselves a great deal of liberty in its practice, retaining only what they have decided is the vital core. They are likely to keep *kashrut* a little more strictly than the "reluctant seculars," they may go to synagogue on Sabbath and the festivals, some may send their children to Jewish religious schools, but judging by the larger picture, their lifestyle can barely be distinguished from that of the "reluctant seculars." They drive on Sabbath, go to sports matches, and have family outings. They fall into the category of religious since the source of their lifestyle is a religious worldview, even if it is not followed through to the end, but they are a long way from Orthodox. It would be most accurate to create for them a new category of religious Jewishness—one which could not have come into being were it not for the fragmentation of ancient unitary Judaism at the end of the eighteenth century and the subsequent decline of a centralized *halachic* and religious authority.

If to be secular is to believe that humans are sovereign over themselves and their world, and to lead a way of life not dictated by religious worldview and doctrine, then the line between religious and secular Jewry passes somewhere through this large body of "tradition maintainers." Displaying a broad spectrum of connectedness to religious tradition, they occupy an area of open ground between the religious and the secular spheres, yet identify themselves with neither of these two ways of being Jewish. They have removed themselves from a fully religious life, from the comprehensive obligation to follow religious dictates, and they reject the right of rabbis to tell them what to do. But they do not see themselves as fully secular, usually because they are under the mistaken impression that to be secular means to have abandoned every scrap of loyalty to Judaism and its religious tradition. We also have to remember that every observant Jewish sect delegitimizes the Judaism of every sect less extreme than itself, so that here we have a fresh source of argument as to where to draw the line between the fully religious and the maintainers of tradition.

Equally far from clear-cut is the line between the "tradition maintainers" and the fully secular. There are plenty of utterly radical seculars and total atheists who can be observed keeping up this or that element of tradition. It is therefore not easy to estimate how large world Jewry's body of maintainers of tradition is, but it is most probably a sizable proportion of the Jewish population. In Israel, this grouping is estimated at a third of the Jewish population.

Messianic Jews

From the time the new Jewish sect of Christians appeared in the first century, until its final and irrevocable divorce from Judaism in the mid-second century, there were Judeo-Christians. The Ebionite sect, who accepted Jesus's messianic mission, but not his divinity, regarded themselves as fully Jewish and were fully *mitzva*-observant. The Christians who did accept Jesus's divinity and the modifications to *mitzva* observance declared by the apostle Paul, still never ceased regarding themselves as part of the body of Jewry. It was Rabban Gamliel II who forced them out by ordering R. Shmuel Hakatan to write in a supplement to the Standing Prayer (*Amidah*)[8] called the Blessing against Heretics: "And for slanderers let there be no hope and may all heretics perish in an instant."

For the next 1,700 years there were no Judeo-Christians until around the turn of the nineteenth to twentieth centuries a number of Jews who had converted to Christianity tried to revive the concept, calling themselves also Messianic Jews. In 1894 they founded their first community, *Bet Sha'ar Shalom,* House of the Gate of Peace, and hundreds more have followed, mainly in the United States but also elsewhere, the best-known is the movement called "Jews for Jesus," founded in 1970. Several groups have set up home in Israel itself, where they preach that accepting Jesus as the messiah does not mean quitting or repudiating Judaism. On the contrary, they say, therein lies Judaism's true fulfillment, since without it Judaism remains incomplete. No Jewish institution, in Israel or the Diaspora, recognizes them as Jews, they are treated as committed Christians. Even the Israeli Supreme Court has dismissed their petition to be recognized as Jews for all intents and purposes.

The claim that Christianity is the authentic, full, and complete development of Judaism, makes relations between Messianic Jews and Judaism problematic. They claim in essence that there is an unbroken line from Judaism to Christianity, but then every Christian, whatever nation he belongs to, or whatever language he speaks is a true Jew, and then what distinguishes Messianic Jews from Christians who are not Jews? One must suppose that, as they see it, their Jewishness stems from their Jewish descent, from the nationalist component in their Jewish identity, since the religious components—faith and religious law—that they profess are the same as all Christians profess.

In practice, Messianic Jews may call themselves whatever they want—even Jews—no matter what the Jewish establishments may say. The only problem they face with this strategy is in Israel, where the issue is an essential one, if at present kept to the margins of politics. The issue will become serious when the question of how Israeli law identifies a Jew is brought to a crisis, for the Law of Return provides benefits in citizenship rights to those who fit its definition of a Jew.

SECULAR JUDAISM

Earlier, we defined secularism as an individual worldview and way of life rooted in humanism and recognizing humans, free of the dominion claimed for any transcendental divinity, and thus free to possess sovereignty over themselves and their world. We have mentioned a few of the individual Jews, who over the course of Jewish history have refused to regard themselves as subject to divine governance. *Akher,* Elisha Ben Avuya in the second century; Khiwi HaBalkhi in the ninth century; and in the seventeenth century, Baruch Spinoza, whose philosophy marks the arrival of non-religious, humanist thinking in early modern Europe, and who exerted such a strong influence over the future course of that aspect of our intellectual development. It is extremely probable that these and others like them were not alone in their refusal to bow down to the conventions of organized religion; there may have been many, but if so, no witness to their stand has come down to us. Jewry may even have known whole movements of deniers but if it did, its record keepers have taken care to wipe the slate of history clean of them.

As a legitimate mass phenomenon, as a current in the mainstream of normative Judaism, Jewish secularism surfaced in the late nineteenth century, with the consolidation of Jewish nationalism and socialism. Although neither the nationalist nor the socialist movements had made themselves a force with a view to establishing secularism, they were completely secularist. Jewish socialists rejected religion and religious practice in line with the pan-European socialist doctrine that religion was a tool manipulated by the upper classes to suppress the workers. Jewish nationalism, in its very conception, raised the national component of Jewish identity high above the religious one, which it held to be superfluous to any Jew's self-definition. The repudiation by no means extended to Jewish tradition and its sources, nor to the Jewish religion as one of the prime sources of the vast inherited culture that informed Jews about who and what they were. As we have seen, the nationalist and socialist movements made free use of this heritage in every sphere of art and culture, in every language that its writers used—Hebrew, Yiddish, Russian, and German, among others.

The secularism of Jewish socialism carried the greater part of Eastern European Jewry with it. By the first half of the twentieth century, the popular image of a community of Jews clinging to its age-old synagogue-dominated lifestyle had lost validity. Of the Jewish masses, most laborers and artisans were *Bund* supporters and most of the remainder were Communists. As for the wealthier strata—the professionals, merchants, industrialists, and the educated youth—they gravitated either to the equally secular Zionism or to assimilation into secular gentile society. Although most of the Jews remaining in the Soviet Union before and after the Second World War jealously maintained their Jewishness, full religious practice was rarely a part of it, and the same was true for the millions who set sail for the Americas. The emigrants were in the main secular and *Bund*-socialist, as is abundantly clear from the flourishing press and rich literature that catered to them in Yiddish and English and, to a lesser extent, in Hebrew, too.

Large-scale Jewish socialist organizations were still actively ministering to North and South America's secular Yiddish culture until the 1950s, but that was the watershed. From then on, the demand for their services fell into continuous decline. Today, throughout the Diaspora the role of community organization has been taken over by synagogue and community center, most of them affiliated to one of Jewry's religious denominations, and most Jewish education and pro-Israel activity is conducted by and within the same framework. Although religious organizations may provide a framework for communal activity, in the home and away from the organized community the way of life for large numbers of families and individuals is to all intents and purposes secular. The same is true of the many Jews who are unaffiliated with any

Jewish communal organization but openly declare themselves as Jews and have preserved ties to their Jewish identity.

As for Israel, the great majority of its Jews lead a secular life. More than half of the Jewish population declare themselves completely secular and, together with those who maintain tradition but do not define themselves as fully religious, they make up 80 percent of Israel's Jewish citizens. The chief reason for this is that Zionism has been secular from the outset. Almost all the Jews who resettled the Land of Israel in the late nineteenth and early twentieth century were secular in outlook and lifestyle. They built the new society and they set the tone for it. Even the hundreds of thousands who, after 1948, poured in from North Africa and the Middle East, where religion dominated, after a time relaxed their religious practices, so that they or their second generation soon lapsed into maintaining tradition. Few kept up the old lifestyle and even fewer affiliated themselves with any variety of organized Orthodoxy. Four decades later, another massive wave of immigrants arrived, this time from the former Soviet Union; these new immigrants arrived fully secularized, since Soviet Jewish society had been almost exclusively secular for many years.

In politics, secular Israelis can be found at all points on the spectrum, left, right, and center. The platforms of a variety of political parties are fully secular in character and profess to oppose religious coercion with equal determination. Nor can Israeli secularism be tied to any socioeconomic class or section of society. In sum, secularism's reach and roots are as wide and deep as those of Israeli society itself. The fact that Jewish secularism originally arose as an adjunct to socialism and Zionism gives it, as a phenomenon of Jewish society, a character very different from that of religious Judaism. Secularism is not, and never has been, organized around its own ideology or contained within its own political movement. Unlike the numerous religious movements for whom the cause of religion is their *raison d'être*, Jewish secularity has not produced movements and organizations proclaiming secularism as their motivation and purpose.[9] Almost all Jewish non-religious settings are open to religious and non-religious alike. Only in the Diaspora, and in particular in the United States, have secular Jews felt the need for some form of community organization to reinforce their Jewishness, and this led in the 1960s' to the founding in Detroit, Michigan, of a community of secular humanist Jews, guided by R. Sherwin Wine. More such communities followed in other cities in the United States, as well as in Canada and in a few other countries. Today they are all united under the International Federation of Secular Humanistic Jews, founded in 1963.

Since the boundaries between the religiously observant, the maintainers of tradition, and the secular are so imprecise, and since secularism is an unorganized phenomenon, the number of secular Jews around the world is hard to measure with any exactness. Two facts are certain, that the great majority of Israeli Jews are secular and that 40 percent of Diaspora Jews deny membership of any religious body or organization and lead a secular lifestyle.[10] A fair estimate would be that considerably more than half of the world's Jews lead a secular lifestyle and hold a humanist worldview, and that the great majority of the remainder, including all non-Orthodox religious congregations, support a pluralist concept of Judaism.

Assimilation and Total Absorption

Jews have been assimilating to the ways of their host nations throughout history. Sometimes this has resulted in a specific Jewish community's total absorption into the local culture, in effect in their slipping out of Judaism and Jewry, but this has by no means been the inevitable result. Jews have also become active members of non-Jewish society, adopting its manners, becoming fixtures in the local scene, without any surrender of their Jewish identity. Assimilation, says the *Aggada*, began even before the Jews left Egypt: "When Joseph died they stopped circumcising their sons, saying, 'We shall be as the Egyptians'" (*Exodus Rabba* 1). In the Second Temple period, large sections of Jewish society in Judea came under the influence of Greek culture, which the sages of the Mishna called "Greek wisdom." Although tradition-observing Jews called these assimilators Hellenizers, *mityavnim*, they did not deny their Jewishness, as the Hellenizers themselves did not. The bitter wars of the Maccabees were fought as much against this invasion of Hellenistic culture and institutions as against Seleucid-Hellenistic rule, and yet no more than one generation after the Maccabean victory and the re-installation of a Jewish royal house, the Hasmoneans, went over to a Hellenistic lifestyle. Hellenism had now firmly established itself alongside the culture of Pharisaic Judaism and even the Pharisees could not remain immune to it.

By the medieval period, it was no longer possible to assimilate without being converted, since this was a time of religious exclusivity in office and society. We know that large numbers of Jews converted, especially in Christian Europe. For many it was a choice between conversion and death, but others took the step willingly and wittingly, pre-

ferring the path of material and social prosperity. Some of these
converts rose high enough in their new church to persecute their ex-
coreligionists with all the zeal of the new convert. Other Jews abandoned Judaism to "marry out," as Shylock's daughter Jessica does in
Shakespeare's *The Merchant of Venice.* We have no way of knowing just
how many crossed over, but certainly, in Europe at least, the proportion
was large—perhaps even the majority of its Jewish population.

With the arrival of the Emancipation, the religious pressure on Jews
lessened. Officially, they could now take their place in the wider society
without hindrance and without having to surrender their religious identity. However, official policy is one thing and reality is another: practical
discrimination did not disappear so easily and conversion—even if it was
no longer the only path to survival—still offered huge advantages to
Jews who aspired to full societal acceptance. From the middle of the
eighteenth to the end of the nineteenth century, some two hundred
thousand or more European Jews chose to "cross over" to Christianity.
Many made a triumphant success of it in politics and finance, in the arts
and in culture. In England Benjamin Disraeli, whose father had him
converted, rose to the leadership of the Conservative Party, to the office
of prime minister of Her Majesty's government, and to the income as
one of the country's best-selling novelists. Heinrich Heine came to be
acknowledged as one of the greatest lyric poets in the German language.
Neither Benjamin Disraeli nor Heinrich Heine, nor many others who
converted, showed any inclination to hide their Jewish ancestry; it was
even a source of pride to them and they made much of it in their writings, which Jewry now acknowledges belong fully to the body and story
of Jewish culture. Other converts did cut themselves off, such as Felix
Mendelssohn-Bartholdy, the composer and grandson of Moses Mendelssohn who had given the *Haskalah* its intellectual inspiration, and Karl
Marx, the philosopher and workers' leader. From the mid-nineteenth
century on, the tide set towards assimilation and emigration, and more
and more, the trend was for Jews to settle into their host societies without converting and openly retain their identity as Jews. For many, this
did not obstruct their path to fame and fortune: for Sigmund Freud, in
psychology; for Albert Einstein in physics; for Franz Kafka in literature;
for Leon Trotsky in revolutionary politics; for Leon Blum and Pierre
Mendes-France in a more sedately conducted form of politics. The list
could go on and on.

Simultaneously, the forces of anti-Semitism gathered strength, apparently in alarm at the ascent of Jews to political and economic heights.
Xenophobia is as old as mankind itself, but this anti-Semitism had new

ammunition. The Jews, it was said, and this included the "purported" converts and the assimilated, were exploiting the "native" population as they pursued their remorseless goal of taking over Aryan-Christian civilization and its economy. In other words, the target had now become Jewish assimilation itself; totally "absorbed" Jews were as unwanted as their unassimilated forebears had been. The slogan that anti-Semites most liked to shout around the turn of the century was "Jews to Palestine!"; ironically, this was the same idea that the Zionists were propagandizing, and for the same reason, the Zionists also despised the strategy of assimilation.

This phenomenon of mass-anti-Semitism convinced many Jews that, as in the Middle Ages, assimilation was no longer an option. Some of them sought a way out in nationalism. Theodore Herzl, the assimilated son of assimilated parents, wrote in his book *The Jewish State:*

> We have honestly endeavored everywhere to merge ourselves in the social life of surrounding communities and to preserve the faith of our fathers. We are not permitted to do so. In vain are we loyal patriots, our loyalty in some places running to extremes; in vain do we make the same sacrifices of life and property as our fellow-citizens; in vain do we strive to increase the fame of our native land in science and art, or her wealth by trade and commerce. In countries where we have lived for centuries we are still cried down as strangers, and often by those whose ancestors were not yet domiciled in the land where Jews had already had experience of suffering.[11]

Indeed, Herzl thought assimilation would have been a good solution to the Jews' problems, had it only been possible.

Once the Holocaust had done its grisly work and racism could no longer be openly voiced in respectable society, European Jews were able to assimilate without further difficulties, without converting and, in most places, without concealing their Jewishness. Nowadays, large numbers of Diaspora Jews regard themselves as Jews and are so regarded by neighbors and colleagues without their maintaining any contact whatsoever with Jewish organizations and institutions of any kind. Nor does marrying a non-Jew—"marrying out" in Jewish parlance— imply a renunciation of all things Jewish. Sometimes each partner keeps up his or her own religio-ethnic identity within the marriage, often the non-Jewish partner takes up the Jewish partner's Judaism. The rate of mixed marriages can no longer be used as an indicator of the extent of assimilation, and proof positive of this very fact was seen recently when hundreds of thousands of mixed couples and their offspring emigrated from the former Soviet Union to Israel, claiming a home and full recognition as Jews under the Law of Return. How did the Orthodox religious establishment react? This body, which spends so much time bemoaning the loss to Jewry by "marrying out" responded by bluntly, brusquely denying them the rights and facilities giving to Jews under the Law of Return and by filling their new life in Israel with as much bureaucratic trouble as possible.

In the United States and other countries of immigration, whose populations are a patchwork of ethnic minorities, total religio-ethnic absorption is the exception rather than the rule, for there is no one predominant ethnic group whose identity all immigrants feel pressured to adopt. Minorities tend to retain their own ethnic identity and even to nurture it. For Diaspora Jews, an additional anti-absorption force has operated—pride in the existence and achievements of the State of Israel, to the degree that these have remained objects of pride. It remains true that many Jews, particularly second and third generation assimilated Jews, have taken the path of absorption into their non-Jewish surroundings. Their right to do so is both unquestionable and blameless. That some or all of a national or social minority will choose the road of absorption must simply be recognized as an inevitable tendency in human nature.

The assimilation and absorption of Jews into non-Jewish society has never taken an organized form. Each individual makes his or her own decision to change identity, persuaded by an individual combination of reasons and motives, large and small, serious and not so serious, carefully considered and more impulsive, so that there could never be, and never has been, an ideology of assimilation or an organized assimilationist movement. This is not to say that external forces cannot influence many people's choices; the *Haskalah*'s advocacy of assimilation was one such force. Huge numbers of Jews, whether they had heard of the *Haskalah* or not, chose the path of "halfway" assimilation—that is, preserving one's Jewish identity as a private matter: "In public a man of the people, at home a Jew." For some, it is no great leap from such a halfway point to the point of abandoning Judaism and Jewry for absorption into the wider society.

Time and again we hear from Orthodox religious establishment figures the claim that the effect of Reform and of Conservative Judaism is to encourage Jews to assimilate and even to desert Judaism through absorption. Israel's former Chief Sephardi Rabbi, Bakshi-Doron, has gone so far as to state categorically that Reform Judaism presents a greater threat to Judaism than the Holocaust did, and when made aware of just what he was saying, he still refused to retract.[12] Let us examine the facts. The great nineteenth-century wave of assimilation was not a consequence of Reform but coincidental with it and played itself out long before Conservative Judaism arrived. Moreover, in the pre-Emancipation period when the unity of Jewry was still intact and rabbinic authority at its peak, conversion to Christianity and other religions was far more common than in the period of Reform and took in a much wider swath of world Jewry than it does today. Events have proven that Reform and Conservative Judaism are neither competitors to Orthodoxy nor have the power to seduce Jews from Orthodoxy to their own ranks. Most Orthodox Jews who make the decision to leave their community leave for a totally secular life. What Reform and Conservative Judaism offer is a home for assimilating Jews who want to give their Jewish identity some institutionalized form. In other words, they constitute a barrier to total absorption, not a gateway towards it.

Assimilation has been a constant of Jewish existence throughout its history. It is legitimate and unstoppable. There are inevitably borrowings and interactions between ethnic groups who live in constant cheek-by-jowl contact with each other. After a time, considerable numbers of assimilators will inevitably find themselves or their offspring far removed from their community of origin. As I have said, that is their decision and their choice. They have the full right to do as they wish with their life, to go where their thinking leads them and to bring up their children in accord with this thinking. Other Jews, no less determined to be full members of the wider society, will combine this with a strong loyalty to Judaism, one that nowadays generally takes the form of Jewish solidarity and ethnic nostalgia, and often somewhat more than this. However, the key point is that by identifying themselves as Jews and being recognized by their neighbors as Jews, they belong to the Jewish people and are part of the body of Jews worldwide. Their culture is Jewish culture in every way and whatever they create belongs to the cultural heritage of all Jews as it passes down from generation to generation.

ISRAELI JEWS

The Jewish population of Palestine in the mid-nineteenth century was a believing population, an agglomeration of small Orthodox country of origin-defined communities. The settlers from the first wave of resettlement (the First *Aliyah*) arrived between 1882 and 1903, and set up the first settlements in Judea and the Galilee. Most of them were religious people, as were the urban Jerusalemites who had left the city in

1878 to found the first new Jewish agricultural settlement in the land, Petakh Tikva, A Gateway to Hope.[13] It was the Second *Aliyah,* beginning in 1904, that brought a different type of settler, the "pioneer," fired by the idea of socialist Zionism, resolved to build a new society that would be an exemplar of justice and equality, and bearing a vision of a new kind of human being. They were secular in belief and behavior and humanist in outlook. They laid the foundations of a new secular humanist Jewish society in the Land of Israel. The Third *Aliyah,* after the end of the First World War, brought tens of thousands of pioneers made in the same mold, who built upon the foundations laid by the Second *Aliyah* and firmly established the character of Jewish society in Palestine as secular and humanist—as it has remained to this day.

Zionism and the Palestinian Jewish community had a right wing, the Revisionists led by Ze'ev Jabotinsky, who were no less secular in outlook and behavior than the socialist mainstream. Jabotinsky himself was a secular liberal, steeped in European culture. His political philosophy declared that nothing was of more importance for the Jews than their sense of nationhood; religion came a distant second. Given that most of his disciples' liberalism was very similar to his own, Revisionism further cemented Jewish Palestine's secular structure. The immigrations of the 1930s from Poland, Germany, and other parts of Europe were equally dominated by secular Jews, for the ultra-Orthodox were prevented from countering the trend to any significant extent by their leaders' still fierce disapproval of Zionism and *aliyah,* it was sufficient to stop all but a few coming. Emigration to the Land of Israel was considered a transgression of the ban on "forcing the walls of exile," one of the four oaths that the People of Israel had sworn to the Creator to keep (Song of Songs *Rabba* 2:18). The most extreme position was taken up by the *Neturei Karta* sect, led by R. Yoel Teitelbaum, the Satmar *rebbe,* for whom Zionism was no less than heresy and a work of Satan, an ordeal sent by the Lord to test His people.

Against all expectations, Orthodox support for Zionism and settlement came from the Ashkenazi Chief Rabbi in Palestine, R. Avraham Yitzhak Hacohen Kook. R. Kook, as we have seen, was a committed Zionist, finding a *halachic* home for his stand in the idea that Zionism is a forerunner for the messiah's own coming. He directed his followers to show tolerance toward the secular pioneers on the grounds that they were "rebuilding the land" and were due, in the fullness of time, to return to a perfect faith. In 1921 he founded a yeshiva, later named in his memory *Yeshivat HaRav,* where he taught not only Jewish Studies and his particular theory of messianic redemption but also general studies.

R. Kook's tolerance of the secular did not for a moment imply a legitimatization of their thinking, but it did have the beneficial effect of enabling Religious Zionism (organized behind the *Mizrakhi* and *Hapoel Hamizrakhi* political parties) to cooperate with the preseminently secular leadership of Palestinian Jewry and to play a full part in the struggle for a Jewish state, building and defending settlements, organizing immigration, and fighting the War of Independence. With the state formally established, Religious Zionism took its place in all state organs and agencies, political, military, and social. Ultra-Orthodoxy, or at least part of it, joined in only when the War of Independence was already being fought. *Agudat Yisrael* had been until then the voice of ultra-Orthodoxy's anti-Zionism and, strictly speaking, the ultra-Orthodox still, to this day, have not accepted Zionism's core concepts. But in 1948 they thought it right to engage themselves in the new state's command structures and their representative, R. Yitzhak Meir Levin, appended his signature to the Declaration of Independence. Since then they have granted the state recognition only *de facto,* and have done so, as they explain it, in order to exert influence from within, to try and steer it in the direction of a theocracy, a state in which *halacha* constitutes the code of law. What they have accepted from the state is its largesse. A partner in every governing coalition (since 1948, no party has been strong enough to govern alone), they have exploited their ministries and committee chairmanships and the frequent happy circumstance of their holding the balance of power between the two largest parties to squeeze as many material benefits as possible for their community from the state treasury. The theological extremists of ultra-Orthodoxy, *Neturei Karta* and the Satmar Hasidim, refuse even to do that. For them the state is a non-entity.

That Israel's secular and the religious leaderships were going to find it hard to agree about anything became evident during the new state's very first step onto the international stage—the formulation of a Declaration of Independence. The Religious Zionists wanted it composed in religious terms, it should praise the Lord for his bounty, allude to the messianic coming that this bounty so obviously heralded, petition the Almighty to take the state under His wing and give it peace. When the seculars would not wear that at any price, they made do with opening the last section of the declaration with the ambiguous phrase, "Trusting in the Rock of Israel . . .," which each side could understand in its own way. The Religious Zionists' understanding of it was made clear in their new *Prayer for the Welfare of the State,* composed for recitation in their synagogues after the Sabbath Torah reading. True to Rabbi Kook's teaching, the prayer pronounced the State to be "the first shoots of our redemption."

Another bone of angry contention between the Orthodox, the non-Orthodox, and the secular camps, a bone still being fought over to this day, was thrown into the arena by the first Basic (constitutional) Law passed by the newly elected Knesset, parliament. This was the Law of Return, giving Israeli citizenship to every Jew arriving in Israel who wanted it. In time, the all-embracing quality of this offer was qualified by restrictions relating to Jews who had converted to another religion, who were wanted for crimes, or whose health was in a certain condition, but as though to counterbalance this, the Law was also broadened to include Jews' non-Jewish family members to the fourth generation. What caused all the trouble was the small question, four words long but enormous in implication and complication: Who is a Jew? Who exactly does the Law with all its legal and material benefits embrace? An amendment was passed stating that a Jew was one born to a Jewish mother or who had undergone formal conversion—an out and out *halachic* definition, flying straight in the face of the secular view that a Jew was anyone who defined himself or herself as one. But it was not enough to satisfy the Orthodox, for conversions were carried out by all sorts of rabbis, including non-Orthodox rabbis. They demanded—and are still demanding to this day—that the Law's definition of a Jew be further amended to read "or who has undergone formal *halachic* conversion," for in Orthodox thinking the only body of *halacha* that exists is Orthodox *halacha*. They also want the Israeli Chief Rabbinate, an Orthodox body, granted exclusive authority within Israel's borders over all conversion-related issues. The consequences of this last demand, if granted, are not small, granting it would do no less than outlaw all non-Orthodox Jewish communities, at least in Israel; it would be the state's formal acknowledgment that Orthodoxy possesses exclusive status, and it would affirm officially that only one form of Judaism exists, the Orthodox form. In personal terms, it would immediately expel from the body of Jewry all those people who regard themselves and are regarded by others as Jews, who conduct their lives as Jews, who even fulfill all their duties and obligations as citizens of the State of Israel, whose fathers are Jews but whose mothers are not, or cannot be proved to have been, or who, having no Jewish parent, have been formally converted to Judaism by a Reform, Conservative, Reconstructionist, or other non-Orthodox conversion program.

Controversies like this, the warp and weft of life in Israel since its founding, are simply off-shoots of the central and fundamental controversy over the basic character of the State. From 1948 on, the religious camp has demanded that Judaism be proclaimed the state's official, established religion. More, they maintain, Israel ought to be a theocracy, a *halachic* state in which authority proceeds from God and the law from *halacha*. Ranged against them, the vast majority of Israel's citizens have taken it for granted that their state will be a democracy on the model of Western Europe and the United States and, with some, perhaps many, glaring exceptions, that is what it has been.

The Declaration of Independence is explicit, that the state shall maintain "equality of social and political rights for all its citizens regardless of religion, race and gender" and it promises "freedom of religion, conscience, language, education and culture." This has not prevented every religious political party, from 1948 till now, from declaring that the vision it is working to realize is that of a theocratic, *halachic* state. Piecemeal, law by law and issue by issue, they are doing their utmost to bring that vision to pass.

For a number of reasons, Israel's first prime minister, David Ben Gurion, refused to accept the apparent solution to this unavoidable state of conflict—the separation of religion and state institutionalized in most modern democracies. He preferred instead to negotiate a status quo, an agreement with the religious leaders, under which the structure of relations between the state and the religious establishment, between secular and religious citizens, would continue as it stood on the day the State was officially established. As it was then was how it would continue. Let it not be naively assumed that this status quo was a sort of golden mean. Every single concession that was made was made by the seculars and that is still the state of affairs. Not even as a hypothetical possibility had it ever been considered that the rights of the religious population to live and practice their faith and to preserve their lifestyle as they saw fit might be in any particle curtailed by law, on the contrary: laws were passed constructing triple protections around these rights. The state allocated huge sums of money to enable its observant citizens to maintain their faith and lifestyle—as it still does today, only more so. Synagogues, ritual baths, *mikvot,* and other religious institutions were built anywhere there was even a whisper of demand. The rabbinic courts of law were given official status within the national legal system. The religious education systems, each enjoying substantial to near-total autonomy from state intervention, were generously funded. Legislation was passed making the observance of *kashrut,* the Sabbath, and the festivals compulsory in every facet of public life, from all government ministries and offices, through to the army and police, to the prisons and schools, all of which were designed to enable the religious to play their part in these institutions without compromising their religious obligations. On Sabbaths and Holy Days, observant neighborhoods were even permitted to close their internal roads to all motor traffic, public and private, and even some main roads that ran next to synagogues were closed.

In contrast, secular life has been beset with limitations and prohibitions. Opening of businesses on Sabbaths and holy days, including restaurants, cafés, cultural institutions, cinemas, theaters, and so forth, is unlawful,[14] and in most cities public transport may not run on Sabbath and holy days. No unleavened food may be offered for sale or bought during the eight days of Passover, or even publicly displayed. The most severe restriction of all imposed on secular freedoms is the placement of all matrimonial law under Orthodox rabbinic jurisdiction, as civil marriage does not exist in Israel. As a result, seculars are forced to suppress their own beliefs and have a rabbi conduct their marriage with full a Orthodox ceremony. A rabbi-regulated theocracy can even have worse consequences. In certain cases, the rabbis refuse to marry some couples, for example, a man considered to be *Cohen,* a descendant of priests, and a divorced woman (on the authority of Leviticus, chapter 21) or couples of two different religions. The Israeli rabbinate still enforces ancient rulings that humiliate women, such as the law of levirate marriage, under which a woman widowed before giving birth to a son must either marry her late husband's brother or undergo the demeaning ceremony of *khalitza* (on the authority of Deuteronomy 25 and Genesis 38), in which the brother releases her to marry someone else, not forgetting on occasion to extort a substantial payment for the favor. Nor will the rabbinate marry anyone it designates a *mamzer,* bastard; in Jewish law, this is anyone born to a married woman by a man who is not her husband. What is more, it maintains a list of these and other persons it labels as unmarriables. When it comes to *halachic* divorce, *get,* rabbinic law favors the husband and discriminates heavily against the wife, in addition to forcing her to undergo a most humiliating ceremony if a divorce is granted. The rabbinate also has a monopoly over the burial of the dead and regularly creates difficulties when it is charged with burying someone it defines as *halachically* not a Jew, or a suicide, both of which under *halacha* may be given only shameful burial. It is also not easy to arrange a burial for someone who has willed parts of his body to medical research, as under *halacha,* all parts of the body must be present in the grave, to await messianic resurrection. The pain caused by these difficulties is of course particularly distressing as they come at a time when a family has just been bereaved.

Such a state of affairs, sustained for such a long time, inevitably regularly provokes conflict between the secular, on the one hand, and the religious and ultra-Orthodox on the other. Modern Israel presents in fact an example of a *Kulturkamf*,[15] fought out in all national and local organs of government and legislation, in print, and even on the streets, when, for instance, rioting ultra-Orthodox demonstrators battle with the police. The religious and ultra-Orthodox political parties have regularly exploited their grip on the balance of power between the main parties to force the Knesset to pass theocracy-oriented legislation, such as prohibiting abortion; prohibiting the import of non-kosher meat; forcing the national airline, El Al, to shut down operations on the Sabbath; refusing to convert an adopted baby unless the parents undertake in writing to raise the child according to Orthodox dictates, including educating the child at religious schools only, and so on. Perhaps the most provocative of these impositions has been forcing the government to exempt tens of thousands of yeshiva students from the military compulsory service. The ultra-Orthodox argument for this exemption is that defense of the country and its Jewish communities cannot be secure if Torah is not being constantly studied; the young men poring over the secrets of Mishna and Talmud are therefore playing their part in the national defense just as much as the soldiers on the front lines. What has never been explained is why it is so vital that this study be undertaken specifically by men of conscription age.

The *Kulturkamf* between the ultra-Orthodox and the secular, and between the religious as a whole and the secular, in fact spills onto the streets quite frequently. On Sabbaths, the ultra-Orthodox block traffic arteries they have not been permitted to close, one tactic being to stone cars trying to get through. They also incinerate bus stops that display what they consider indecent advertising. When the coercion is extreme, the secular community has recourse to the High Court to protect its rights. One intervention of the court, for example, ordered the government-appointed broadcasting authority to reverse a directive canceling television broadcasts on Sabbaths. There have been many others, to the point that the High Court has become the ultra-Orthodox *bête noire*, an obstacle they try to circumvent by legislation in the Knesset, once again manipulating the majority by their hold on the balance of power between the major parties. This is a tactic most of the country regards as blatantly anti-democratic, designed to undermine the separation of powers and remove an obstruction on the road to a general imposition of *halacha*. The religious parties claim to be fighting to protect the Jewish character of the state, to prevent its Sabbath from being publicly desecrated, to stop its restaurants serving non-kosher food, to extend the place of Jewish education in non-religious schools. What they are in essence and in fact arguing is that Orthodox Judaism is the only true Judaism and no other form of Judaism has the right to life.

I have treated this issue extensively and have made my own position clear. Not only is secular Judaism legitimate, but it is a far broader and richer construct than religious Judaism. The Jewish character and appearance of the present secular State of Israel is not a whit less Jewish than it would be under some future *halachic* regime. Its Jewishness is in the Hebrew spoken in its streets; in the Hebrew names of its rivers, mountains, towns, streets, and squares; in its national symbols; and in the festivals celebrated by its people, not necessarily by religious ceremonial, and most of all in the way that the majority of its citizens define themselves culturally and nationally. This does not mean that I in any way question the right of the religious population to give their own neighborhoods and communal life what meets its understanding of Jewish character. In other words, it is obvious that this campaign by religious Jewry for the Jewish character of the state is a coercive campaign against secular Jewry and an invasion of its legitimate territory.

RETURNING TO THE FAITH

Around the Jewish world for some time now voices can be heard, some triumphant, others apprehensive, calling on people to take note of the increasing number of Jews making the choice to "return to the faith," not merely to the faith, but to its ultra-Orthodox sub-variety. The returnees are mostly young, a few are celebrities and they all make the choice to spend the greater part of their day sitting in a yeshiva, peering into the ancient wisdom of Torah and Talmud. This internal migration to ultra-Orthodoxy is in fact a small part of a wider phenomenon that has been affecting the whole Western world in the last three decades or so, the core of which is the movement of certain religious sects and denominations toward more extreme doctrinal-political positions, harking to what they perceive as the fundamentals. We know these movements as Fundamentalism. Another facet of this trend is a renewal of popular interest in religious matters, especially in mysticism and the esoteric enigmas of remote, arcane and exotic faiths. At the extremes of this new interest, individuals and sometimes whole groups have

attached themselves to eccentric cults and withdrawn into fundamental-
ist enclaves. Jewry has been no exception. We have our own fundamen-
talist trend, one stream, *Chabad,* even deranging itself, recently and
disturbingly, into a mass messianic hysteria. Young Jewish "returnees to
the faith" are part of this wider trend. Others try to find themselves in
strange cults, from the *Hare Krishna* to *Bratzlav* or *Chabad* Hasidism.
In the wider public, the trend assumes the form of all manner of people
from all sections of society taking renewed interest in a scattering of
activities lumped together as Judaism, Bible and Talmud study groups,
Hasidic music-making, the exploration of Kabbalah, indeed anything to
do with Jewish mysticism.

   This worldwide back to basics phenomenon seems to be an offshoot
of social changes that have revolutionized all elements of our existence.
The economic component in the revolution is evident: It began with
the collapse of classic capitalism in the 1930s. Its scientific-technological
component is central—from the revolutionary inception of a world-wide
telecommunications system, to the restructuring of our lives by car and
plane, and later, by computer and Internet. Politically and historically,
the same social revolution, after bringing down the great colonial empires, established on their ruins new nations struggling for identity as
well as new socio-economic-political confederations of states. The structure of Western society was thrown into upheaval; minorities and repressed sections of society gained status and power, centuries-old
conventions went out the window, and a new cultural perspective began
to establish itself, still not entirely clear as to its content but definitely
alive and kicking, and labeled for the interim post-modernism.

   Social revolutions awake disturbing anxieties, a deep sense of uncertainty, and doubt about the very nature of our world; they shake the
ground under our feet. Some sort of foothold, something to grip hold
of, becomes an urgent necessity. In such situations, the past begins to
seem a land of stability and calm certainties. At these moments in history, there are always some groups who will attempt to halt the advance
of the new movements and who wish to cling to old securities. We saw
this during the 1980s in the socioeconomic sphere, when there was a
revival of conservative free trade policies in the United States and Europe. In social life, people attempt to return to pre-revolutionary traditions, values and conventions, to former principles and methods of
education. Religio-cultural fundamentalism is the most characteristic of
all these reactions. Whether the proponents are Christian, Muslim, Jewish, Hindu, they are all driven by the same impulse. Fundamentalism is
simply a reaction, a deep need to stop the clock of the last three hun-

dred years, a clock whose hands have been marking off the uninterrupted progress of secularization.

The tendency to return to religion may dry up soon or it may continue
for many more years. Religious reaction and fundamentalism are clearly
supported and fostered by powerful politico-historical factors. However,
the wider trend of history is clearly towards a deeper and more pervading secularism. In Israel, certainly, returnees to the faith are outnumbered by the numerous groups and individuals moving in the opposite
direction, former *mitzva*-observant people who, as I would describe
them, have found enlightenment.

In secular Israel, crossing over to ultra-Orthodoxy still makes news
and never more so than when the new convert is a celebrity, whether a
film actor, an artist, a footballer, or someone in a profession enjoying
high social prestige, such as a fighter pilot, army officer, or university
professor. The cross-over is often the triumph of professional missionaries, who broadcast a constant flow of propaganda and information designed to convince those seculars who are hesitating on the brink and to
offer a path to people who have lost theirs, a path through religion to
personal redemption. Convicted criminals, drug addicts, and the desperately poor are among some of the other groups targeted by the missionaries. To the poor they offer financial assistance, cheap education,
free school meals, and other real benefits. But every benefit is also a
vehicle and channel for pro-faith propaganda that is often shocking in
its primitiveness: promises of supernatural solutions for daily troubles,
threats that the faithless will be visited with hellfire, a cult of Holy Men
and Kabbalist sages with a blessing and amulet to distribute for every
category of anxiety. Even a cult of dead Holy Men, who from the grave
will render assistance to the believer prepared to prostrate himself or
herself over their tombs, new wonder-working gravesites are "discovered" with remarkable frequency. This last cult is a strange growth, particularly since Deuteronomy 18:10–11 expressly forbids the practice:
"there shall not be found among you anyone that . . . inquires of the
dead." According to the Bible, Yahweh Himself expressly set a counterexample with respect to Moses: He concealed his place of burial and
"no man knows his burial place to this day" (Deut. 34:6). The poor or
the ignorant are drawn into an ultra-Orthodox lifestyle with tactics like
these. A different stream of propaganda is directed at the educated.
Books are composed to "prove" from selected texts of the great Jewish
rationalist philosophers that there is no contradiction between the tenets of Judaism and modern science. Study groups and advanced lectures
are arranged in educated secular neighborhoods.

The ultra-Orthodox missionaries to the non-Orthodox and the secular protest the "missionary" label on the grounds that their target population does not belong to another faith, but the propaganda they use is the same as Christian missionaries have been taking to the "natives" for hundreds of years, the tactics they deploy and the incentives they offer are the same, and when their assessment of their target's current spiritual state is also just as contemptuous, it is impossible to believe their protestations.

In Ben Barabash's novel, *My First Sony*, we have an account of what happens when a young man from a completely secular family returns to the faith. The narrator is a young boy and the returnee is his uncle Nimrod:

> Dad went to visit Nimrod trying to understand how he'd let himself go like this, and Nimrod got excited and explained that he was searching for better answers to questions like what made him a Jew and what was the connection between the Jewish religion and the Land of Israel, because how did you throw away your religion and in the same breath choose to renew the Jewish people's covenant with this land, made sacred to the Jews by God's command, and before Dad could begin to answer him he asks why did Dad have Sha'ul circumcised . . . Dad said he hadn't come all the way to hear that in the end there were questions to which he didn't have the answer, . . . but he wasn't ready to make God an exclamation mark to put after all the question marks that break life up into islands of uncertainty.[16]

However, as we have noted, the returnees are countered by a steady stream of emigrants from religion coming the other way. The way of life that secular society offers—freedom of ideas and thought, a medley of social groupings and freely chosen lifestyles, pluralism—is clearly visible from many religious and ultra-Orthodox neighborhoods and draws many young observant people to it. In some localities there is even a degree of interaction between the two camps. The internal migration in this direction, however, is not organized; there are no missionaries at work to publicize it, and so it does not make the news, even though it is certainly larger than the migration in the opposite direction. We have only to remember that secularization has been the trend in the Jewish world for over two hundred years now, ever since Jews began to adopt the ideas and ways of the gentile Enlightenment, and that the influence of the gentile world has not grown any weaker since then. The returnees to the faith, we may say, are a surface current that stirs up lots of froth and foam, but the tide underneath is pulling the other way.

The factors and motives drawing the religiously observant over to "enlightenment" are many and varied and, without doubt, the influence of the fashion of the times is the most powerful of them. Without that we would still be talking of scattered individuals. For each "émigré" from *halacha*, the weight and mix of motives will differ. Some will be attracted to the lifestyle that, from "the other side," may appear free and easy and seem to promise all sorts of earthly delights. Some leave an observant home to marry out, others to find answers to their questions about faith and scripture that Orthodox rabbis and teachers cannot or will not give, still others out of disgust with intellectual oppression and constraint. Quite a few recent "finders of enlightenment" have described their experiences to us in newspaper articles, autobiographies, and novels. Indeed, loss of faith has been a common theme in Hebrew literature since the nineteenth century. Two of the most celebrated accounts are in Mordechai Zeev Feuerberg's "Lean" (*Whither?*) and Mich Yoseph Berditchevsky's "Kalonimos and Naomi." Here is a passage from the latter:

It is a question of someone who has not been taught the basics of Judaism . . . ideas are a product of reasoning . . . His head was in turmoil; he thought of the *Guide,*[17] . . . the words stand strong and clear in front of him: "The premises we require in treating the existence and reality of God, blessed be He" . . . He felt only that all of a sudden everything had vanished . . . Man was created in the image, and the image was the original but not the original, only an approximation . . . Who said to the universe Be? Who set the elements of nature into a whole? . . . Suddenly a thought struck him: Who knows if there is one God? If there is any God, an "Ultimate Cause"? . . . He jumped back as though bitten by a snake, but the idea would not leave him: that was it, there is no Almighty God in Heaven, there is no Heaven, it's all air rushing to and fro, day after day . . . The terrible idea would not go away and was clearly not some momentary thought. He fought it, he tried to push it away; he would have given his soul to be able cut out this "root bearing gall and wormwood" but nothing availed . . . there was only void and desolation. His room contained no Ultimate Cause . . .

Of course, there is nothing wrong with changing one's mind if one is truly convinced that another way is better, but "converting" from secularism to religion, and even more so from religion to secularism, entails far more than a change of mind, especially in Israel where secular-religious relations are so adversarial. One's whole lifestyle is transformed, including one's social network, cultural needs, day-to-day routine. The change and the rift are likely to split apart the convert's whole mental-emotional world and that of their family too, if the family is not part of the change. The daily life of a married couple when one is secular and the other religious can be extremely difficult and painful; the same can be true for the secular child of religious parents, or vice versa. The family unit is the most embittered of all arenas of conflict between secularism and religion. It is almost inevitable that the unit will suffer extreme stress, and may well fragment. Israeli seculars regularly charge the ultra-Orthodox with "soul trapping," with their hunter-missionaries being happy to detach children from home and family. The missionaries retort that they are not trapping souls, but saving them.

The conflict over Israel's future character is at a crisis. Although the secular constitute the great majority of the population, the religious are much more organized and work more actively to extend their influence. This the secular perceive as a threat to their right to live as they choose within the society that they choose, the religious perceive secularism as a threat not only to their status and view of the world but to their very existence. By preaching that the State of Israel ought to look like a Jewish state—according to their definition of Jewish, of course—they are pursuing a sustained effort to impose *halachic* norms and externals on its public life. Their favorite tactic is parliamentary legislation, since the *Knesset* is where they can wield their strongest weapon, which is their grip on the balance of power between the blocs of left and right. To seculars this is religious coercion, pure and simple. Israeli Jews have been embroiled in this war of cultures for decades now, to the point that there is now barely a single facet of Israeli life, public or private, that does not suffer from it.

6

Secular Reading of Jewish Culture

SOURCES OF JEWISH CULTURE

"Judaism"

THE WORD "JUDAISM" WAS COINED IN GREEK AS A TERM TO DESCRIBE the culture of the Jews. Its first known usage appears in the second book of the Maccabees (probably dating to the second century BCE), the first version of which was written in Greek: "Judah, also [known as] Maccabee, and his men would secretly go around among the villages calling out their kinsmen and those who had remained in Judaism [*Ioudaismos*] they took with them" (8:1). *Ioudaismos* here refers both to religious and ethnic loyalties, but even after this coining, the word was seldom used by Jewish authors, who preferred to use the term "the Law of Israel" (*torat yisrael*). Not until the eighteenth century CE was the word brought back into use, in the German *das Judentum,* meaning Jewish civilization and culture as a subject of scientific research.

There are two problems with using the English term "Judaism" to mean "the civilization and the culture of the Jews," as I have done throughout this book. The first is that Judaism's first and most commonly understood meaning is "the religion of the Jews" and only secondly does it denote "the Jews collectively." The *Oxford Dictionary* admits these meanings. *Webster's*[1] does allow the one used in this book, namely, "the total complex of cultural, social, and religious beliefs and practices of the Jews," but this denotation is in third place. The second problem stems from the eighteenth-century German re-invention of the term. *Das Judentum* (Judaism) was coined as a parallelism to *das Christentum* (Christianity), both signifying the totality of each religion, belief-system, practice and associated lifestyles. The problem is that "Judaism" is also a national-linguistic culture and we do not talk of "Englishism" or "Russianism" to signify the complete culture of the English or Russian peoples and their national language. Despite this, I propose that we stay

185

with *Webster's* definition of "Judaism," which is a comprehensive term that encompasses the rich and complex civilization, culture and being of the Jewish people in its entirety, in all its languages and across all its generations, from the earliest beginnings to the present day.

The Bible: Myth and Law

Every religion and civilization we know, and the Judaic-Jewish civilization-religion is no exception, dresses up its origins in sacred myths, stories of the earliest days of the world's inception. The Hebrew myths that are sacrosanct to the Judaic religion tell of the emergence of the universe (in Jewish tradition, "the creation of the world"); of the creation and early history of humans; of the origins of the Hebrews and of Yahweh's self-revelation to Abram (later Abraham), who is the primal ancestor and progenitor of the people of Israel; of the birth and divine election of the people of Israel and its early history; and of the giving of the divine law code, the Torah, into the hands of Moses, "first among the prophets," who then delivered it to the people of Israel, assembled at the foot of Mt. Sinai. These myths were, at various points in time, told and re-told, embellished and restructured, adapted to fit changing social conditions, and interleaved with the code of divine law, and then inscribed in the five books, also known by the names "the Torah," "the Five Books of Moses," and "the Pentateuch." This intertwining of law and myth is unique, without parallel in ancient literature. Because the law is derived from divine sources, it becomes absolute: unfaultable, unquestionable, fixed, and unalterable. The adapters' superb literary skills enabled them, over many generations, to weld sections of law-cataloging passages into the mythological narrative, making their legal expositions into plot elements of the ongoing story. Upon these myths the Israelites raised the first pillars of their faith, slowly creating a Judaic theology. Over hundreds of generations and three thousand years of change, both this faith and this theology have evolved into what we have today. On the foundation of the law code set out in the Five Books, *halacha* arose, that now vast edifice of law and practice, which each generation of rabbinic judges has interpreted, adjusted and added to in the light of contemporary needs.

The Five Books of Moses, or the Torah, are the Jewish religion's holiest text and the first of the Bible's[2] three divisions. From whose initials—*Torah* (Law), *Nevi'im* (Prophets), *Ketuvim* (Writings)—comes the Bible's Hebrew name, *TaNaKh.* The second division is in two parts. The first comprises the books of the "First Prophets," in which, book by book, the history of the people of Israel, during and after it settled the land of Israel, is narrated—from the conquest under Joshua Bin-Nun, through the period of nation formation under the Judges (local leaders who, when summoned, led Israelite tribal coalitions into battle), up to the unification of the tribes and the establishment of the first monarchy under Saul, a monarchy that King David then expanded and unified into a strong kingdom. From the reign of his son, Solomon, we enter the First Temple period. In this period, Solomon built a great temple to the Israelites' God, Yahweh, and other temples to the gods of his many wives, in Jerusalem, the new capital city that his father, David, had established on an ancient existing village. In this same period, David's grandson presided over the formal breakup of the kingdom into two: Israel in the north and Judah (with Jerusalem as its capital) in the south. The First Temple period lasted for some three hundred and fifty years. It ended in 586 BCE by the armies of Nebuchadnezzar of Babylon, who pulled down the Temple and marched the elite of the population of Judah off into exile (the northern kingdom, Israel, had been conquered and depopulated long before, by the Assyrians in 720 BCE). The second part of Prophets comprises the books and teachings of the Latter Prophets, fifteen all told, some of whom were active towards the end of the First Temple period, others of whom prophesied the exile to Babylon. The remainders, the last of the line of recognized prophets, were those who accompanied the exiles on the Return to Zion (which began in 538 BCE) and the rebuilding of the Temple. With the rebuilding, the Second Temple period opens. The Bible's third division, *Writings,* comprises a medley of genres, works of poetry, of wisdom, proverbs, legendary narratives, and historical chronicle.

The first division, *Torah,* is accorded a rank of holiness far above that of the other divisions: according to tradition, God dictated it to Moses, who wrote it down himself. The other parts are also sacred: They were all composed, believers say, "in the spirit of holiness," that is, under divine inspiration, and each is an instance and promise of God's true self-revelation. For the Jewish religion, all the books of the Bible are "Scripture of the Holiness" *kitvei hakodesh.* Other languages of the world know them as "the Book," "the Bible," "the Holy Book," "the Good Book." The twenty-four (or thirty-nine) books of the Old Testament (depending on which counting and division one is using) were composed over a span of a thousand years. Parts of Genesis, the first of the Five Books, are estimated to be written more than three thousand years ago, whereas the latest books in *Writings* were written some 2,200 years ago, possibly even later. The Bible is therefore an anthology, a collection whose books, eras, subjects, genres, and styles illustrate the development of Israelite religious thought and of Hebrew language and literature over those years of its composition and editing. Yet the long cycle of adaptation, revision, and canon formation displays a consistent search for coherence, a steadfast endeavor to bring the books into line with the theocentric conception which makes God's will the prime mover of world history and human acts, and above all the prime mover of the history of the people of Israel.

The Bible's assemblage, editing, sanctification, and its final closure as the *Tanakh*, the biblical canon, was a long and gradual process. The Five Books, or perhaps only parts of them, are estimated by some to have reached the form in which they have come down to us by the end of the First Temple period; others say that the version we now have dates from the early Second Temple period or later. All the other books belong wholly to the Second Temple period, composed not before the second century BCE even three or four hundred years later on. In the second century of the Common Era, we read in the *Mishna* and *Talmud* that the leading scholars were still arguing whether Ecclesiastes and the Song of Songs were of sufficient sanctity to be included in the canon (Mishna *Yadayim* 3; BT *Shabbat* 30b). The *Tanakh* may be an anthology and a collection but it is also a selection. Works far older than Ecclesiastes and the Song of Songs, some so well-known that the Bible can refer to them in passing by name, were not even candidates for inclusion in the canon, having attracted, apparently, no aura of holiness. *Sefer Hayashar*, Book of Poetry, *Sefer Milkhamot Yahweh*, The Book of Yahweh's Wars, and *Sefer Divrei haYamim leMalkhei Yehuda veYisrael*, Chronicle of the Kings of Judah and Israel, are only three of these works, but the titles are all that have come down to us. During the period when the biblical canon was approaching closure, and for some time after it, other works were composed that were also refused admittance, despite being similar in character to works that had been canonized. The four *Books of the Maccabees* recount the wars of the Maccabees, each from its own religio-historical point of view; the *Wisdom of Ben Sira* is a compilation of proverbs and wise sayings after the model of the biblical *Proverbs*; *Tobit* is a legendary tale with a moral; *Judith* recounts a dramatic but legendary episode from Jewish history; sequels were composed to canonized works; and so on. In most cases, we have their titles and translated versions, in Aramaic or Greek usually, but not the original Hebrew.[3] Some were apparently originally composed in Aramaic or Greek. These works, all rejected from the canon, are known as the Apocrypha, Excluded Books or the Latter Writings.

The first Century CE is also the period when the famous Jewish historian, Josephus Flavius (Yosef ben-Mattityahu), and the philosopher, Philo (Yedidya) of Alexandria, and many others too were active. They wrote in Greek for Diaspora Jews, who by then knew no Hebrew or Aramaic, and for Greek-speaking non-Jews. Josephus's *Jewish Antiquities* retells the story of Jewish history from the Creation to his own time, according to his own interpretation of the biblical narrative. *The Jewish War* is his detailed account of the genesis and course of the Great Revolt against Rome (67–73 CE), a disastrous undertaking that ended in mass slaughter, bitter flight, and the demolition of Jerusalem and its Second Temple. The two works together are our prime source of information on the Second Temple period. Philo's contribution is to lay the basis for an understanding of Judaism in the light and language of Greek philosophy. The framework for most of his writing is commentary on the Torah but he departs radically from the pattern of rabbinical commentary by supplementing his comments on the biblical text with the teaching of the great Greek thinkers. At the same time the New Testament was written, which narrates the revelation of Jesus of Nazareth as messiah. In form, content, and especially in spirit, most this book belongs directly to the Judaism of the time. However, the rabbinical establishment had nothing but contempt for this sort of commentary on Judaism; observant Jews were forbidden even to read it.

By the late second Century CE the Bible was translated to Aramaic, the language used by Jews in Mesopotamia and other eastern countries. One such translation was the work of the proselyte, Onkelos (perhaps the same man referred to elsewhere as Aquilas); another is erroneously attributed to Jonathan Ben Uzziel. These texts are more than translations, they also expound and elaborate on the original. Later they were awarded the stamp of sanctity. The Hebrew Bible had been translated into Greek long before, in the third Century BCE in a translation we know as the Septuagint.[4] Many famous later translations of the Bible were derived from this Greek-language version and not from the original Hebrew.

THE ORAL LAW: *HALACHA* AND *AGGADA*

The books of the Bible, and the five books of the Torah in particular, have provoked numerous thinkers and teachers into seeking to explain them, enlarge on them, supplement them, or realign them to meet changing realities and new conceptions. The books' sacrosanct position, the absolute ban on altering as much as a dot on an *i*, has only served to open the door to unrestrained interpretation, of a kind called in Hebrew *derash,* from a root meaning "to probe," "to study." The idea is to probe the holy words for implied, concealed meanings that a plain or surface reading would miss, but that are there waiting to be found at deeper levels of understanding. Without changing an iota of its outward form, the sacred text can in this way be filled with radically new content and meanings. The sages had a clear understanding of what was being done: "'To interpret a verse of the given text literally is to fabricate'" (BT *Kiddushin* 49a). But it is these texts of commentary and interpretation on biblical myth that are the source of the articles of the Israelite faith and it is on the basis of the "God-given" laws set out in the Five Books that the elaborate construction of *halacha* has been built. By far the most important compilation of commentary and interpretation is the *Talmud,* comprising the *Mishna* and the commentary on the *Mishna,* known as *Gemara.* All three names mean "learning, study."

Another name for the *Talmud* is the Oral Law, to distinguish it from the Written Law, the Five Books. By tradition, the huge tomes of the *Talmud* are held to do nothing more than bring to light meanings that are hidden deep in the original text. It is believed, indeed, that no oral exposition of the Written Law can be made that was not in fact implicitly within the written text from the very moment it was dictated to Moses on Mt. Sinai, and thus the Oral Law partakes of the holiness of the Written Law.

The volumes of the *Talmud* are essentially compendia of law and legal rulings, which elaborate, expand, and update the biblical code. What differentiates them from a standard text of jurisprudence is that they go to great pains to set out not only the final rulings but also the wide-ranging debate and dispute that the scholars of all preceding generations have pursued over each point, which applied the law to current circumstances and to the conditions in different Diasporas. Over the centuries the rulings accumulated in study houses and law courts and were passed down orally from generation to generation, until around 200 CE they were collected together, collated by subject matter, and compiled in writing in a canon of six volumes, known as the *Six Orders of Mishna,* (abbreviated in Hebrew to *Shas*). The *Six Orders* are: *Zerayim,* Seeds, which regulates agriculture and the treatment of agricultural produce; *Mo'ed,* Fixed Times, which concerns all aspects of time, the calendar and the festivals; *Nashim,* Women, which lays out matrimonial and family law; *Nezikin,* Torts, which determines civil law with regard to dealings between individuals; *Kodashim,* Sacred Matters, which deals with religious ritual and divine worship, in the Temple in particular; *Taharot*, Purity, which sets out the law on ritual uncleanness and methods of purification. The *Six Orders* are subdivided into tractates and the tractates are further divided into sub-sections called *mishnayot* (plural of *mishna*). There were *mishnayot* that did not find their way into the compiled *Mishna*, but which the scholars of the *Gemara* knew well and called *beraitot*, outside *mishnayot*. By tradition, the compilation of the *Mishna* is the accomplishment of Rabbi Yehuda ha-Nasi, president of the Sanhedrin, known as Rabbi (135?–220 CE). But it is far more likely that the collation and closure of the *mishnaic* canon was only the final stage of a prolonged process of collection and editing begun early in the Second Temple period, six or seven hundred years before. The generations of the sages of the *Mishna* are known as *tanna'im*. Almost all were ordained in and served in Judea and in Galilee. As a mark of veneration, their names came to be prefaced by the honorific, Rabbi.

After the closure of the *mishnaic* canon, the need to interpret and adjust the law in response to new issues and developments continued. The significant change was that from this point on, the main object of the sages' elucidation was not only the Biblical law but also the *Mishna*, now second in holiness and immutability only to the first great source. A new body of rulings and refinements slowly accumulated, the *Gemara* (Aramaic for "learning") on the *Mishna*. Towards the end of the fifth century CE, in the great centers of learning of the Babylonian Diaspora, this *Gemara*, in its turn, was collected, edited, and organized into a third canon of Judaic law and wisdom that for religious Jews, is the third holiest book, after the Bible and the *Mishna*. According to tradition, the Babylonian *Talmud* was edited and compiled by Rav Ashi and Rabbina. Their organizing principle followed the structure of their revered predecessor. Each of the *Mishna's* subsections (*mishnayot*) was quoted verbatim and then the accumulated and arranged *Gemara* materials were juxtaposed with it. The *Mishna* plus the *Gemara* form the Babylonian *Talmud*, also known, like the *Mishna*, as *Shas*, the *Sixty Books*. Sages quoted in the *Gemara* are called *amora'im* (Aramaic for "interpreters"); their honorific is Rav.

The great bulk of *Mishna* material was produced and edited in Judea and mainly in the Galilee, in Hebrew. Minor contributions came from *tanna'im* who lived in the Babylonian diaspora. By the second century CE, the political and economic situation of the Jews in *Eretz Yisrael* had so deteriorated that large numbers left to join the Babylonian community, including many of the greatest sages. The Babylonian diaspora took over the leadership of the Jewish world and the newest pronouncements on *halacha* now emerged from its great yeshivas. The work of the *Gemara* on the *Mishna* was dominated by Babylonian sages, and their *Talmud* was composed not in Hebrew but in Aramaic, the vernacular of the Babylonian diaspora. However, significant *Talmudic* study and debate continued in *Eretz Yisrael* well into the sixth century CE, when it was compiled into what we know as the *Jerusalem Talmud*, a work of smaller scope and lesser authority than the Babylonian *Talmud.*

The Babylonian *Talmud* is the rock upon which the edifice of *halacha* stands and its prime source. But it is also, as we have noted, a book of law and judgement that not only sets out the current state of the law but also the process of debate and negotiation, of which the current rulings are the fruition. In many instances, where the process is not considered to have reached a stage allowing a single consensual statement, the conclusion is dissent and consequently, divergent practices are permitted, each protected by the sanction of a particular sage or school. A great deal of space and attention is given to this process of debate and negotiation, so that that the process is evidently intended to be part of the message. The very design of the *Talmud* makes the point that controversy and debate are healthy, a way to clear up impediments that might otherwise obscure a truth of each issue. There are times at which some readers might feel that the pursuit of exactitude and possible variants has been carried too far, when the text delves into nuances and details that lack any practical significance.

Interspersed in these thickets of *halachic* investigation and negotiation are other types of material: Statements concerning the core tenets of rabbinic Judaism and glosses on biblical myths and prophetic ideas that are intended to adjust such original notions to new thinking and to new ways of thinking. But the warp and weft of the *Talmudic* text has yet another strand to it—the *Aggada*. The *Aggada* is a collection of legends, of fictional and semi-fictional tales, and folklore introduced by the sages for a variety of purposes. Some *Aggadic* material, elaborating on a biblical myth, interprets it by illustration. Other material explains the law by means of parable and practical instance. There are tales and legends about the deeds of the renowned sages, reports of their striking dicta and the pearls of their wisdom; yet other parables or *midrashim* are intended to enlarge upon an article of faith. New myths are woven by creative exposition of biblical passages. *Aggadic* material was apparently so abundant that what did not enter the two *Talmuds* was used to fill separate volumes of *Aggadic* compendia, of which the most important is *Midrash Rabba,* The Great *Midrash.* Two other collections are *Midrash Tanhuma* and *Yalkut Shimoni.*[5]

In many cases the *Talmud* left contentious issues open for a later consensus, so the work of interpreting and adjusting the law to the realities
of new times continued. One of the main vehicles by which the process
continued was the institution of Questions and Responsa, written questions submitted to a scholar of recognized authority for his written answer. Several attempts were made to impose that closure which
tanna'im and *amora'im* had not presumed to do, to lay down final answers to all the issues that the *Talmud* had left undecided. Rabbi Isaac
Alfasi composed his *Sefer HaHalakhot*, The Book of *Halkhot*, from the
mid-eleventh century), Maimonides his *Mishne Torah*, Second to the
Tora, from 1180), and Rabbi Jacob Ben Asher his *Arba'a Turim*, Four
Columns, from the early fourteenth century). Then in the sixteenth century Rabbi Joseph Caro drew up his *Shulkhan Arukh*, The Laid Table,
with the express intention of providing for all Jews everywhere a settled
and firm statement of *halacha* as it stood at the time. He succeeded to
a notable extent, for since then the *Shulkhan Arukh* has been the starting point for all *halakhic* discussion and the text to which Orthodoxy
looks for final authority.

Rational Thought: Philosophy

As with the *halacha*, the articles of the faith itself were also the subject of continuous debate, particularly when Judaism was confronted by
Greek philosophy and later, in the early Middle Ages, by the theologies
of an aggressive Christianity and Islam, many of their core concepts borrowed from the great Greek thinkers. The tenets of Judaism, deriving
their inspiration from biblical mythology, raised countless problems.
The Bible itself was full of contradictions; for example, chapters one and
two of Genesis present divergent, in places directly conflicting, versions
of the Creation. Flouting the principle that God has no shape or form,
some biblical passages depict an anthropomorphic deity. One instance
is verses 26–27 of Genesis 1, which inform us that man was created in
the image and likeness of God. Under the force of philosophical logic,
fundamental Jewish tenets—the divine creation of the world, for example—seemed to totter on the brink of refutation, for if God possessed
the absolute perfection attributed to Him then there was no place for
change in His universe.

Answers were needed that were capable of satisfying philosophical
reason without shaking the pillars of the faith, and accordingly, Judaism's great minds sought such solutions, but in two very different
spheres. Rationalism looked for ways to reconcile logically the internal

contradictions both within Judaism's belief system and between that system and the dominant philosophical approach to key contemporary issues. Mysticism, however, responded by creating a new mythology and a new myth-based literature, Kabbala. Both tendencies had their origins in the Second Temple period and had developed side by side within Judaism over the centuries since then, each responding and adapting in its own way and to different degrees to the changes occurring within Judaism and in the world around it.

While Jewish philosophy took its first steps in the late Second Temple period, when Josephus and Philo began to pursue some of the challenges presented by Greek thought, and the period of its true flowering came much later, beginning in the tenth century C. E. The most important achievements were: R. Saadiah Gaon's *The Book of Beliefs and Opinions*, which argued the case that reason and divine revelation are perfectly compatible (tenth century); Bakhya Ibn Pekuda's *The Duties of the Heart*, which aimed to strengthen the elements of faith and spirituality (eleventh century); Maimonides' *Guide for the Perplexed*, which stated firmly that God is conceivable only in terms of reason and that all anthropomorphizing depictions are merely illustrative, that God's intervention in the world came in the form of the laws of nature, and that man, by virtue of his possession of free will, also possesses the power of choice (late twelfth century); Yehuda Halevi's *Kuzari*, which apportioned philosophy and religion to separate domains: philosophy's validity was confined to logic and mathematics, while religion's domain was the human spirit and metaphysics—and only religion could give man happiness (twelfth century). Levi Ben Gershom's *The Book of the Lord's Wars* undertook to provide a logic-based explication of several of Judaism's central tenets (fourteenth century). All these men, in particular Saadiah Gaon and Yehuda Halevi, were convinced, and determined to demonstrate in their work, that Judaism possessed significant advantages both over other monotheistic religions and over Greek philosophy.

In the modern period Jewish philosophy has continued to probe the central articles of religious Judaism but its focus has now turned to the role and uniqueness of the Jewish people in this world. Early in the nineteenth century Nakhman Krokhmal's *Guide for the Perplexed of Our Own Time* offered a history-based theory, explaining the biography of the Jewish people in terms of a cycle of birth, maturity, and decline. A century later, Hermann Cohen's *Religion of Reason: Out of the Jewish Sources*, declared that God was the source of both reason and morality and that the Jewish people had been sent by Him to realize justice and peace on earth within the framework of a prophetic morality. About the same time Franz Rosenzweig wrote *The Star of Redemption* setting out his theory of a world formed upon two triangles. The vertices of the one are God, the world, and humankind, and of the other, creation, revelation, and redemption. The two triangles, one placed over the other, form a Star of David, the star of redemption. Martin Buber's contribution was to describe relations between one human being and the other as a dialogue and God as "the permanent Other." He saw the Hebrew Bible as a record of relations between humanity and God, and the laws of religion as the constantly changing human response to this never-ending dialogue. The French-Jewish philosopher Emmanuel Levinas made ethics the center of his philosophical teaching. With those philosophers who were taking religious Judaism in new directions, the visionaries of Reform, Conservatism, and Reconstructionism, the nature, role, and uniqueness of the Jewish people in the modern world also took center place.

Jewish Mysticism: Kabbala

The alternative path to achieving a satisfying understanding and interpretation of Scripture is mysticism, known in Hebrew as Kabbala.[6] Like rational philosophy it began in the latter part of the Second Temple period, but later, under the influence of mysticisms from other parts of the ancient Eastern world, underwent a period of intense development in the second and third centuries CE. A thousand years later, in the twelfth-fifteenth centuries, a second, even higher peak of development and elaboration occurred. Mysticism explains the articles of the faith by means of myths and legends, which are themselves elaborations on and extensions of early biblical myths and *Talmudic midrashim.* Core mysteries—the nature of the Godhead and the universe, the fate and mission of the people of Israel—are treated and answered in symbolic terms.

The central text of the Kabbala is the *Zohar,* attributed to R. Shimon Bar Yokhai, who had taught in second-century. Modern researchers have found that the author was Moses de Leon, a Kabbalist who, at the time the book appeared, was living in Castille, Spain. Throughout the next several centuries, the book's stature rose so high in Kabbalist circles that it began to achieve as much sanctity as the *Talmud* itself. Written in Aramaic, its structure follows the sequence of the Torah portions read each week of the year; the *Zohar* is made up of *midrashim* and mystical commentary on these Torah portions. Piece by piece it weaves an imaginative mythology, encompassing and explaining the creation of the world, the interrelation of the several divine forces, the structure of all existent worlds, and how messianic redemption is destined to unfold. Yet the *Zohar* was only the culmination of a long tradition of Jewish mystical writings, which like the *Zohar* were mostly pseudo-epigraphic, the real author hiding behind an attribution to some venerable historical or even mythological figure. From as early as the second century CE we have the fragmentary *Heikhalot*, Celestial Palaces, texts and *Ma'aseh Merkava* texts, literally The Work of the Chariot, that is, the celestial chariot reputed to carry God's throne. These were ascribed respectively to R. Akiba and R. Ishmael and offered visionary depictions of the celestial worlds, the architecture of the heavens, the throne of glory, and so forth. From the third or fourth century we have the *Sefer Yetzirah,* Book of Creation, from the pen, purportedly, of Abraham himself; this work describes how the world was created by the power of numbers and of the letters of the Hebrew alphabet. From the same period comes the *Sefer Raziel Hamalakh,* Book of the Angel Raziel, with its depictions of the heavenly hosts and carefully conducted census of the corps of angels; this book is ascribed to no less an author than Adam, the world's first man. Another of Kabbala's core texts, *Sefer Habahir,* Book of Luminosity, was composed in the twelfth century. Comprising passages of parable and imaginative commentary attributed to a range of famous *tanna'im,* its main purpose is to name and describe the attributes of the Godhead.

The aura and fame of the Zohar by no means daunted the flow of further Kabbalist composition. New speculation, new structures of Kabbalist thought continued to appear, the most important among them being the theories of Moses Cordovero and his disciple, Rabbi Isaac Ashkenazi Luria. In *The Pomegranate Orchard* Cordovero portrays the universe as a construct and system descended from the Divinity. His disciple's conceptualization of God, the world and the Jews' place in it, known as the Lurianic Kabbala, laid upon Jewry the duty of the reparation and restoration, *tikkun,* of the world from the mythic crisis of "the shattering of the vessels," *shvirat hakelim,* brought about in the upper worlds by the divine act of creation itself. By fervent prayer and *mitzva* observance, it was in the Jews' power to rescue the Divine Presence or Immanence, *shekhina,* from its exile. Prayer and piety could gather up the "sparks of holiness," now dispersed among the "shells," *klipot,* and vessel shards and fallen into the clutch of the "other side," that is, Satan, and return them to their Divine origin. Once the *tikkun* was accomplished, redemption would come. Humans would return their souls to their source in God's spirit, and the corporeal world would come to an end. In Luria's system it was not God's part to redeem Israel but Israel's duty to deliver the *shekhina* to redemption.

The reverberations of the Lurianic Kabbala have resonated throughout the generations. In our very own time the ideas still have the power to excite. In the seventeenth century Luria's conceptions provoked Shabtai Tzvi to announce himself as the Messiah, causing a despairing Jewish world to explode into a frenzy of exultation. In the eighteenth century came Hasidism, motivated at its heart by Kabbalist ideas and aspirations and founded upon Lurianic elements, to which it added the role of the *tzaddik* as mentor and guide between the lower and upper worlds. Around this time, the Kabbalist teaching of the Italian, Moses Ha'im Luzzato, appeared—he too proclaimed himself a Messiah—and messianic speculation has continued to be alive, powerful strand in Jewish hopes and experience across the world. We have already noted R. Kook's theories in early twentieth-century Palestine, and as recently as the 1990s a significant Messsianic tendency emerged in Chabad Hasidism, sparked by the conviction that around their own Rebbe, Menachem Schneerson, head shone the invisible aureole of the King-Messiah.

Taken as a whole, the aim and claim of Kabbala is to probe and uncover the secrets of Divinity, to grasp the very nature of godhead and creation and unravel the purpose assigned to the Jewish people within creation. All these, so Kabbala insists, lie concealed within the biblical text, hidden by many devices and at different levels, residing in the text's overarching meaning as much as in its visible content, to be discovered in sentences and in the order of sentences, in single words, even in individual letters, even in the letters' shape and ornamentation. But secrets as profound as these are not to be uncovered by anyone. It requires the instructed, inspired vision of masters of the hidden wisdom; it takes complex decipherings, super-subtle penetration, an ability to appreciate the text on its mythic, symbolic level to conjure the secret depths out of the printed page. The ability to function on this plane is the preserve only of a handful of masters found worthy of the honor.

With time, Kabbala developed another phase, a plane of functioning called "practical *Kabbala*," whose masters presumed to supernatural powers, which allowed them to bend the higher forces to their will for the sake of good deeds. To the sick and disabled they promise cures, to the poor prosperity, to the young a successful match, to the childless fertility, to expecting mothers children who would be geniuses. Magic is in their knapsack, together with blessings, spells, invocations; they inscribe charms and remedies of exceptional virtue and supernatural power. It is a facet of Kabbala that has dragged it into kinship with sorcery and the black arts. In the Hasidic world the *tzaddik* is said to command the same supernatural authority, empowered, through his links to the upper worlds, to enable his followers to partake of God's loving kindness. He, too, is a source of spells, special prayers, amulets and suchlike. Even Israeli politics is now an arena for the black magic of practical Kabbala, with the amulets, blessings and promises of the "sainted Kabbalists" distributed wholesale among those sections of the electorate willing to believe in them.

Biblical Commentary

The accumulated body of biblical commentary, interpretation, and explanation has now attained gigantic proportions. This was bound to happen, for each generation is further removed from the language of the sacred text and the ways of life that engendered it. The need for some explanation of both the language and the content changed as the language and mores of readers changed. Of all the commentaries, the most celebrated and widely-used by both Bible and *Talmud* scholars is that of the renowned twelfth-century scholar R. Shlomo Yitzhaki, who lived most of his life in Worms and is known throughout the Jewish world as Rashi. His commentary is lucid and easy to understand, rooted in a deep knowledge both of biblical Hebrew and of the exegeses of all the *tanna'im, amora'im* and other scholars who preceded him. Another famous name is R. Abraham Ibn Ezra, who also lived in the twelfth century; his commentary always seeks out the logic in a given passage, while his knowledge of biblical Hebrew and its grammar is encyclopedic. During the sixteenth century in Venice, the most important commentaries were collected together, edited, and printed alongside the biblical text upon which they commented. These were compiled into a celebrated edition of the Hebrew Bible, called *Mikra'ot Gedolot*. Since then, and up to our present time, edition after edition of this famous undertaking has been issued.

A very different school of commentary arrived on the scene after the emergence of the *Haskalah* in eighteenth-century Germany. This approach became known as "textual criticism," in which comments and elucidations proceeded from the scientifically investigation of the history, archeology, anthropology, and linguistics of the Hebrews and of their ancient Semitic and non-Semitic neighbors as well. It is this form of commentary that is now practiced in most universities and research institutes around the world.

Jewish Literature

History, philosophy, and biblical commentary are not the only spheres of writing to have attracted learned Jews, our heritage also includes a rich creative literature. As far as is known, at the end of the first millennium CE creative writing was confined to *Talmudic Aggada* and religious poetry, called *piyyut* (from the Greek *poietes*, meaning poet). The first masters of *piyyut* were heirs to the biblical poetic tradition, whose glory is the book of Psalms. The poetry of the *piyyutists* consisted of praise and exaltation of God, supplication and petition, lament, and appeal for forgiveness. A favorite device was the acrostic; another was to decorate the verse by making the lines rhyme—they were, inasmuch as we know, the first poets to do so. They improvised freely with the biblical tongue, making nouns from adjectives and adjectives from nouns, putting verbs into conjugations that lacked any biblical precedent, to the point of making their poetry difficult to understand. Hebrew at this time, we must remember, was a language of texts, not a spoken tongue. Many of these poems were so loved as to be absorbed into their communities' prayer services, chanted at religious ceremonies, and festive meals or recited on the days of fasting and mourning. The *piyyut* tradition remained strong into the middle of the second millennium and in every part of the Jewish world, in Europe, North Africa, and Western Asia. The Yemenite community enjoyed an especially rich *piyyutic* tradition; their greatest artist was Shalom Shabzi, who lived in the sixteenth century.

From the eleventh century onward, the boundaries of *piyyut* opened to include secular themes and the poets' virtuosity scaled new heights. Spain, Provence and Italy were the main centers of this new flowering. While the poets continued to practice the devices invented by their Jewish predecessors, they also borrowed heavily from secular verse in Arabic and from Italian poets of the Renaissance, introducing genres and themes in poetry and prose that had been unknown to post-Biblical Hebrew literature such as drinking songs, nature poetry, love poems, and even war poems. The best known poets of this new poetic development were, in Spain, Samuel Hanaggid, Solomon Ibn Gvirol, Moses Ibn Ezra, Yehuda Halevi, and Abraham Ibn Ezra; in Italy, Immanuel of Rome; and many more elsewhere. They enriched Hebrew with new words and new linguistic formations, which led them into notable philological studies. As early as the tenth century R. Saadiah Gaon had composed the *Egron*, the first dictionary of the Hebrew language. Following the example set by Arab scholars in Arabic, Menachem Ibn Saruk (tenth century) and Yonah Ibn Janakh (early eleventh century) laid the foundations of grammatical research into Hebrew. Much more religious *piyyutim* have survived than have secular poetry because only the former were absorbed into the synagogue service and enshrined there. Of the secular *piyyut*, we have almost only what was discovered in the late nineteenth century in the *geniza* of the Cairo synagogue.

Another type of Jewish literature of rare beauty and great depth are the legends and folk tales of Hasidism, most of which recount the deeds and sayings of famous *tzaddikim*. R. Nakhman of Bratzlav, an important *tzaddik* himself, had a store of wonderful stories, which he would recite to his disciples. These stories were modeled upon folktales, but they articulated a mystical concept of human actions.

The Observant Jew's Bookcase

As we have seen, the Jewish religion and its culture have their source in the Bible and in the huge corpus of writings inspired by it. On the second rank of sanctity stand the *Talmud* and *Zohar.* Immutable as all three are in their sanctity, each generation has composed reams of commentary and exposition to mold them to its needs and interests, so that by now the accumulation of commentary and exposition has reached daunting dimensions. Some two hundred years ago, the evolution of *halacha* brought to a sudden stop by rabbinic Judaism and, with it, the evolution of Judaic doctrine, the articles of the Jewish faith. The lifestyle and beliefs of Orthodox Jewry have not altered since. They have proved impervious to every change in internal or external realities. Another outcome has been that Orthodox Jews have almost ceased to compose fine literature. It has been left up to the other communities of Jewry, and particularly to the secular community, to take responsibility for Jewish culture's development and to shape it to the needs of new times, without waiving the immense heritage bequeathed to all Jews by earlier generations.

Not every book in this "bookcase of observant Judaism" was revered at all times by all observant Jews. The authority or sanctity of some works was always being questioned by one or another section of Jewry. On occasions the questioning touched matters so central to the nature of Judaism and Jewry at the time as to result in the questioners being ejected from the community of normative Judaism, they became one of Jewry's outside sects. The Samaritans, for instance, Israelites who had remained in the territory of the Northern Kingdom of Israel after its conquest and depopulation by the Assyrians (720 BCE), refused to extend the sanctity of the Five Books of Moses to the later Prophets and Writings, on the grounds that these latter works had been sanctified by Pharisee rabbis only in the period of the Second Temple, after the Samaritans' overtures of reunification with the main body of Jewry (exiled to Babylonia) had been curtly rebuffed by Ezra and Nehemiah, leaders of the returnees from exile. In the eighth century CE, in the Babylonian Diaspora, arose the Karaite sect, led by Anan Ben David; it refused to admit the *Talmud* to a share in the Bible's holiness. By the tenth century the sect had grown to such numbers that the then acknowledged leader of Jewry, R. Saadiah Gaon, felt it necessary to formally denounce them in his writings. As time progressed, they were gradually distanced from normative Jewry and marriage with them was eventually forbidden. To this very day, Samaritans and Karaites regard themselves as the bearers of the true Judaism and consider rabbinic Judaism as a deviant form. Even within rabbinic Judaism, certain volumes of the "observant bookcase" have been challenged, sometimes violently so. Maimonides' philosophy and codification of halacha provoked bitter dispute and defamations, particularly in Spain during the twelfth to fourteenth centuries, to the point where Jews were forbidden to read Maimonides' books and his works were even burned in the public square. Rabbi Gershom Ben Levi's *The Book of the Lord's Wars* was renamed by some Jews *The Book of the Wars Against the Lord,* after certain passages had been condemned as heretical. Hasidic writings of all kinds, from biblical commentary to popular legends, to the tales of R. Nakhman of Bratzlav were dismissed by the *mitnagdim* as valueless trash and were banned at various times.

A Secular Reading of the "Observant Jew's Bookcase"

The Bible is the foundation and sovereign source of Jewish culture, and together with the texts inspired by it—the *Talmud, Zohar,* and the volumes of explanatory, *midrashic,* philosophical, and mystical commentary—it constitutes what is known as the observant Jew's bookcase. Judging by the range of form and genre on its shelves, it is a bookcase of very broad content, it contains works of law and ethics; literature of rules and regulations for daily life; theology and other explorations of the faith; philosophical, theoretical, *midrashic,* and mythological studies; books of poetry and prayer; and also legends and folk tales of all kinds. In essence, these works address the three core components of the religion: the faith rooted in biblical myth; *halacha* constructed on its platform of biblical law; and the messiah, the concept that carries Jewry's sense of nationhood. All the works are sacred, mantled in sanctity by the belief that all were composed under divine inspiration in the spirit of holiness. Solid evidence supports the position that they were composed by humans and declared sacred in order to put their authority beyond question. What *is* beyond question is that many of them are masterpieces and their cultural authority is immense. Also beyond question is the fact that they carry a message of great hope to humanity, but certainly not a divine message.

This potency and this message are, of course, as conspicuous to us seculars as to anyone. These works have so much to say to us that we would never think of belittling their value, but we read them with a critical eye, trying to understand them in the spirit of the humanity they breathe, to absorb from them what is worth absorbing and leave aside what is not. Some believers insist that the texts in their bookcase have no meaning for those who have no faith in God. We do not think so; on the contrary, those believers belittle our cultural treasures because compared to the all-embracing human significance of many religious texts, far outweighs their importance as divine self-revelation. We treasure the Hebrew myths as cultural artifacts of rare beauty and complex meanings but we do not believe in them; similarly, we may admire the mythologies of other peoples and civilizations yet set aside their supernatural elements as aspects of faith for their originators. Mythologies are part of the culture of most peoples; they are devices by which the human spirit symbolically represents, encompasses, and comprehends his place in the universe. We secular Jews prefer the Hebrew myths because they belong to the origins of our culture, not because they contain any greater truth than those of other cultures.

This is true, too, of our approach to the biblical law that mythology ascribes to God. As a legal system that fit the conditions of those early times and had its parallels, with variations, in other civilizations of the ancient East, it is a cultural and historical phenomenon of immense interest and a tribute to the breadth of the Israelite mind and vision. Without question, the biblical legal code, embodying ethical values previously unknown, was far ahead of its time. So, too, within limits, was much of its subsequent expansion. This is a matter of great pride. However, does it follow that today we must regulate ourselves by that law and its many interpreters and make it our daily practice? Over the centuries, and particularly during the last two, European civil law has advanced immeasurably, to the great benefit of society and the individual, while Jewish religious law has not. In fact, it has been left far behind.

To apply *halachic* law now to the modern secular reality that we inhabit is to go back in time to the patterns of thought and behavior of ancient and medieval worlds, surrendering all the advances in liberty, equality, and democracy that have been achieved in the modern period.

At the very least, evaluating the sources of Judaism in the light of secular concepts cannot impair our Jewish identity to the slightest degree because that identity is neither rooted in the Jewish religion nor is it a product of it. It is rooted in the fundamentals of our Jewish culture—and Ahad Ha'am has already said all that is necessary on this point:

> I know perfectly well "what keeps me a Jew," or more correctly, I do not understand what the question means at all, just as I should not understand were I to be asked, "What keeps you your father's son?" I may utter whatever statement my fancy takes me on the beliefs and opinions bequeathed to me by my ancestors without fearing lest by that I sever the bonds tying me to my people. I may equally profess the "scientific atheism bearing the name of Darwin" without there stemming from it the smallest risk to my Jewishness.[7]

A Secular Reading of Hebrew Mythology

Every believing Jew accepts Judaism's mythology and law code, and all their multitudinous theocentric interpretations as exclusive and absolute truth; he regards each mythical story as factual, as an accurate account of exactly what happened, in terms of plot, characters, time, place, and so on. Yet a critical reading reveals that the biblical myths evolved and changed over time: from an anthropomorphic conceptualization of *Yahweh* as one of numerous gods presiding over the Semitic heartlands to the monotheist and universal conception of the God of Israel as the One God and the God of All. We also now know that modern science has found the majority of the myths to be just that, flights of the human imagination.[8]

Religious establishments have closed their eyes down the ages to scientific discoveries and theories that contradict the truth of their sanctified myths. For hundreds of years the Roman Catholic Church, having bound itself to the third-century Ptolemaic theory that the earth is the stationary center of the universe and having elevated this theory to the status of a dogma, absolute truth, had to dismiss Copernicus's theory that the sun is stationary and the earth revolves around it. Having closed its own eyes to the scientific theory, it also had to force others to close theirs, or at least their mouths. Astronomers whose observations con-

firmed the Copernican system were burned at the stake, the most notorious instance being Giordano Bruno in 1600 CE. Others were
compelled to recant publicly; Galileo is the most famous of them. To
this very day, both Jewish and Christian church establishments reject
the Darwinian theory of evolution. How could they make peace with a
doctrine that describes how plant and animal life on earth evolved, how
it changed and adapted, and died out over hundreds of millions of years
of competitive survival to become the forms we see today, when the
book of Genesis say that all these same forms were created together in
a single week of time at the command of God?

Modern research has revealed that the biblical myths derive to a considerable extent from earlier mythologies invented by other peoples, the
Sumerians, Akkadians, the peoples of Mesopotamia, and the Canaanites
of the Mediterranean coast. A particular debt is owed to the myths of
Ugarit, discovered during excavations in present-day Syria in the early
1930s, which, pre-dating the biblical stories, recount the deeds of the
gods of Canaan, sometimes in the same language as the Bible uses in
recounting the acts of *Yahweh*, God of Israel.

All scientific research and analysis of the origins of the Bible's theocentric mythology, does not mean that the stories have nothing to say
to us. Whether they actually happened as narrated is of little concern.
Numerous events have happened or could have happened over the
course of time, and only a tiny fraction of them have been handed down
to us. The point of the mythical narratives is that the human race has
recounted them across hundreds of generations; their significance lies
in that, not in their factuality. For us, these myths rank among our peoples' supreme creations, an amazing record of their struggles with the
primal questions of human existence and of their attempts to explain
the world in symbolic terms. We have already noted that by regarding
the myths as spiritual explorations and not as sanctified truth, we grant
ourselves the best opportunity to understand and make sense of them.
Even the sages of old allowed themselves the liberty of wide-ranging—
not to say far-fetched—exposition and in so doing, further complicated
an already complex mythic structure with legends of their own invention. This shows that for them, too, the myths were parables, allegories,
important for what they implied, not for their factual veracity. But even
the sages' expositions were perforce bound to the articles of the faith
and to Scripture's fundamentally God-fearing vision. Their object was
to reconcile inconsistencies, particularly biblical verses that clashed with
later religious thought, and to reconcile contradictions between the sacred text and their own theosophy.

Once we are free of such anxieties and limitations we can give our humanism free rein, even if it brings us into conflict with what religion insists is true. We read the text as written, clearing away as much as possible of the interpretive augmentation that has adhered to it, whether in the body of the text or in later Oral Law tradition. Inconsistencies do not disturb us as we have no preconceived system into which we must fit them. For example, we accept anthropomorphic depictions of *Yahweh* as an influence from pagan sources and we feel no need, as the sages did, to bend over backwards to explain away verses in Genesis, such as: "the sound of *Yahweh-Elohim* walking in the garden in the cool of the day" (3:8); "[*Yahweh*] will go down now, and see whether they have done all together according to the cry of it, which is come to me" (18:21); "When *Yahweh* went his way as soon as he had left communing with Abraham" (18:33). We are able to read the Song of Songs as a masterpiece of secular poetry, intensely erotic, and of a rare beauty, rather than a theological allegory of the love between God and his Chosen People, which is indeed very sharp, but reduces the poetical magic that we enjoy in reading it in its literal meaning.

Not only can we allow ourselves to decipher the myths' original meaning in light of our own understanding and knowledge; we can also rework them as mythic representations of our own grasp of the nature of human existence. For example, Genesis chapters one and two offer two disparate renderings of the Creation. We treat them not as contradictory but as the juxtaposition of two different sources. Chapter one describes the creation of the world and of man in it in philosophical terms, as a sequence of acts of speech. Then chapter two offers a materialist account. We can appreciate chapter one as expressing the very deep and complex idea that man's consciousness of reality is conditional upon the language and things can exist for him only after he has named them: light exists for us as a perceived phenomenon only when we can say "light."

In the second Creation myth (Gen. 2:4), humans are faced with choosing between an existence of mindless, morality-less calm in God's Garden of Eden and an existence of unceasing struggle, but illuminated by a high awareness of self and of the consequences of their choices and their actions. Luckily for us, as the myth tells us, Eve chooses to eat from the Tree of Knowledge and so launches us on the path of never-ending struggle with God and with ourselves over our continued existence. Similarly, we can appreciate the Sacrifice of Isaac not only as a denunciation of human sacrifice on pagan altars but also in the later extended meaning of human sacrifice as death for the sake of upholding

God's glory, *kiddush hashem*. Abraham passes the test not by obeying the summons to sacrifice his son, but on the contrary, by overcoming the instinct toward blind obedience and by listening to his heart: "Lay not your hand upon the lad" (Gen. 22:12).

We also allow ourselves the right to question and, if necessary, reject images of biblical figures woven by centuries of manipulated tradition, and in so doing, we are able to return to the way in which the Bible itself originally portrayed them. For example, we can regard Ishmael with empathy (Gen. 21) and sympathize with his mother Hagar's anguish when she is thrown out into the desert by Abraham to appease Sarah. In concert with many modern poets and authors, we can take a poor view of Sarah's spite and Abraham's indifference. Here is Itzik Manger's response to Hagar from his *Midrash Itzik:*

> Hagar stands there weeping,
> The baby heavy in her arms.
> For the last time then
> Her eyes wander over the walls. . . .
>
> "Don't cry, my little Ishmaelikl,
> This is to be our fate, it seems.
> This is how pious fathers behave
> When their beard is long and sleek." . . .
>
> And Hagar, calling heaven
> And all its hosts to witness:
> That is how pious fathers behave
> When their beard is long and sleek.[9]

Manger has displaced the myth from its biblical setting to the nineteenth-century *shtetl*. Abraham—*Avroom* in Yiddish pronunciation—is a respectable and pious local notable, his beard long and sleek who, having "got entangled" with one of his servant women, now wants to get rid of her and her child, perhaps without even caring about how she is suffering. In the same spirit we can now reproach or even condemn the deceit that Jacob practices on Esau when he steals his birthright (Gen. 27), and we can respect the "wicked" Esau's willingness later to forgive him (Gen. 33). We may even come to understand the Korakh episode, in which Korakh heads a group of Israelites in a challenge to Moses's exclusive authority—until *Yahweh* caused the earth to open up and swallow them (Num. 16), as a story of sociopolitical rivalry and not of rebellion against *Yahweh*. We might feel less than admiration for the

zeal of Pinkhas ben Eliezer, son of Aaron the High Priest, when he murders Zimri ben Salu for his adultery with a Midianite woman (Num. 25).
Could even *Yahweh's* jealous fury in slaughtering twenty-four thousand
Israelites for that same offense not seem somewhat exaggerated? Modern Hebrew literature has not been able to make its peace with the totalitarianism of biblical law, as our myths portray it. The stories in David
Frishman's collection *In the Wilderness* describe how the lone individual attempts to defend his portion of individuality against the all-inclusive absolutism of the new religion's demands:

> Then everybody heard a strange and wonderful thing: In this very place,
> these very people were to be given the Torah, and laws and judgments. . . .
> But Puah and Mooshi understood nothing. What was this Torah for? What
> were the laws and judgments for? . . . The Torah was to conquer the whole
> world around, to the very ends of the earth, and the laws and judgments
> were to subdue to their rule every dweller in that world. . . . Why was the
> Torah to be like a nose-ring to lead people around by; why could they not
> let life flow as it was and as it always had done? . . . "Torah has captured the
> flow of life and subdued it . . ."[10]

As Itzik Manger cast a new eye on Abraham, so other authors in modern Hebrew have reappraised our famous heroes. Whereas religious tradition has not dealt kindly with Samson, modern writers and readers
have found him a very attractive figure, not for his great strength or his
heroic deeds or his slaughter of Philistines, but for his very weakness—
his irresistible desire for Delilah, caught so beautifully by Leah Goldberg in her "Samson's Love":

> The rod of commander is given him,
> Tribes and nations all tremble,
> In battle and feast rings out his name—
> Hero! Governor! Ruler!
>
> Yet perhaps he did not know either
> That his fate was of the *nazirite*[11] and dreamer
> That the answer quite simple to all riddles
> Was the defenseless heart in his breast. . . .
>
> He knew very well she betrayed him,
> But he could not resist that smooth tongue,
> He knew he would die by her hand—
> The Philistines are on you, Samson.

Could not lie on her bosom,
His reflected face in her eyes,
A traitoress in treachery so delightful—
The Philistines are on you, Samson.

In similar vein, we can discard tradition and agree with Sha'ul Chernikhovsky and other authors in feeling sympathy, not to say respect, for the tragic figure of King Saul, founder of the Israelite monarchy; we might even take his side in his running battle with Samuel the Seer. Nor do we now see King David shining with the clear radiance in which the tradition-bearing texts enshrine him. A courageous and cunning warrior, a powerful king, certainly, let that suffice. And what of Elijah the Prophet? The biblical account has him inciting the massacre of four hundred and fifty prophets of *Ba'al* and four hundred prophets of *Aserah* for promoting a rival faith. Chernikhovsky, who had considerable respect for the pagan culture, puts the following words in the mouth of a *Ba'alist* prophet who has survived the bloodbath, in his poem "*Hazon Nevi Ha Asherah*" "Vision of a Prophet of Asherah" (1932):

Don't boast, you slaughterers: "How we have slaughtered them!"
Worshipers of *Ba'al* are gone, cut down every one.
Look how you have blunted your knives,
Your swords are bent and useless from so much killing,
But Him, *Ba'al*, you cannot defeat, your strength comes not near Him.

One of the most useful outcomes of our critical reading of biblical mythology, a reading not subordinated to a pre-constructed belief system, is how much we learn about the way monotheism developed out of the pagan view of the world that our ancestors held, down to the end of the First Temple period. We learn respect for pre-biblical Canaanite-Phoenician culture which reached such levels of achievement that Greeks and Romans borrowed deeply from it, and through them it passed into Western culture. We accept these pagan sources as a potent strand in our own Israelite-Jewish culture no matter how much the religious establishment is outraged by such an idea.

A piquant comment on changing attitudes to our biblical history is the names that Israeli-Jewish parents have been giving their children in recent decades. As we saw earlier,[12] from the Second Temple period until late into the modern period Jewish parents avoided giving their children the names of historical characters with traditionally bad reputations. The only exception was "Ishmael," a popular choice in the *Mishnaic* period. Today, however, Israeli-Jewish society is full of Nimrods,

Avirams, Omris, Hagars, Athaliahs, Avishags—and many other Biblical names of "infamous" characters.

A Secular Appreciation of Halacha

Believing Jews accept the biblical code of law, together with its vast accretion of interpretative rulings, preventive rulings, and restrictions, as one single body of God-given *mitzvot*. As such, they are to be obeyed to the letter, that is all that is required, not explanation, not consent, only obedience. It is easy to demonstrate that whereas numerous biblical and *talmudic* laws more or less successfully addressed the needs of their own times, in other eras—the present one, for example—these same laws possess neither logic nor justice. By the end of the *talmudic* period, some biblical laws had already been amended, using the method of *midrashic* exposition. The Bible's stipulation of "an eye for eye, a tooth for tooth," (Exod. 21:24–25) is only one of many laws that the sages found illogical. The Babylonian *Talmud* amends it as follows: "'An eye for an eye'—this means a money payment" (*Baba Qama* 83b). Yet other laws have survived to become too anachronistic to allow any useful amendment. Some scholars, perturbed by this, have seen fit to set out the grounds for *mitzva*-observance; one of the first such attempts at explanation—justification was made in the thirteenth-century *Sefer HaKhinukh*, "Book of Education".

To our secular way of thinking, *halacha* is neither a divine code of law nor the decree of Heaven. Compiled by men, it was then ascribed to *Yahweh* in order to suppress counterarguments. In the early twentieth century, another ancient code of laws was discovered, the text of which attributes authorship to Hammurabi, who ruled Babylon some four thousand years ago. Since large sections of the Hammurabi code bear a striking resemblance to the biblical code, it is evident that the biblical code derives from an earlier one possessed by more than one people of the ancient East,[13] even if in its ethical qualities the biblical code surpasses them all.

It is frequently claimed that it was *halacha* that for two thousand years of exile preserved the Jewish people from extinction by assimilation and absorption. It is considerably more likely that a smallish section of Jewry observed *halacha* while the large majority did not, and thus their preservation cannot be ascribed to it. The Torah and *halacha* neither preserved the Jewishness of the millions who converted to other religions nor the lives of the millions who were murdered for their faith or for merely being Jews. In his short story, "Drabkin," Ha'im Hazzaz mocks this quaint thesis of the *"halacha* as savior" by using the *talmudic* study itself as ammunition. Drabkin, a disillusioned Zionist, is in conversation with Gideon, a young man born in Palestine to parents who had arrived with the First Aliyah:

> Drabkin now began in the sing-song of *Gemara* exposition: "A man who had two sets of daughters from two wives said: "I have just betrothed my eldest daughter and I don't know if she is the eldest of the older ones or the eldest of the younger ones or if the youngest of the older ones is older than the oldest of the younger ones . . ." And before he could get to the end of that hoary old disputation between Rabbi Meir and Rabbi Yose,[14] he dissolved into a bubbling laughter, . . . "That is a *mishna*, exactly as set down and for two thousand years sage after sage, early ones, later ones, has worked it over, ha-ha-ha . . . And this is how Torah and *mitzvot* have guarded us, and this is how exile and torment have preserved us!

Amos Oz says: "In every generation Jews have made the choice to be Jews, some by keeping the *mitzvot*, others in other ways. The People of Israel has lasted these thousands of years by dint of millions of personal decisions taken by millions of Jews for scores of generations, Jews who all chose to live their identity."[15]

Over and above the issue of our response to *halacha* stands the two issues of *halacha's* effect on Jewish community life and the function of *halachic* study in Jewish communities through the ages. By largely ignoring the changes and innovations that time has brought, *halacha* held back almost all social development in the communities whose pattern of life it controlled. More than this, it erected and cemented in place a strict hierarchy, with the rabbi and *dayan* at the top—doing the bidding of the communal leaders, the notables and rich men whose money maintained the religious institutions and paid the rabbi's and *dayan's* salary—and at the bottom, poverty-stricken and degraded, Jewry's toiling masses of artisans and manual laborers.

In the nineteenth century, Jews of *Haskalah* persuasion denounced both the social discrimination institutionalized by Jewry's leaders in the name of religion and of *halacha,* and *halacha* itself for legitimating that discrimination and providing it with ideological backing. The *Haskalah's* poets and authors assailed the stony hearts of the rabbis and their patrons who turned their eyes away from their people's poverty. They lambasted *halachot* that injured the simple man's rights, degraded women's status and, in the final analysis, held the people down in a state of privation, backwardness, and ignorance of everything modern. They railed against the status of Torah study as the central, almost the only, activity of Jewish community life and against *halacha*'s preoccupation with issues totally disassociated from real life, such as the notorious "unwitting resignation to loss" (BT *Baba Metzia* 21b) and "eggs laid on Holydays" (BT *Beitza* 2a). They held up to shame the absence of any training in crafts and occupations capable of lifting the people out of poverty. It was a central pillar of *Haskalah* teaching that Diaspora Jewry's degradation and parasitic status was the outcome of this debasement of manual labor and of the fixing of absolute priority on Torah study and Torah students. Here is Yehuda Leib Gordon's statement of the thesis in his 1879 poem *Zidkiyahu Beveit Hapkudot"* "Zedekiah in Prison":

And lo, another new testament was concocted for Judah:
All the people of the land from high to low
Are to study the words of Torah and Scripture.
Everyone—from peasant to president
All are to be scribes, teachers and speakers of prophesy. . . .
Each man and man will say: Not for me to plough and thresh,
For I am born into a kingdom of priests, a holy nation,
Therefore, no more shall be heard the voice of men at their work,
But the voice recites of prayers and psalm and blessing,
And bands of prophets shall swarm the land
Naked beggars, dreamers and babblers,
Pursuers of vanities, herders of the wind and clouds.
Could there ever be such a people under heaven?
And if there could—could it endure for a day or two?
Who is to plough its fields, bake its bread,
And when the enemy presses who will fight for it?
A people like that can never create government,
But only descend from disaster to ruination . . .

Some fifty years later, Sha'ul Chernikhovsky, in his *"Hazon Nevi Ha Asherah"* "Vision of a Prophet of Asherah," described the consequences of a *halacha*-governed community life in the very same vein, emphasizing how out of touch *halacha* was from real life and powerfully conveying the degradation inherent in Jewry's economic parasitism:

O you wretched priests of the God *Yahweh*,
Get out and think, take stock, make a reckoning:
When will *Adonai* ever reign alone
Through the word of his prophets and the teaching of his priests
Through the bonds of a covenant of believers,
If not when you have all been rooted out from this earth,
Torn out like couch grass from good soil.

Laws you have compiled, prescripts and proscripts,
For tithes and offerings from a non-existent harvest;
Rite and ritual you have endlessly elaborated—
For sacrifices and oblations you can never celebrate;
The Days of Rest you have bound about with edict and ban
For what working days have you? All your days are rest.
The gentile ploughs—and you eat;
The gentile herds—and you fill your bellies;
The non-Jew builds—and you sit.
What do you bring to this *Elohim* your God
But your incarceration and schematization of men's lives.
No fields, no useful labor,
No sovereign state, no people's government. . . .

A no-less-vexed issue was the methods of Torah study. Century after century *halacha* had been the one and only subject taught in Jewish educational institutions, especially in Eastern Europe. Not a thing that was not directly connected to the study of *halacha* ever crossed the threshold of *cheder*[16] and yeshiva. Since the beginnings of the *Haskalah* movement in the mid-eighteenth century, Jewish voices demanded more and more insistently that this obsession with the Babylonian Talmud and its commentaries had to stop. A progressive *cheder* was needed that would teach the Bible and Hebrew grammar, as well as outside studies, that is, secular science. The issue was of concern not only to *maskilim*. The great poet Chaim Bialik, who watched the decline of Jewish tradition with great sadness, spoke very severely of the content and methods of education in the Orthodox schools of his day, and even today they have hardly changed. His autobiographical story, *Safiah*, Aftergrowth, paints *cheder* education in grotesque colors:

> In *cheder* I had gone up in the meantime to the Hebrew Composition class. From now on, my duty and that of all the little boys in the class was to chorus together, in the traditional sing-song and at the tops of our voices, any sage-like comment of whatever odd concoction the teacher felt like making after each verse of the passage of Written Law we were reading in the Five Books. . . . In the end it was all diktat, and diktat you do not question. I resigned myself to the diktat, rocked back and forth with all my strength and joined my voice to the band of yellers. . . . Such it seems has been the nature of Hebrew Composition from the six days of the Creation and it is not to be changed. . . . The only words that stuck in my head, strangely enough, of all those bizarre *melamed*[17] concoctions were the words my ear had never heard before. Not that I had any idea what they meant for the teacher never took the trouble to explain.

At the close to his great poem, *"Hamatmid,"* The Devoted Student, Bialik also laments the fate of *yeshiva* students, who spend their entire youth poring over "dry as dust" *halacha,* "discussions of Abaye and Rava,"[18] seeing neither light nor love:

> Every crease and stare told me without words
> Of emotions stifled, of sparks snuffed out;
> Every crease and stare stirred me deeply,
> My heart tightened, my stomach knotted.
> Every time I recall those voices, O those voices
> Crying in the nights like the agonies of wounded soldiers,
> I want to scream: Lord God Almighty!
> For what, on what have all those energies gone to waste? . . .
> What great fortune they could have brought us
> If only a ray of light had warmed them with its heat;
> What sheaves of corn we could have harvested singing
> Had only one gust of a big-hearted spirit breathed into you,
> Blown away the "path of Torah," our oppressor,
> And opened up a road of life up to the *yeshiva* doors; . . .
> How arid that soil must have been and how accursed
> If seeds like these could have moldered within it!

Secular Research into Jewish Philosophy and Kabbala

In the eyes of certain sections of Orthodoxy, the Zohar's sanctity rests on its attribution to the great second-century *tanna,* Rabbi Shimon Bar Yokhai, who is supposed to have composed it—inspired by the Spirit of Holiness, while hiding from the Romans in a cave with his son, Rabbi Eliezer, after the failure of the Bar Kokhba uprising. Today, careful examination of the text and its language, supported by a few surviving documents, as well as by the fact that the book is not referred to by any writer in any form before the thirteenth century, all prove that the book was composed in thirteenth-century Spain by Moses de Leon. Some other holy books of the Kabbala derive their sacredness from the belief—obviously from the fallacy that they were penned by biblical figures, such as Adam and Abraham, or by venerated historical figures, such as Rabbi Akiva and Rabbi Ishmael. But even later Kabbalist works, published under the real author's name—for example, by Moses Cordovero or Ha'im Vital in the sixteenth century (the latter claimed to have put down on paper the spoken thoughts of his master, Rabbi Isaac Ashkenazi Luria)—are deeply problematic. For all the magnificence of their language and the subtlety of their argument, their mystical conception of the world is far removed from the scientific logic with which we now try to understand the universe. The Lurian Kabbala—the conceptualization of the world that Hasidism made one of its central tenets—was anachronistic even in its own day, even as a mythic, symbolic representation of the nature of the Godhead, His creation and Israel's destiny, while on these days the European Renaissance flourished, and the medieval mythological logic was superseded by scientific thinking.

The issues taken up by classic Jewish philosophy are also no longer the issues that concern us. Certainly, the rationalist approach taken by most Jewish philosophers appeals to us and we occasionally find them coming very close to our humanism, occasionally even going beyond it, denying individual providence or questioning the notion of a Creation. But the problems they are endeavoring to solve are the problems intrinsic to religious faith and the sanctification of the Bible and *Talmud,* problems our humanist thinking has solved or dismissed by an objective critical reading of these holy texts, as we have already seen.

Yet the interest we think that the branching streams of Jewish thought is a development of great historic-cultural significance. Most Kabbalist research nowadays is pursued by secular researchers and with a critical frame of mind, and they are uncovering for us myths of surpassing imaginative beauty as well as an important stage in Jewry's cultural evolution that is capable of teaching us a great deal about phenomena in our own society. In them we find an explanation for twentieth and twenty-first-century messianism, and insight into the cast of Lurian Kabbala dominated *Hasidic* thought, so central nowadays to Jewish Orthodoxy, they confront us with the grave dangers posed by messianic thinking in our current political climate and circumstances. Studies in Jewish philosophy, by contrast, show us the development of Jewish free-thinking, how rationalist philosophers broke the shackles of a coercive yoke-binding faith, opening the way for the secular humanism now central to modern Jewish thought.

JEWISH CULTURE OUTSIDE AND BEYOND RELIGION

In the library of Judaism, the bookcase of the observant Jew is a part of the Jewish bookcase. Religion is indeed a most important part in Jewish culture, but not the only one. In the constantly expanding, swirling tapestry that is Jewish civilization and culture, religion is but one motif, itself subject to continual modification, its historical evolution hardly ever stationary, its endless feuds, schisms, and factions always to some extent punctuating, to some extent propelling, the three-thousand-year history of the Jewish people. We seculars can stand aloof from the succession of internal religious feuds, from past to present, and allow ourselves the appreciation to all the creations of the Jewish spirit of every generation; the creations of its early paganism and of its later pure monotheism, of Hellenizing Sadducees and of tradition-clinging Pharisees; of rationalist philosophers and Kabbalist mystics; the story-telling of Hasidim and the traditional Torah learning of Hasidism's opponents, *Mitnagdin*. Moreover, now that we have cast off the blinkers of preconceived belief and of a sanctified text, our secular reading of the sources can uncover more profound depths and wider ramifications than any believer's reading, that no matter how rhapsodic a midrashic excursion from the printed verses, it remains within the narrow limits fixed by the articles of the faith.

What are the other sections in the whole of Judaism's culture? We start with the pre-biblical Hebrew civilizations; go on through the excluded books, rejected for one reason or another by the rabbinic establishment; secular works, many of them lost to us, and finally the huge section of modern writing, all of which Orthodoxy pretends does not exist.

To go into a little more detail: The Jews are the only people to have preserved and developed the Hebrew language and culture. Therefore, we are the direct heirs to the cultural treasures of the ancient Hebrew speaking peoples, including the pagan, pre-Biblical Hebrew epics of Ugarit,[19] that have an especially important place in our cultural evolution. The excluded books are the writings of Jewish sects expelled by the rabbinic leadership and operated outside established *halachic* jurisdiction, including the Samaritans, the Dead Sea sects and the early Christians, Karaites, Sabbateans, as well as the works of Hellenized Jews in Hebrew and Greek, works of Jewish philosophy and theology repudiated by the official rabbinate. The labeled secular works is a rich corpus of secular literature composed in Italy and Spain in the medieval and Renaissance periods, including nature poetry, drinking songs, love poems, and even pornography. In negative form only we have the writings of Jewish atheists, considered so delinquent that they are all lost or destroyed and survive only in the denunciations of their rabbinic opponents. The section that houses the second great period of secular creation's, the two-and-a-half centuries of the modern period, in all spheres of life and art, in Hebrew and in other languages in which Jews spoke, in Palestine-Israel, or in the Diaspora. Jewish artists have been composing work on Jewish themes, creating a culture completely unknown to the ultra-Orthodox and to most Orthodox Jews too, an increment to our cultural heritage of incalculable importance and perhaps, in terms of volume, forming the largest section of the library.

JEWISH CULTURE: EXTENT AND FRONTIERS

The frontiers of Jewish culture expand and contract with our definition of Judaism. Stipulating that the heart, soul, and substance of Judaism is its religion narrows Jewish culture to the culture of its religion and religious practice. Accepting that being Jewish and a Jewish life have ethnic and national dimensions extends the frontiers of Jewish culture to include all manifestations of Jewish existence, whatever and wherever they are. Since we detect Jewish existence by evidence of Jewish culture, I might be in a circular reasoning here, but in practice, Jewish life and Jewish culture are two sides of the same coin. Declaring that Jewish life is present and active is a cultural act. Jewish life is carried on within a context of cultural behavior and practice. Every manifestation of life that is perceived as being Jewish belongs, therefore, within the frontiers of Jewish culture, from the earliest Hebrew civilizations to the rich Hebrew culture now brewing in Israel and the equally rich contemporary Jewish culture being generated in the Diaspora.

Having maintained continuity from its ancient origins to the present day, our Hebrew–Jewish culture possesses a longer time-span than any other Western civilization. Only in the Far East, the Chinese and Indian cultures can boast a longer ancestry. This continuity has been sustained for more than three thousand years. For much of that time the religious conceptualization of the world was indeed the heart of Jewish existence: Jewish life was the day-to-day practice of the faith and its traditions. Jews' lives, both in the home and in public, were totally suffused with religion; in this aspect, Jews were no different from the Christians and Muslims of the time. The passing of the Middle Ages marks the passing of religion's centrality and totality. The Jewish civilization of the time reflected this real predominance of religion, but at all times there was also a parallel stream of secular and humanist culture that expanded in influence through the ages, until in the nineteenth and twentieth centuries it had become the major driving cultural force in the Jewish world.

The place and role of secular culture in Jewish daily life is of paramount importance in all parts of the contemporary Jewish world, particularly so in Israel, where it is an integral part of the Hebrew vernacular of the street, of school and university syllabi, of the intense cultural life of cinema and theater, music, literature, philosophy, and journalism. It constitutes a cultural enterprise and edifice that, in its depth and range, has no precedent in the whole of Jewish history. Outside Israel too, Jewish culture is a highly visible ingredient of Jews' daily lives. It shows itself in strong local community bonds, in solidarity with Jews worldwide, in wide-ranging scholarly and artistic Jewish creativity that reaches into all parts of the Jewish world, and in an amazingly strong Jewish presence in all fields of science and the arts.

Jewish culture traces its origins all the way back to early Canaanite–Phoenician civilization, a pagan culture of great splendor and attainments on land and which, on the seas, navigated its way to all parts of the Mediterranean, founded thriving overseas colonies, established trading links with all the other civilizations of its time, developed the alphabetic system, composed a magnificent mythology, and housed its kings and princes in resplendent palaces ornamented by fine painting and sculpture. In Egypt, in the islands of the Mediterranean, and in Greece, its imprint is clearly visible, but it also knew how to fill its pockets, culturally as well as commercially, and enrich its own civilization with borrowings from others. From this great pagan culture emerged the Hebrew–Israelite culture of the biblical period, as we have noted its obvious traces in the Hebrew Bible, and from centuries of conflict with its paganism arose the Judean culture, which gave the world the concept of a single transcendent god and the idea of human freedom.

Struggling to contain a remarkable variety of genres and of divergent points of view, the Bible's redactors have edited it to conform overall to a vision of the world that presupposes men's acts to be overseen and directed by a divine providence. Yet, in amongst the books inspired by an authentic faith are others in which religion is conspicuous by its total absence. The authors or redactors may ascribe the Song of Songs to King Solomon, but actually it is a choice collection of nuptial-bridal verse, preoccupied to the exclusion of all else with the love of a young man and woman. God and religion receive not a single mention, not even by implication. Ecclesiastes is also ascribed to King Solomon, but its linguistic style and areas of concern suggest that it most probably dates to the end of the Second Temple period. Its philosophy is a melancholy one, suffused with pessimism about the human condition, very far from the tone of mainstream rabbinic preaching of the time, although the book does close by affirming: "The conclusion of the whole matter: fear God and keep His commandments! For this is the whole duty of man" (12:13). The epilogue is most likely a late addition, which enables the inclusion of Ecclesiastes in the biblical canon. As we have seen, the books of the Bible make many explicit references to other books that did not survive, whose message and purpose apparently did not conform to the message and purpose of the Bible's redactors. The works they did select for inclusion must be a small part of what was composed and written by the Hebrews over the thousand years before the Second Temple fell; much of the greater part of this output has been lost, mainly because the Pharisee scholars controlling religious practice in those days, did not see fit to preserve it. The debate recorded in the *Mishna* and the *Talmud* (Mishna *Yadaim* 3; BT *Shabbat* 30b), whether to include the Song of Songs and Ecclesiastes in the biblical canon, a debate previously cited, confirms that this was the case.

A fundamental premise of the *halacha* scriptures, the *Mishna* and the *Talmud*, is that the law is divine in source and that the text of the Bible mediates between us and the word of God: The making of *halacha* is thus, in essence, a religious act. Yet the *Talmud* and its commentaries also deal with matters of daily life not directly connected to religion or rite; nor are many of the tales and legends that its compilers thought right to include. It is also perfectly clear that the Jewish sages had read Classical Greek and Roman literature, despite regarding them as "books of heretics," *sifrei minim*, as the influence of and the borrowings from those gentile sources are very evident. A midrash on the Creation, for example, runs: "When the Holy One Blessed Be He created the first man He created him with two faces, and then cut him in two so that He made two backs, separate from one another" (Gen. *Rabba* 8:1). This is directly lifted from Plato's *Symposium*, which relates that originally man had four legs, four arms, and two faces; Zeus cut him in half to make two separate beings, who from the moment of division longed to rejoin each other, which accounts for human beings' intense sexual drive. Some hundreds of years later, the *Tosefot*, a commentary on *Gemara*, plagiarizes the tale of the Widow of Ephesus from Petronius's *Satyricon*, of the first century CE:

> A woman was weeping and wailing over her husband's grave and in the same place was a man whose duty was to guard the corpses of hanged men, whom the king had ordered to be kept hanging. Now this man approached the woman, tempted her and she gave herself to him. But when he went back to the hanging corpse it was not there and he was terribly afraid of what the king would do. But the woman said to him: "Don't be afraid, take my husband out of his grave and hang him up instead." (Tosefot *Kiddushin* 80b)

Nor let us forget that the Sadducees, one of the two major divisions of Jewry in the Second Temple period, wanted to broaden Jewish culture by incorporating the philosophy and creative work of the Ancient Greeks. The *Mishna* tells: "The Sadducees said, 'We complain against you, Pharisees, for you say, Holy Scriptures impart uncleanness to the hands,'[20] do not the works of Homer impart uncleanness to the hands?'" (Mishna *Yada'im* 4:6). In other words, the Sadducees so admired Homer that they wished to accord his work the same degree of holiness as the Bible. But it is clear that the Pharisees, too, must have been well acquainted with Homer's work, even though they presumably did not find it to their taste.

We have no idea just how many Hellenistic, Greek, and Latin works were translated into Hebrew. Certainly, during the Second Temple period and over succeeding centuries, excerpts from them found their way into *talmudic aggada*, to make another strand in the complex fabric of Jewish culture. We do know that a large amount of Jewish writing was translated into Greek and Latin and some Jews even composed in those languages—another extension of Jewish culture's frontiers and evidence of a cordial embrace of the Hellenism that was dominant in cultured circles in the Eastern Mediterranean. Within this new cosmopolitanism Jews created a most impressive body of work that included philosophy, historiography, fine literature, architecture, and more.

The trend toward cultural assimilation continued into the medieval period. Jewish scholars and littérateurs were thoroughly at home in the language and culture of their host nations, particularly so in the Islamic Arabic-speaking world, and enjoyed a considerable reputation. Yehuda Ibn Tibun writes in the introduction to his translation of the most important text on Hebrew grammar, *Sefer HaRikmah* that "[Jewish scholars'] tongues are used to the fluency of the Arabic language." The influence and interaction of the two cultures, Hebrew and Arabic, was mutual and marked. Most Jewish philosophy was written in Arabic and, although written for Jews, was well known to both Arab and Christian scholars. The Jews' reputation as poets also spread far beyond the frontiers of the Jewish world. Jewish poets composed in both Hebrew and Arabic and won fame in both languages and both cultural communities. Cultured Italian Jews responded in the same way to the coming of the Renaissance. Alongside their *piyyut* on sacred themes they composed secular verse, love songs, comic and satiric verse, drama, and other genres. Jews even played an indirect part in the great voyages of discovery of the fifteenth and sixteenth centuries, for they were acknowledged to be the best map-makers available. The maps that Columbus took with him on his famous 1492 voyage were commissioned from Jewish cartographers.

The frontiers of Jewish culture have always been porous, conspicuous as much in their infringement as in their observance. Even Jewish communities that turned their backs on their non-Jewish surroundings could not seal the breaches. The Hasidim of Eastern Europe, for example, found their now famous "Hasidic" music and dance among the local Ukrainian peasantry. Hasidic legend even admits it, albeit in its own way: R. Zusia was walking in the fields when he saw a swineherd playing a flute. The *tzaddik* listened until he knew the tune and thus redeemed the tune of David the shepherd-boy from its long exile.[21]

In the nineteenth century, these porous cultural borders changed from being a matter of fact to a matter of calculated policy. It is hardly necessary to mention that thousands of Jews made great names for themselves in all genres of gentile culture, but the movement in the opposite direction is equally significant. For the first time in centuries, great numbers of non-Jewish works were translated into Jewish languages, first into Hebrew and later Yiddish. The intellectuals of the *Haskalah* called this enterprise "opening a window onto Europe." By the early twentieth century, Jewish translators were also working in the opposite direction, translating Hebrew and Yiddish Jewish writing into its host languages, particularly Russian and German. Since then, any notion of frontiers between Jewish and non-Jewish culture has dissipated.

Since the eighteenth century, Jewish religious writing and culture had become more and more marginalized within the Jewish world, partly because all development and innovation in its own sphere had been halted by rabbinic decree, but more because it was overwhelmed by a flood of secular creativity and exploration. Only in the twentieth century was there somewhat of a resurgence of important original theological and philosophical thought, written mainly in German and English for German and English-speaking Jews, but some also in Hebrew. The impetus for this resumption of development was the need to explain and expound the ideas of Reform, Conservatism, and Reconstructionism. The leading minds of non-Orthodox Judaism, Wise, Einhorn, Kaplan, Schechter, and others, took up the task. But Orthodoxy also produced a few important thinkers, two of the most prominent of whom were R. Abraham Yitzhak Hacohen Kook and R. Joseph Dov Halevi Soloveitchik.

One beneficial and extremely influential change riding on the secularist tide was the new status of Jewish women as authors and creators of Jewish culture. In the traditional sources and throughout the whole history of Jewish culture, the role granted to women as creators was minuscule, indeed usually non-existent. Only one work in the Bible, the Song of Deborah (Judges 5), is attributed to a woman author. They are recognized as singers and dancers and we hear of them weaving and sowing, especially in the eulogy of the "capable wife" (*Eshet Hayil,* Prov. 31). That is almost the total sum of women's acknowledged contribution to biblical events, and thus it remained for more than fifteen hundred years after the closure of the biblical canon. An exception comes in the seventeenth century, with Glickl of Hamelin's *Book of Memoirs,* a precious mine of information on the lives of German Jews at the time. By the time of the *Haskalah,* only one woman poet, Rachel Morpurgo of Trieste, is credited with carving out a name for herself. From Abraham to the opening of the twentieth century of the modern era, Jewish culture remains the culture of its men. Secularization has changed that. The beginnings were small: Writers such as the novelist Nechama Pukhachevski in Palestine became renowned, as did the poetess Elisheva, a Russian woman who wrote Hebrew poetry first in Russia and then in Palestine. By the 1920s and 1930s, however, the flow gathered strength and in Palestine alone, writers such as novelist Dvora Bron, poetesses Rachel Blobstein, Esther Raab, Yokheved Bat-Miriam, Leah Goldberg, and others appeared. Women have been central to the development of the performance arts, particularly dance, theatre and song. In the second half of the twentieth century their role has gone from strength to strength in Hebrew literature, the more prominent names being novelists Yehudit Hendel, Amelia Kahana-Carmon, Orly Kastel-Blum, Savyon Librecht and poets Dalia Rabikovitch, Tirtza Attar, Yona Wallach, and many others.

Today, Jewish culture's frontiers are limitless. Hebrew literature has been translated into a score of languages and its authors are known all over the world. Conversely, the best world literature, translated into Hebrew, has become an essential ingredient of Israeli culture. All over the world, Jewish literature is being written in English, French, German, Russian, and so on. Jewish musicians, including many Israelis, are to be found almost everywhere, working in every form and genre, regardless of whether there is any tradition of Jewish involvement in that particular genre. Hebrew theater, lacking an established dramatic tradition before the twentieth century, emerged in Moscow in the early years of the century and achieved extraordinary international success. Today it is central to Israeli and Jewish culture. Important original drama is being composed in Hebrew, English, and other languages. In dance, similarly, we have witnessed a rich flourishing after centuries of inactivity. Jewish predominance in the new twentieth-century genre of the musical is well known. The plastic arts of painting and sculpture and architecture, also marginal to Jewish culture for centuries, are now at the center of Jewish culture worldwide and Jewish painters, sculptors and architects are respected and celebrated and their works are exhibited worldwide. Yet, despite this eradication of previous frontiers, Jewish art in Israel and in the Diaspora still maintains the strongest bonds to its sources in the millennia of Jewish tradition.

This is the immense and thriving culture that our own generation and all the generations before us have created, the culture of the Jewish religion and the dynamic secular culture that embraces it, yet also extends far beyond it. This is the full cart of secular humanist Judaism.

Notes

INTRODUCTION

1. See William James. *The Varieties of Religious Experience, a Study in Human Nature*, Cambridge MA, Cambridge University Press, 1902; Otto Rudolph. *The Idea of the Holy*, trans. by J. W. Harvey, Oxford University Press, 1958; Mircea Eliade, *The Sacred and the Profane*, trans. by W.R. Trask, New York Hartcourtine, 1959.

2. In Jewish history "emancipation" is the act of granting civil rights to the Jews in central and western Europe in the eighteenth and nineteenth centuries.

3. Yeshayahu Leibowitz, "Datiyim ve-hilonin" *(Religious and Secular Jews)* *Yahadut, Am Israel u-Medinat Israel Judaism, the Jewish people and the State of Israel* (Jerusalem and Tel Aviv, Shocken 1976) 268.

CHAPTER 1. IDENTITY

1. Zelda, "Each Man Has A Name." "Lekol ish yesh shem."

2. Sha'ul Chernikhovsky "Shirim le-Ill-il" "Poems for Ill-il"

3. Aharon Megged, "Yad Vashem."

4. Further reading (in Hebrew): Sasha Vitman, *Shemot pratiyim kemedadim tarbutiyim* "First Names as Cultural Indicators," in *Nekudat Tatzpit, Culture and Society in Israel*, ed. Nurit Graetz, 141–151 Tel Aviv, 1987; Gid'on Turi, *Ivrut shmot mishpacha beIsrael ketargum tarbut;* "The Hebraicization of Surnames in Israel as 'Social Translation,'" in *Nekudat Tatzpit,* 152–172.

5. Two works setting out different theories are: Edward Evans Pritchard, *Theories of Primitive Religion* (Oxford University Press 1965); and: Claude Levi-Strauss, *The Savage Mind* (Chicago: University of Chicago, 1966.)

6. James Bennet Pritchard, *Ancient Near Eastern texts relating to the Old Testament,* (Princeton University Press, 1969) 60.

7. Ted Hughes, *Tales From Ovid* (New York: Farrar, Straus and Giroux, 1997) 4–5.

8. See *Shorter Oxford Dictionary,* 1993

CHAPTER 2. SECULAR IDENTITY

1. Bertrand Russell, *A History of Western Philosophy* (New York, 1945), 77.

2. From the Greek: *a* (without) + *theos* (god).

3. Greek: *a* + *gnosis*, without knowledge.

4. Protagoras, *On the Gods,* quoted by Russel, 93.

5. Blaise Pascal, *Pensees,* trans. by Martin Turyell (New York, Harper, 1962), 418

6. Here, a Hasidic rabbi.

7. See: Martin Buber, 'Perhaps?', *Tales of the Hasidim,* trans. by Olga Marx (New York: Schocken, 1975) 228

8. Israel Davidson, *Polemics Against Hivi al-Balkhi* (New York: Jewish Theological Seminary, 1915).

9. See: Yirmiyahu Yovel, *Spinoza and other Heretics* (Princeton University Press, 1988); Lewis S. Feuer, *Spinoza and the Rise of Liberalism* (Boston: Beacon Press, 1958); Bertrand Russell, *A History of Western Philosophy* (New York: Simon & Schuster, 1945) 569–580. White Lewis Beck, *Six Secular Philosophers* (New York: Harper, 1997) 23–40.

10. See Walter Kaufman, *Existentialism From Dostoevsky to Sartre* (New York: Meridian, 1956.)

11. Friedrich Nietzsche, "Thus Spake Zarathustra," in *The Portable Nietzsche,* ed. and trans. Walter Kaufman (New York: Viking Press), 1954.

12. Titus was the Roman emperor who destroyed Jerusalem and its Temple in 70 CE.

13. An oven constructed as a snake-like linked chain of units: *akhnai* in talmudic Hebrew is a snake. Some say that in this case, it was the name of the oven builder.

14. Nihilism — from the Latin *nihil,* or "nothing," meaning the total rejection of all laws, principles, customs and traditions.

15. On humanism and its history see Myron P. Gilmpre, *The World of Humanism,* (New York: Harper, 1952); Robin W. Winks, *Western Civilization: A Brief History* (Englewood Cliffs, NJ: Prentice-Hall, 1979).

16. Israel's Basic Laws have superior status to ordinary laws, require a much larger parliamentary majority to repeal, and will, in the fullness of time, when more has passed, combine to make up a written constitution.

17. See Isaiah Berlin, *Four Essays on Liberty* (Oxford University Press, 1969).

18. On political toleration see Michael Walzer, *On Toleration* (New Haven: Yale University Press, 1997); David Hyed, ed. *Tolaration: An Elusive Virtue,* (Cambridge: Cambridge Univeristy Press, 1996); Raphael Cohen-Almagor, *The Boundries of Liberty and Tolerance,* (Gainsville: University of Florida Press, 1994).

19. On Renaissance culture, see Jacob Burckhardt, *The Civilization of the Renaissance in Italy* (New York: Random House, 1954) Denys Hays, *The Italian Renaissance and its Historical Background* (Cambridge: Cambridge University Press, 1977). On Jews in the Renaissance see Robert Bonfil, *Jewish Life in Renaissance in Italy* (Berkeley: University of California Press, 1994).

20. Sha'ul Chernikhovsky, Immanuel Ha-Romi, *Immanuel of Rome: A Monograph* (Berlin: Eshkol, 1927), 14 .

21. *Tophet* is a site near Jerusalem where pagan rites, including child sacrifices, were made to the god Moloch; in Hebrew it is another name for Hell.

22. From the Latin *libertas,* or freedom, liberty; capitalism is from "capital" in the sense of invested wealth; socialism is derived from the Latin *socialis,* meaning allied and *socius,* friend, companion.

23. Utopia: (Greek no place) an imagined perfect society. *Utopia* was the title of a book by Sir Thomas More, in which he describes a land of ideal, flawless government.

24. After the Communists' victory, the government of the empire was put in the hands of councils (in Russian, *soviets*) of workers, peasants and soldiers, which the Communist Party set up in all parts of what had been Russia.

CHAPTER 3. JEWISH IDENTITY

1. The *Concise Oxford Dictionary of Current English* (Oxford: Oxford University Press, 1990), 636

2. On Jewish faith, see Martin Buber, *Two Types of Faith*, trans. Norman P. Goldhawk (New York: Macmillan, 1951); Isidore Epstein, *Faith of Judaism*, (London: Soncino Press, 1954). On the Israelite religion, its birth and development during the First Temple period, see Georg Fohrer, *History of the Israelite Religion, trans. David E. Green* (London: Abingdon Press, 1975). On the faith of the mishnaic-talmudic period and later, see: Ephraim E. Urbach, *The Sages: Their Concepts and Beliefs*, (Cambridge: Harvard University Press, 1978.)

3. Quoted by Menachem Becker in his column, "Tales of the Hasidim," *Yediot Akhronot,* October 1, 1999.

4. Valley of Hinnom in southern Jerusalem, also called Tophet, was a place where sacrifice of children was practiced in honor of the god Moloch. Tophet was borrowed for "next world's Hell."

5. Rashi's commentary: "Where the Holy Blessed Be He summon them to judgement as to why they had not complied with what they had taken on themselves, they would have the answer that they had accepted it under Duress."

6. *Halacha* forbids sowing one field with two kinds of seeds, cross-breeding animal species *('kil'ayim)*, and wearing clothes made of both wool and linen (*Shaatnez,* Lev. 19:19; Deut. 22:9–11).

7. Quoted by Rashi in his comments on Leviticus 20:26.

8. From the Greek *synedrion,* for a council.

9. On the messianic idea, its significance and development, see Joseph Klausner, *The Messianic Idea in Israel* trans. W. F. Steinspring (New York: Macmillan, 1955); Gershom Scholem, *The Messianic Idea in Judaism and Other Essays on Jewish Spirituality* (New York: Schocken, 1971).

10. *Khristos,* Greek for "the anointed one."

11. On the Sabbatean movement, see: Gershom Scholem *Sabbatai Sevi: The Mystical Messiah* tran. Zwi Werblowsky (Princeton University Press, 1973).

12. A quotation from Dan. 12:6, understood as referring to the time of redemption. Haim Shirman, *Hashira Haivrit bi Sfarad ube Provonce (Hebrew Poetry in Spain and Provence)* (Jerusalem 1955: Dvir, 244.

13. See: Gen. 15:10.

14. Medieval religious poems.

15. A special group of psalms recited on days of the new moon and on festivals.

16. Pre-*bar mitzvah* school.

17. The name comes from the Italian *ghetto,* meaning "a foundry," as the first of these closed Jewish quarters was established in 1516 in Venice near a group of foundries.

18. Jean Paul Sartre, *Reflexions sur la Question Juive* (Paris: Gallimard, 1954). On Anti-Semitism, see Leon Poliakov, *History of Anti-Semitism* (Oxford: Oxford University Press, 1985).

CHAPTER 4. JEWISH PLURALISM

1. Pharisees, Hebrew *Perushim,* separatists; Sadducees, Hebrew *Zedokim,* followers of the Hellenizer high priest Zadok.

2. Ascetic, from the Greek *essenoi*.

3. Josephus Flavius, *The Jewish War*, trans. G. A. Williamson (Harmondsworth: Penguin Books, 1959). See also his *Jewish Antiquities*, William Winston (Peabody, MA: Hendrickson, 1987).

4. Ezer Kahanov, "Patterns of Secularization in the Western Sephardi Diaspora in the seventeenth Century" *Encyclopedia Judaica Year Book* (1988–1989) 189–195.

5. *Hasid*, pious, righteous. On the history and teachings of Hasidism, see: Martin Buber, *The Origin and Teachings of Hasidism* (New Jersey: 1988); Safra, Bezalel, ed., *Hasidism: Continuity or Innovation* (Cambridge, MA: Cambridge University Press, 1988).

6. On the Messianic idea and the Sabbateans see chapter three.

7. All these concepts and terms (*kavannah, dvekut, sefirot, klipot, tikun*) are drawn from the Kabbalist system developed by R. Isaac Ashkenazi Luria of Tzfat, "the Holy ARI" (Ashkenazi Rabbi Isaac—"Ari," meaning "Lion" in Hebrew). See Gershom Scholem, *Major Trends in Jewish Mysticism* (New York: Schochen, 1961).

8. Phylacteries, in Hebrew *tefillin:* small boxes of prayer texts bound to a man's forehead and arm with narrow leather straps.

9. From J. Blocker, ed., *Israeli Stories*, trans. Walter Lever New York: Schocken, 1962).

10. On the *Haskalah* see Jacob Katz, ed., *Toward Modernity: The European Jewish Model* (New Brunswick, N.J.: Transaction Books, 1987); Moshe Peli, "The Age of Haskalah" in *Studies in Hebrew Literature of the Enlightenment in Germany* (Leiden: E. J. Brill, 1979); Simon Halkin, "The Dilemma of Haskalah Literature" in *Modern Hebrew Literature: Trends and Values* (New York: Schocken, 1950).

11. *Maskilim*, Jews who adopted the *Haskalah* approach to Judaism.

12. Ruhama, a woman's name meaning "obtained pity"; see Hosea 1:6.

13. Itzik Manger, *Lid un Balade* (New York, 1952) 17. *Kaddish* means "holy" in Aramaic and is the name of the Jewish mourner's prayer.

14. The "Canaanite Movement," especially in the 1940s, argued that a diferentiation should be made between the "Hebrew Nation" in the "Kedem [Eastern] territories" and the Jewish people in the Diaspora. In addition, they maintained that the ancient Hebrew pre-Biblical culture should form the basis for the new Hebrew civilization. See Boaz Evron, "Canaanism: Solutions and Problems," *Jerusalem Quarterly* no. 44 (Fall 1987): 51–72.

15. See note 8 in this chapter.

16. See, for example, Chernikhovsky's "Mot Hatamuz" *(The Death of Tammuz)* and "Hazon Nevi Ha-Ashera" *(Vision of the Asherah Prophet)* and Zalman Shne'ur's "Luhot Gnuzim" *Hidden Tablets*, and other writings. This tendency is evident also in Yonatan Ratosh's "Et Nishmat" *To The Soul*, "Mot HaBaal" On Death to Baal, "HaHolhhi; BaHoshech" The Walkers in Darkness, and other works.

17. See in chapter 3 of this volume "The Messianic Idea."

CHAPTER 5. JEWRY TODAY

1. "Orthodox", from the Greek: the correct faith.

2. Yiddish nickname for a small Hasidic *Bet-midrash*, (study house-cum-syna-

gogue). The *siddur* (order of prayers) used by *Hasidim* was arranged by the Kabbalist Isaac Luria, and it is called "Sepharadi Version."

3. The founder of *Chabad* Hasidism

4. According to 1998 World Jewish Congress survey.

5. From the Greek: *syn* meaning going together.

6. Shoshana Silverman: *Siddur Schema Yisrael,* United Synagogue of Conservative Judaism, 1996.

7. According to a 1998 World Jewish Congress survey.

8. The Standing Prayer is the core of all three daily prayer services. Originally, it comprised eighteen blessings and so came to be known as *Shmone-esre* (Eighteen). There are small differences between the version recited on Sabbath and that recited during the festivals.

9. Except for a few politically oriented organizations founded in recent years to protect the rights of Israeli seculars, such as League Against Religious Coercion, the Secular Movement for a Humanist Judaism, the Free People Association, the *Shinui* and *Or* political parties.

10. According to a 1998 World Jewish Congress survey.

11. Translated by Sylvie D'Avigdor, American Zionist Emergency Council, 1946.

12. See Israeli press, late January 1999.

13. See Hos. 2:17.

14. Lately, in many towns and suburbs, more and more businesses, especially groceries, restaurants and cafes, cinemas and theaters are open on Sabbaths, against the law, answering the demand of the secular population of these towns.

15. The concept *Kulturkampf* is a German term coined to describe the campaign waged by Chancellor Bismarck in the early 1870s to impose the authority of the civil state upon the religious establishment.

16. Tel Aviv: Hakibbutz Hameuhad, 1994) pp. 195–97.

17. Maimonides' famous *Guide for the Perplexed.*

CHAPTER 6. JEWISH CULURE

1. *Webster's 3rd New International Dictionary,* 1993.

2. The "Old Testament".

3. The original Hebrew of most parts of *Ben-Sira* and some other fragment were found in the *Cairo Geniza. Geniza* is a chest or cupboard in a synagogue for the disposing of worn-out sacred books and sacred objects. In the late nineteenth century two hundred thousand fragments were found by Professor Solomon Schechter in the *geniza* of the ancient synagogue of Fostat in Cairo, Egypt. This treasure is now stored in the Cambridge University, England.

4. After the story that Ptolemy II Philadelphus, king of Egypt, reportedly gathered seventy-two Jewish wise elders to make the translation for his great library at Alexandria. See Henry G. Meecham, *The Letter of Aristeas* (Manchester: Manchester University Press, 1935).

5. See William G. Braude, *The Book Of Legends* (New York: Schocken, 1992).

6. On the Kabbala and mystical writing see Gershom Scholem, *Major Trends in Jewish Mysticism* (New York: Schocken 1961) and *On the Kabbalah and its Symbolism,* (New York: Schocken, 1969.)

7. From the essay, *Avdut mitoch Herut, Subjection Within Freedom.*

8. On the historicity of the Bible, see: Zecharia Kallai, (ed.), *Biblical Historiography and Historical Geography* (Frankfurt am Mein: Peter Lang, 1998) Richard Eliot Friedman. *Who Wrote the Bible?* (New York: Simon & Schuster, 1987).

9. Itzik Manger, "Hagar farlozt Avram's Hoiz", "Hagar Quits Abraham's House."

10. David Frishman, *Be-Har Sinai* "At Mount Sinai," *Bamidbar, In the Wilderness* (Berlin: Hasefer 1922.)

11. A person dedicated to God, not allowed to drink wine or to cut his hair. See Numbers 6:13.

12. See chapter 1.

13. See James B. Pritchard, *Ancient Near Eastern Texts Relating to the Old Testament* (Princeton: Princeton University Press, 1969).

14. Mishna *Kiddushin* 3:9.

15. "Full Cart, Empty Cart?", *"Kol Hatikvot," All our Hopes, Essays on the Israeli Condition,* (Jerusalem: Keter, 1998.

16. School for pre-bar mitzvah boys.

17. *Melamed,* lowest grade of teacher.

18. Two of the greatest *amoraim,* who argued out numerous issues, some of which were utterly insignificant.

19. An ancient town in northern Syria, where a library of clay tablets from the fifteenth cen. BCE was found in 1929. See Frank M. Cross *Canaanite Myth and Hebrew Epics* (Cambridge, Mass.: Cambridge University Press, 1973).

20. A regulation introduced in the first century BCE in order to prevent damage to sacred scriptures (see *Mishna Shabbat*).

21. See Martin Buber, "The Shepard's Song," *Tales of the Hasidim* (New York: Schocken 1975), 250.

Biographical Notes

Abrabanel, Isaac (1437–1508): Leader of Spanish Jewry at the time of the 1492 expulsion. Diplomat to kings of Portugal, Spain, and Italy. Philosopher and biblical commentator.

A'Costa Uriel (1585–1640) A marrano who returned to Judaism in Amsterdam, but then rebelled against certain commandments and other elements of Oral Law doctrine. His community declared him ostracized, (*kherem*). He repented and returned to the faith but later committed suicide.

Adler, Alfred (1870–1937) Austrian–Jewish psychiatrist who, having studied under Freud, parted company with Freudian psychoanalysis to establish his own school, Individual Psychology.

Agnon, S. Y. (1888–1970) Hebrew novelist and short story writer, whose work conveys an atmosphere of Jewish life ridden with crisis. His writing is suffused with the influence of the classical sources of Hebrew language and culture and his Hebrew style is rooted for the most part in the pre-*Haskalah* Hebrew of "God-fearing" biblical commentators, theologians, and ethicists. His books include: *Sippur Pashut*, A Simple Story, *Oreakh Nata Lalun*, A Guest for the Night, *Tmol Shilshom*, The Days Before, *Hakhnassat Kala*, To the Bridal Canopy.

Ahad Ha'am—see Ginsberg, Asher.

Akiva Ben Yosef (50–136 CE) Third-generation *tanna* and one of the most revered of Jewish sages. The innumerable stories told of his life say that he was forty years old before he dedicated his life to Torah study at the urging of his devoted wife, Rachel. His halachic method employed far-reaching, casuistic interpretation to make the link between established halachic rulings and biblical texts when text and ruling seemed far apart. A fervent supporter of Bar Kokhba's revolt against the Romans, to the point of proclaiming Bar Kokhba King-Messiah. After the revolt's crushing, he was one of the ten sages selected by the Romans to be executed as an example.

Albo, Joseph (1360–1444) Spanish-Jewish philosopher who, in his *Sefer Ha'Ikarim*, Book of Principles, propounded the central tenets of the Jewish faith.

Alexander Yannai (126?–76 BCE) A king of Judah of the Hasmonean dynasty. Extended the boundaries of the kingdom by persistent military campaigning. A great builder. His constant conflict with the Pharisee rabbis who commanded the loyalty of the mass of the people led in the end to a popular uprising against him.

Allen, Woody (1935–) Multi-talented American Jewish film-maker, script-writer, director, and actor, many of whose films portray the problematic Jewish life in the United States. Among his most famous films are *Annie Hall, Hannah and Her Sisters,* and *Manhattan.*

Alkalai, Yehuda ben Solomon Khai (1798–1878) Herald of Zionism and a leading rabbi of Serbian Jewry. Preached that redemption would come only after a return to the Land of Israel. Not having succeeded in organizing a resettlement movement, towards the end of his life he settled in Jerusalem himself.

Amichai, Yehuda (1924–2000) Poet, writer, playwright, one of the post–1948 generation's supreme poets. His works include: *Shirim* 1948–1962; Poems 1948–1962, *Akhshav beRa'ash*, Now in the Storm; *Miakhorei Kol Ze Mistater Osher Gadol*, All This Conceals a Great Joy; *Lo MiAkhshav VeLo MiKan*, Not From Now or From Here; and the collection of plays *Pa'amonim VeRakavot*, Bells and Trains.

Armstrong, Louis (1901–1971) American jazz trumpeter and singer, a key innovator in jazz and popular music.

Asch, Sholem (1880–1957) Novelist, story-writer, and playwright in Hebrew and Yiddish, a star in the Yiddish literary firmament. His books include: *Salvation, The God of Vengeance, Moshe, The Nazarene, Mottke the Thief*. His most famous story is "A Village Tzaddik."

Ashi, Rav (335–427 CE) A Babylonian *amora* of the sixth generation of *amora'im* Head of the great Sura Academy and one of Babylonian Jewry's greatest champions. Considered one of the greatest halachic authorities. According to tradition it was under his and Ravina's tutelage that the Babylonian Talmud was brought to closure.

Attar, Tirtza (1941–1977) Poet, songwriter, and translator. *Ir HaYareakh*, Moon City, is a collection of her poetry.

Avtalion—See Shemaya and Avtalion.

Baal Shem Tov (*Besht*), Rabbi Israel ben Eliezer (1698/1700–1760) The founder of Hasidism.

Bach, Johann Sebastian (1685–1750) German composer whose music is considered a summit of European civilization and the greatest achievement of Baroque polyphony. A main part of his output was choral works on religious themes.

Bacon, Francis (1561–1626) English statesman, philosopher, and essayist. Contemporary of Shakespeare. Impassioned advocate of rationalism.

Bakhya ben Joseph ibn Pakuda (eleventh century CE) Spanish–Jewish philosopher. His *Khovat HaLevavot*, The Duties of the Heart, draws a cardinal distinction between practical obligations and the obligations of the heart deriving from the individual's inner spiritual life.

de Balzac, Honoré (1799–1850) French novelist, among the most important of the nineteenth-century realistic school.

Bar Kokhba, Shimon (second century CE) Leader of the Jews' revolt in 132 against Roman overlordship of the Land of Israel. Proclaimed by Rabbi Akiva as King-Messiah but the revolt ended in total disaster.

Bat Miriam, Yokheved (1901–1980) Hebrew poet whose main body of work dates from the period of the Third Aliyah (1919–23).

Beckett, Samuel (1906–1989) Irish author and playwright who wrote both in French and English. His *Waiting for Godot* is a landmark of the Theater of the Absurd.

van Beethoven, Ludwig (1770–1827) German composer, one of the greatest in all musical genres. His symphonies especially are of the immortal glories of Western civilization and culture. An immense influence on nineteenth-century music.

Bellow, Saul (1915–2005) One of the leading American and Jewish novelists of the twentieth century. Many of his books treat the issues of American Jewish life, in particular *Herzog* and *Mr. Sammler's Planet*.

Ben-Gurion, David (1886–1973) Zionist and Socialist politician. Israel's first prime minister. Headed a series of Israeli governments between 1948 and 1963.

Berlioz, Hector (1803–1869) French composer of the Romantic school. A great innovator in orchestration.

Bernstein, Eduard (1850–1932) German-Jewish socialist, both practical leader and theoretician. Proposed a revision of socialist theory which would have allowed its goals to be achieved by socio-political reform. Held opinions close to those of *Poalei Tzion*, Workers of Zion Party, and took an interest in the situation of the Jews.

Bernstein, Leonard (1918–1989) American–Jewish composer, pianist, and conductor and a central figure in American twentieth-century music. A frequent visitor and performer in Israel. His works include the *Jeremiah* symphony, *Kaddish,* and the musical, *West Side Story*.

The Besht—See Baal Shem Tov.

Bialik, Ha'im Nachman (1873–1934) Poet, author, editor, and essayist. One of the foremost artists to emerge from the revival of Hebrew as a spoken and literary language. Made a huge contribution to the renewal and expansion of the language. Active in the Zionist movement and a powerful force in Jewish artistic/intellectual life, especially after his emigration to Palestine in 1924.

Bin Gorion (Berditchevsky), Micah Joseph (1865–1921) Hebrew novelist and thinker and a luminary of the New Hebrew Literature. Called for a reconceptualization of Judaism and new Jewish values, with the aim of freeing the Jews from the shackles of *Galut*, exile, tradition. Among his best-known works are *Me'ever LeNahar,* Across the River; *Makhanayim,* Two Armies; *Beseter Ra'am,* Under Cover of Thunder; *Miriam*.

Blum, Leon (1872–1950) French-Jewish politician, a leader of European Socialism and prime minister of France from 1936 to 1937. A supporter of Zionism, he was bitterly opposed by the French Right and made the target of anti-Semitic vilification.

Boccaccio, Giovanni (1313–1375) Italian Renaissance author, one of the first to compose in Italian instead of Latin. His most famous work is *The Decameron*.

Borges, Jorge Luis (1899–1986) Argentinian poet and author. Some of his thought and writing were influenced by Kabbala. Winner of the Jerusalem Prize. Among his works are *The Aleph and Other Stories, The Garden of Forking Paths, Fictions, Dr. Brodie's Report*.

Borokhov, Dov Ber (1881–1919) Leader and ideologue of the *Poalei Tzion*, Workers of Zion, movement. His fusion of Zionism and Marxism had a great influence on the direction taken by the labor movement of Jewish Palestine.

Brahms, Johannes (1833–1897) German composer, one of the greatest in symphonic music.

Brecht, Bertolt (1898–1956) German poet, playwright, and man of the theater. Sworn opponent of Nazism. Among his greatest works are *The Threepenny Opera, The Caucasian Chalk Circle, Mother Courage and Her Children, The Good Woman of Setzuan*.

Brenner, Yosef Ha'im (1881–1921) Author and thinker, one of the most important writers of the Hebrew Revival period and a great innovator in Hebrew prose-writing.

His works include *Bain Mayim leMayim*, Between Water and Water; *Mikan UmiKan*, From Here and There; *Misaviv LaNekuda*, All Around the Point; *Bakhoref*, In Winter; *Shkhol VeKishalon*, Breakdown and Bereavement.

Breuer Joseph (1842–1925) Austrian-Jewish psychiatrist, his research was the source of the early theoretical development leading Freud to psychoanalysis.

Broch, Hermann (1886–1951) Austrian-Jewish novelist, poet, and essayist who fled Austria in 1938 for the United States of America. His novels, *The Death of Virgil, The Sleepwalkers*, and others together constitute a landmark in the development of the European novel.

Brunelleschi, Filippo (1377–1446) A leading light of Italian Renaissance architecture and architect of the celebrated dome of Florence cathedral.

Buber, Mordechai (Martin) (1878–1965) Philosopher and researcher whose philosophy of religious existentialism was based on the idea of continuous dialogue between the individual and his others, and between him and his world and God. An active Zionist. In 1938 he left Germany for Palestine to take up a professorship at Hebrew University. Advocated a bi-national state of Arabs and Jews.

Byron, Lord George Gordon (1788–1824) English poet, one of the most celebrated of the Romantic era. Author of a cycle of poems on Jewish themes, *Hebrew Melodies*. Of liberal opinions, volunteered to fight alongside the Greeks for independence and met his death there.

Camus, Albert (1913–1960) French-Algerian born author, playwright, thinker, journalist, and polemicist. Active in the Second World War French Resistance. His philosophy is essentially an ethical existentialism. His novels include: *The Stranger, The Plague*, and *The Fall*. His philosophical work appeared in *The Rebel* and *The Myth of Sisyphus*.

Cézanne, Paul (1839–1906) French post-Impressionist painter. A precursor of Expressionism. Used geometric shapes to construct landscapes and still lifes.

Chagall, Marc (1887–1985) Russian–Jewish painter who lived and worked in Paris, a leading figure of modernism. After a period of Cubist influence, most of his work was in a Surrealist mode. His paintings portray symbolically the world of Eastern European Jewry. Also made several sets of stained-glass windows, for the Metz Cathedral, a Jerusalem synagogue, and the United Nations Building in New York. Also painted the ceiling of the Paris Opera and a wall of the Metropolitan Opera in New York.

Chekhov, Anton Pavlovitch (1860–1904) Russian playwright and short-story writer, an early practitioner of modern drama, whose plays such as *The Seagull, Uncle Vanya*, and *The Three Sisters*, are never off the contemporary stage. His realistic short stories are also modern classics.

Chernikhovski, Sha'ul (1875–1943) One of the leading poets of the Hebrew Revival as well as a celebrated and important translator and qualified doctor of medicine. His poetry displays the tension in him between his Jewishness and his aspiration to achieve universality and a place in European culture.

Cohen, Hermann (1842–1918) German–Jewish philosopher who perceived Jewry as an exemplary society and resisted the message of Zionism as a disowning of Jewry's mission to the gentiles. His works include *The Religious Concept in Philosophical Method* and *A Religion of Reason: Out of the Sources of Judaism*.

Copernicus, Nicolaus (1473–1543) Polish astronomer who detected the Earth to be a planet revolving on its own axis and, with the other planets, orbiting the sun, the center of our planetary system.

Cordovero, Moses (1522–1570) A kabbalist, his *Pomegranate Orchard* is one of Kabbala's basic texts.

Crescas, Khasdai (1340–1412) Philosopher, biblical commentator, and leader of Jewish community in Christian Spain. In religion a determinist, he rejected Maimonides's conception of Judaism and in particular the articles of the faith as set out by Maimonides, proposing articles of his own devising.

Dalí, Salvador (1904–1989) Spanish painter and star of the Surrealist school.

Dante Alighieri (1265–1321) Italian poet, one of the first to compose in Italian. A great innovator in poetic form and a sharp critic of contemporary society. His great work, the *Divine Comedy,* describes a journey through the world of the dead, through Hell and Purgatory to Paradise.

Darwin, Charles (1809–1882) English biologist whose *The Origin of Species* proposed that all current species of animal and plant life are the outcomes of an extremely long process of evolution, propelled by natural selection.

da Vinci, Leonardo (1452–1519) Italian painter, sculptor, architect and inventor. The supreme instance of the Renaissance man. Best known for the paintings *Mona Lisa* and *The Last Supper.* His long list of inventions includes siege engines and flying machines, the latter an example of how far his conceptions flew ahead of his time.

Descartes, René (1596–1650) French philosopher and mathematician. Believed that sense-derived knowledge was dubitable and knowledge was best built up by a process of logical reasoning, proceeding from the axiom "I think, therefore I am."

Degas, Edgar (1834–1917) French painter and sculptor, a late Impressionist. Best known for his paintings and sculptures of dancers.

Disraeli, Benjamin (Lord Beaconsfield) (1804–1881) British politician, whose father had converted the family to Christianity. Leader of the Conservative Party, who as prime minister, crowned Queen Victoria Empress of India and bought England control of the Suez Canal. His Jewish ancestry was central to his persona and he maintained a belief in Jewish racial superiority. His novel, *Alroy,* deals with Jewish themes.

Dostoevsky, Fyodor Mikhailovitch (1821–1881) Russian novelist, one of the greatest of all time. Distinguished by penetrating psychological insight. An influential force on later novelists as well as on the development of Existentialism. His main works are *Crime and Punishment, The Idiot,* and *Brothers Karamazov.*

Dubnow, Simon (1860–1941) Russian-born Jewish historian and social thinker. Believed that the continued existence of the Jewish people required social and ideological autonomy but not political or territorial sovereignty.

Einhorn, David (1809–1879) Theologian and religious thinker, advocate of the radical reform of Judaism. Pioneer of the Reform movement and one of its foremost leaders. The book of prayer he compiled, *Olat Tamid,* The Daily Offering, formed the basis for Reform Jewry's *siddur.*

Einstein, Albert (1879–1955) German–Jewish physicist who moved to the United States of America in the mid-1930s to escape the advent of Nazism. The creator of the Theory of Relativity which revolutionized theoretical and experimental physics and opened new lines of nuclear research. Deeply involved in Jewish affairs, especially in helping European Jews in difficulties and in the development of Zionism.

Eisenstein, Sergei (1898–1948) Russian-Jewish film director, one of the leading theoreticians and most creative practitioners of the cinema. Among his most celebrated films are *Battleship Potemkin, Alexander Nevsky,* and *Ivan the Terrible.*

Eliezer ben Hyrcanus (70–120 CE) Also known as Rabbi Eliezer the Great, a second-generation *tanna* and disciple of Rabbi Yokhanan ben Zakai, the founder of the Yavneh Academy and leader of the "first generation" of *tanna'im,* who rehabilitated and recast Judaism after the devastation of the Great Revolt. Known for his stringent halachic rulings and opposition to leniency of interpretation. *Pirkei Rabbi Eliezer* is a collection of *midrashim* attributed to him.

Elisha ben Avuya (70–140 CE) One of the leading *tanna'im* of the "third" generation. Came to voice severe objections to aspects of the great sages' doctrine and to question the actuality of divine providence, for which he was contemned as a denier of God and to be referred to in halakhic writings only as *Akher,* "the other one."

Elisheva (Bikhovsky-Zhirkova) (1888–1949) Russian-born poet in Hebrew who emigrated to Palestine.

Ellington, Edward "Duke" (1899–1974) One of the foremost American jazz pianists and composers.

Epicurus (341–270 BCE) Greek philosopher, founder of a school that taught that happiness and the pleasures of life, spiritual and physical, constitute a cardinal value.

Feierberg, Mordechai Ze'ev (1874–1899) Hebrew author, an early contributor to the Hebrew Revival. His stories convey the waverings of Jews between tradition and European culture. His most important story: "Le'an?".

Flaubert, Gustave (1821–1880) French novelist, whose novel *Madame Bovary* is one of the acknowledged masterpieces of world literature.

Fourier, Charles (1772–1837) French philosopher and utopian socialist who envisioned a future egalitarian society based on cooperatively-owned property, cooperative labor, a common education system, and direct democracy.

Frankel, Zecharia (1801–1875) Rabbi who founded and directed the Jewish Theological Seminary in Breslau, Germany, from which emerged the leaders of Conservative Judaism in the United States. Frankel's position on the future direction for Judaism was a midway one between Reform and Orthodoxy.

Freud, Sigmund (1856–1939) Austrian–Jewish psychologist, the father of psychoanalysis, a body of theory and practice that locates the source of mental problems in emotions repressed in the subconscious and the solution to the problems in raising those emotions to the conscious level by means of an experiential therapist-patient dialogue employing the technique of free association. Repressed sexuality is also perceived as a prime cause of mental disorder. Freud's theories and concepts have exercised strong influence on twentieth-century thought and literature.

Frishman, David (1859–1922) Author, translator, critic, editor, and scholar of literature, an eminence of the Hebrew Revival. Made many translations of European literature into Hebrew in order to open Jewish eyes to aesthetic concepts. A posthumously-published collection of his short stories, *BaMidbar,* In The Wilderness, depicts the opposition between Torah's all-encompassing demands and the small world of the individual.

Galilei, Galileo (1564–1642) Italian astronomer and mathematician. Used the telescope he developed to observe for the first time sunspots, the satellites of Jupiter, and the phases of Venus, proving that the planets in our system, including Earth, revolved around the sun. Forced by the Church to publicly recant his discovery, but according to legend insisted on his deathbed, "Despite everything, [Earth]) does move."

Gamliel, Rabban (first century CE) Grandson of Hillel and president of the Sanhedrin. The title Rabban passed down to his heirs and successors.

Gamliel II, Rabban (first century CE–132) Grandson of Rabban Gamliel and also president of the Sanhedrin. A colleague of Yokhanan ben Zakai in the effort to rehabilitate Jewry as a religio-cultural entity after the destruction of the Second Temple.

Gaon of Vilna, Elijah ben Solomon Zalman (1720–1797) Rabbi and halachic authority, one of Jewry's greatest spiritual leaders. Though he advocated Jews studying mathematics and the natural sciences, he opposed the teachings of the *Haskalah*. A sworn enemy of Hasidism, which he regarded as trivializing Judaism and even bordering on idolatry, he ordered its persecution and issued ostracism orders against its leaders.

Gauguin, Paul (1848–1903) French painter and forerunner of the Expressionist school.

Geiger, Avraham (1810–1874) Rabbi, Jewish Studies scholar, and one of the leaders of the Reform movement. Advocated the integration of Jews into European society, and therefore opposed Jewish nationalism and Hebrew as the language of prayer, within the basic structures of Judaism and Jewry.

Gershwin, George (1898–1937) American-Jewish composer, most famous for his popular songs but also the composer of more classical orchestral works, showing a strong jazz influence. His opera *Porgy and Bess* is based on jazz rhythms and folk melodies.

Ginsberg, Asher (Ahad Ha'am) (1856–1927) Thinker and essayist. Laid the intellectual foundations of Judaism as nationality, both historically and in the present day. Advocated a spiritual Zionism as against Herzl's political Zionism. To him the aim of resettling Israel should be to make it a spiritual-cultural center capable of uniting world Jewry on a basis of common nationality and culture.

Gnessin, Uri Nissan (1881–1913) A leading figure in the Hebrew Revival and one of the first psychological authors in Hebrew. Made wide use of the interior monologue, the stream of association, and the stream of consciousness some twenty years before Joyce. His works include: *Hatzida*, Aside; *Beterem*, Before; *Beinta'im*, In the Meantime.

von Goethe, Johann Wolfgang (1749–1832) German poet, playwright, novelist, and essayist, the father of modern German literature. Initiated the romantic *Sturm und Drang* literary-artistic movement. His philosophical play, *Faust,* is one of the supreme achievements of European culture.

Goldberg, Leah (1911–1970) Poet, playwright, editor, translator, and scholar of literature. Among the greatest of poets in modern Hebrew. Her works include the poetry collections: *Tabaot Ashan*, Smoke Rings; *Al HaPrikha*, A Flowering; *Barak BaBoker*, Lightning in the Morning, and the play, *Ba'alat Ha'Armon*, Lady of the Manor.

Gordon, Aharon David (1856–1922) A thinker on sociopolitical issues, mentor to the Pioneers of the Second Aliyah (1904–14). Preached the liberating virtues of manual work. Strongly influenced by Tolstoyan thinking.

Gordon, David (1831–1886) Author, essayist, and editor of the *Haskalah* journal, *Hamagid*.

Gordon, Yehuda Leib (1831–1892) Poet, essayist, and critic, considered the most outstanding of the Haskalah poets. Lashed out at the religious leaders of Russian Jewry and the *halachic* shackles the rabbis held them in. Advocated Jews integrating into the life of the Russian Empire, changing the way they educated their children, freeing their women, and "productivizing" themselves, moving from "parasitic" trades, such as money-lending, to the society-building occupations of agriculture, manufacturing, and construction.

Graetz, Heinrich (1817–1891) German–Jewish historian and pioneer of Jewish historiography. His thirteen-volume *History of the Jews* exercised immense influence on the Hebrew literature of his time and on Jewish historiography since.

Greenberg, Uri Tzvi (1896–1981) A supreme artist of Hebrew poetry. The subject matter of his early verse, especially the collection, *Anacreon al Kotev Ha'Itzavon*, Anacreon at the Pole of Sorrow, is full of man's solitude and the terrors of existence. Later he became mystical, messianic, and developed a fierce nationalism. His collection on the Holocaust, *Rekhovot HaNahar*, is one of the summits of Hebrew literature. He also wrote in Yiddish.

Gropius, Walter (1883–1969) German architect, who in 1937 moved to the United States. As a pioneer of the International Style, he exerted a major influence on modern architecture. Founder and director of the Bauhaus school of architectural design.

Hadrian (76–138 CE) Emperor of Rome from 117 to 138 whose memory is reviled in Jewish tradition. Started out as a benign ruler but, after crushing the Bar Kokhba revolt, enacted draconian decrees against *mitzva*-observance.

Hazzaz, Ha'im (1898–1973) Hebrew novelist, the bulk of his work dating to the interwar period. A central theme is the profound fracture in the history of Judaism and Jewry during the modern period. Many of his books describe the life of Yemenite Jews. His two most important novels are *Ya'ish* and *HaYoshevet BaGanim*, You Who Linger in the Garden.

Hegel, Georg Wilhelm Friedrich (1770–1831) German philosopher. Conceived reality and human consciousness as a unity, or Idealism. Human society, in his view, was a historical process, advancing by the clash of opposing forces, the thesis and antithesis, resulting in a new unity, or synthesis.

Heidegger, Martin (1889–1976) German philosopher. Focused on the nature of human existence, "how it is to be." Anxiety, dread about death, and the necessity of living under its constant threat are seen as essential elements of that existence.

Heine, Heinrich (1797–1856) German–Jewish poet who converted to Christianity. His poetry is romantic and lyrical, his journalism wickedly satirical. Many of his poems, set to music by Schubert and Schumann, have become part of the German folk song heritage. Gave considerable thought to Jews and Judaism, and his novella *The Rabbi of Bachrach*, is evidence of his interest in the theme. His works were banned under Hitler.

Hendel, Yehudit (1925–) Israeli novelist of the "1948 literary generation." Her books include: *Rekhov HaMadregot*, Stepped Street; *Anashim Akherim Hem*, They are a Different Kind of People; *Hakoakh Ha'Akher*, The Other Power; *Arukhat Boker Temima*, A Complete Breakfast; *Kesef Katan*, Small Change.

Herod (first century BCE) Roman-appointed king of Judea. An active builder, his projects including the enlargement and beautification of Jerusalem Temple, and the founding of the cities of Tiberias and Caesarea, both named for his overlords.

Herzl, Theodore (1860–1904) Author, playwright, journalist, and essayist, the "visionary of the Zionist state." His book, *The Jewish State*, put forward a politico-diplomatic solution to the "Jewish Question." He summoned the first Zionist Congress to Basel, Switzerland, where, in 1897, among its other outcomes, the World Zionist Federation was founded, which, since then, has been the primary international agency for Zionism.

Hess, Moses (1812–1875) German–Jewish philosopher and social thinker, among the earliest European socialists and a herald of Zionism. Saw socialism as essentially a moral position. His *Rome and Jerusalem* describes the Jews resettling the Land of Israel and a revitalization of Jewish culture in the spirit of socialism.

Hildesheimer, Azriel (1820–1899) Rabbi and leader of German Orthodoxy. Opposing the Reform movement, he was one of the founders of Modern Orthodoxy, which looked for ways to "modernize" Judaism within the framework of Orthodoxy. A supporter of the *Hibbat Tzion*, Love of Zion, movement for the resettlement of the Land of Israel.

Hillel (70 BCE–10 CE) Leader of the Pharisees during Herod's reign. President of the Sanhedrin for many years, and the greatest of the sages of Mishna in the Second Temple period. Instigated many *takkanot*, some even running counter to explicit biblical commandments. In the long-running dispute-filled dialogue with Shammai, the chief justice of the High Court and, as such, Hillel's partner in the official leadership of Jewry, Hillel usually took the more lenient approach. His fame became such that the presidency of the Sanhedrin passed down to his descendants, collectively known as *Beit Hillel,* House of Hillel.

Hirsch, Samson Raphael (1808–1888) German rabbi and founder of Modern Orthodoxy. Defended traditional Judaism but demanded Jewish participation in Western culture. Withdrew from official Orthodoxy and its institutions to set up his own community where his influence persuaded many assimilationist Jews to return to *mitzva-* observance.

Holdheim, Samuel (1806–1860) Leader of the Reform movement in German Jewry. Proposed separating the moral-religious elements of Judaism from the nationalist elements and observing only commandments of which the essence was moral, not ritual.

Homer (seventh century BCE) Greece's greatest poet, perhaps historical, perhaps legendary. The authorship of the two monumental epics, *The Iliad* and *The Odyssey*, as well as other epic compositions of the seventh century BCE, have been attributed to him.

Ibn Ezra, Abraham (1089–1164) Biblical commentator, poet, philosopher, and Hebrew grammarian. Despite the fame of his great learning and breadth of knowledge, he suffered throughout his life from poverty and enforced displacements.

Ibn Ezra, Moses (1055–1135) A star of the Spanish golden age of Hebrew poetry, both secular and sacred. Wrote a book on the subject in Arabic. His philosophical studies are also outstanding.

Ibn Gvirol, Solomon (1020–1057) Among the greatest of Jewish poets and philosophers of the Middle Ages. A prolific composer of secular verse, love songs, drinking songs, poems to friendship and parables, as well as important sacred poetry. His key work, *Keter Malkhut,* The Royal Crown, is a long philosophical poem on the nature of God and the universe.

Ibn Tibbon (twelfth–thirteenth centuries) Yehuda ben Samuel (1120–1190), Samuel ben Yehuda (1160–1230), Moses ben Samuel (d. 1283), Jacob ben Makir (1236–1307)—a family of translators, mainly from Arabic to Hebrew. They gave European Jewry access to the greatest Greek, Arabic and Jewish philosophers, mathematicians, astronomers, and physicians. Translated Maimonides' writings from the original Arabic to Hebrew. Extended the Hebrew language by coining a terminology for philosophical writing.

Ibsen, Henrik (1828–1906) Norwegian poet and playwright, whose dramas were a critical factor in the development of twentieth-century theater. Among his works are *Peer Gynt, Ghosts,* and *Enemy of the People.*

Immanuel of Rome (1260–1330) Jewish poet of Renaissance Italy who introduced new forms into Hebrew-language prosody. Composed both religious poetry and light-hearted secular verse. Also composed in Italian.

Ishmael (second century CE) A renowned *tanna.* Known for his inclination to accept a literal, *pshatt,* reading of the biblical text.

Jabotinsky, Zeev (1880–1940) Novelist, journalist, essayist, and a Zionist leader. Founder and leader of the World Zionist Federation's Revisionist wing, later named the New Zionist Federation. A gifted novelist and poet. Translated masterpieces of world poetry into Hebrew and Hebrew literature into Russian, particularly Bialik's verse.

Jacobson, Israel (1768–1828) A pioneer of Reform Judaism in Germany. Established schools and synagogues that followed his conception of Jewish education and religion, a key element being the integration of Jews into gentile society.

Johns, Jasper (1930–) American painter of the pop-art school. Best known for his "Stars and Stripes" series.

Josephus Flavius (Yosef ben Matityahu) (37–100? CE) Military commander, author, and historian. Appointed commander of a section of the Jewish forces participating in the Great Revolt against Roman rule of Judea but having surrendered to the rival general Vespasian Flavius in order to prevent a general slaughter, he lived the rest of his life as a citizen of Rome. Wrote a history of the Revolt in Greek, *The Jewish War,* a history of the Jewish people, *Jewish Antiquities,* and works of Jewish philosophy. A glittering product of Hellenized Jewish culture.

Joyce, James (1882–1941) Irish author. His *Ulysses* introduced the stream of consciousness technique, following the thoughts and emotions of its protagonists throughout a single day. A huge influence on twentieth-century modernist literature.

Jung, Carl Gustav (1875–1961) Swiss psychologist and disciple of Freud. Theorized that primitive cultural elements of the collective unconscious, archetypes, were a cause of mental disorder. Drew up a systematic distinction between the introvert and extrovert types of human personality.

Kafka, Franz (1883–1924) Czech–Jewish novelist and an extraordinary influence on twentieth-century literature. Lived in Prague and wrote in German. His novels portray a delusive, nightmarish reality taking place in an undefined time and place and lacking all logic or explanation. Man is helpless against forces encompassing him and condemned to the inexorable dissolution of his personhood. Kafka's works include novels *The Trial, The Castle, America* and short stories.

Kahana-Carmon, Amalia (1929–) Israeli novelist of the "post-1948 generation." Her works include: *Bakfifa Akhat,* Stuck Together; *Yareakh BaEmek Ayalon,* Moon in the Ayalon Valley; *Lema'ala BeMontifer,* High Up in Montifer; *Sadot Magnet'im,* Magnetic Fields.

Kalisher, Tzvi Hirsch (1795–1874) Orthodox rabbi and an early proponent of religious Zionism. Believed that messianic redemption would come only after Jews had returned to the Land of Israel and the commandments relating to the settlement of the land were fulfilled.

Kandinsky, Wassily (1866–1944) Russian–born pioneer of abstract painting who lived and worked in Germany and France.

Kant, Immanuel (1724–1804) German philosopher whose teaching has had immense influence. His theory of knowledge drew a fundamental distinction between "things as they are in themselves," into which reality human beings have no direct insight, and "the world as we see it," which we can have some descriptive knowledge of thanks to the presence in us of certain pure intellectual concepts. Kant also made significant contributions to ethics and esthetics.

Kaplan, Mordechai Menachem (1881–1983) Rabbi and religious thinker, founder of Reconstructionist Judaism in the United States.

Karelitz, Avraham Yeshayahu (*Khazon Ish*) **(1878–1953)** One of the great Torah scholars and *halachic* judges of the modern period. Is famous for his likening of secularism to an "empty cart" which, as such, must give way to the "fully laden cart" of observant Judaism.

Katzenelson, Berl (1887–1944) Essayist, editor, and leader and ideologue of the Labor movement in Palestine. Saw the Labor movement as the key vehicle for the realization of Zionism. An activist of workers' settlement and cooperative movements in addition to his work in the educational and cultural fields.

Kautsky, Karl (1854–1938) German political theorist of moderate Marxist persuasion. An important figure in the history of Social Democracy.

Keats, John (1795–1821) English, one of the foremost of the Romantic poets.

Khatam Sofer—See Sofer, Moshe.

Khazon Ish—See Karelitz, Avnaham Yeshayahu.

Khiwi Habalkhi (ninth century CE) Gave public voice to two hundred questionable points in scripture and publicly questioned the actuality of Divine Providence and the holiness of Holy Writ.

Kierkegaard, Søren (1813–1855) Danish philosopher regarded as the founder of existentialism, considered from a religious point of view.

Klee, Paul (1879–1940) Swiss painter of the Expressionist tendency, one of the most original artists of the twentieth century.

Kook, Avraham Yitzhak Hacohen (1865–1935) Chief rabbi of Palestine during the British Mandate and an important religious thinker. Saw in Zionism a messianic movement signaling the coming of divine redemption and, as such, gave it his support, the secularism of its activists notwithstanding. After the Six Days' War his teachings encouraged religious Jews to settle the occupied territories, "Judea" and "Samaria." The chief religious settlement movement, *Gush Emunim,* Bloc of the Faithful, takes Kook as its mentor.

Krokhmal, Nakhman (1785–1840) Religious philosopher and one of the founders of the Jewish Studies movement, which set out to conduct scientific investigation into the history and development of Judaism and Jewry. An early spokesman for *Haskalah*. His *Guide for the Perplexed of Our Own Time* sets out the essence of Judaism from a historiosophical point of view.

Lassalle, Ferdinand (1825–1864) German–Jewish author, political thinker, and revolutionary socialist. Founder of the German Socialist Party.

Lebensohn, Micah Joseph (1828–1852) One of the foremost poets in Hebrew of the Haskalah period. His poetry collections include: *Kinor Bat-Tzion*, Lyre of Zion, and *Shirei Bat-Tzion*, Songs of Zion. Translated European poetry into Hebrew and also part of Virgil's *Aeneid*.

Le Corbusier (Charles-Edouard Jeanneret) (1887–1965) Swiss architect, one of the greatest innovators of modern architecture, for example, in the use of reinforced concrete as a design element. One of the designers of the United Nations building in New York. Among other celebrated achievements include government buildings in Chandigarh, India, a low-income residential complex in Marseilles, and a chapel at Ronchamp, France.

Leibowitz, Yeshayahu (1903–1993) Israeli chemist, biologist, neuropsychologist, and philosopher. Perceived the essence of Judaism to lie in the practical commandments. Faith and science, guided by different goals, to him are not in contradiction.

Lenin (Vladimir Ilyich Ulyanov) (1870–1924) Russian political theorist, writer, and revolutionary leader. As leader of the Bolshevik Party he headed the 1917 revolution and subsequently the new Soviet Union.

Lessing, Gotthold Ephraim (1729–1781) German philosopher, dramatist, and essayist. A theorist on art. Friend of Moses Mendelssohn, who served as the model for the Jew, Nathan, in Lessing's play, *Nathan the Wise*.

Levi, Ben Gershom (1288–1344) Rabbi, philosopher, biblical commentator, mathematician, and astronomer. He followed the rationalist example set by Maimonides. Best known for his *Sefer Milkhamot Adonai*, Book of the Lord's Wars.

Levi Isaac of Berditchev (1740–1810) A Hasidic tzaddik of the third generation of European Hasidim. Stressed that at the basis of the "Worship of the Creator" is joy and exhilaration. Especially famous for his love of Israel, insisting that every Jew has good in him.

Levi, Primo (1919–1988) Italian–Jewish author whose experiences in Auschwitz engendered *If This Is a Man*. Also wrote *The Periodic Table*.

Levin, Yitzhak Meir (1894–1971) A leader of the *Agudat Yisrael* ultra-Orthodox political party and signatory in its name to Israel's Declaration of Independence. A minister in a number of Ben-Gurion governments.

Levinas, Emmanuel (1905–1995) French–Jewish philosopher of ethics and educator. His works include *Ethics and Infinity: Conversations With Philippe Nemo, Totality and Infinity*, and *Other Than Reality, or Beyond Being*.

Lichtenstein, Roy (1923–1997) American artist who specialized in reproducing newspaper comic-strip images on an enlarged scale.

Lieberman, Aaron Samuel (1845–1880) Pioneer of Jewish socialism. Established the Hebrew Socialist Union and a Hebrew-language socialist monthly, *The Truth*. Published numerous articles calling on Jewish workers to unionize.

Locke, John (1632–1704) English philosopher, argued that the only source of knowledge available is human experience.

Luria, Rabbi Isaac Ashkenazi (The Holy ARI) (1534–1572) One of the greatest of medieval Kabbalists, founder of Lurian Kabbala. Deviser of an elaborate system explaining in mystical and mythological terms the nature of Creation and the fate and divinely-ordained role of the people of Israel. Introduced the concept of *tikkun* to be brought about by the Jews' self-dedication to *mitzva* observance, whose ultimate end was universal redemption.

Luther, Martin (1483–1546) German religious reformer and a founder of Protestant Christianity.

Luzzato, Moses Ha'im (1707–1747) Kabbalist, poet, and playwright who lived and worked in Italy, The Netherlands, and Palestine. His lyrical verse and dramas are considered by some to mark the inception of Haskalah literature. His plays include *Ma'aseh Shimshon,* A Story of Samson; *Migdal Oz,* Tower of Strength; *LeYesharim Tehila,* Glory to the Upright.

Magritte, René (1898–1967) Belgian painter and leading Surrealist.

Mahler, Gustav (1860–1911) German–Jewish composer and conductor who converted to Christianity. A great innovator in symphonic music.

Maimonides, Moses (R. Moses Ben Maimon—RaMBaM) (1135–1204) Physician, philosopher, and codifier of halacha. The greatest intellectual and halachic authority in Judaism and especially so in the medieval period. His great philosophical opus, *Moreh Nevokhim,* Guide for the Perplexed, and his codification of halacha, *Mishne Torah,* A Recapitulation of Torah, are constructed on two levels, for general readers and for the small stratum of learned Jews. His philosophy is rationalist and draws deeply on Aristotelian concepts.

Manet, Edouard (1832–1883) French painter, forerunner of Impressionism.

Manger, Itzik (1901–1969) Yiddish poet. The prime source for his poetry, saturated in millennia of Jewish tradition, is Jewish folk culture. In his collection, *Midrash Itzik,* Itzik's Midrash, he re-enacts biblical figures in a *shtetl* setting.

Mapu, Abraham (1808–1867) Author and pioneer of the Haskalah in Eastern Europe. Wrote the first novel in Hebrew, *Ahavat Tzion,* Love of Zion. Other works are *Ayit Tzavua,* Painted Eagle—the hypocrite, *Ashmat Shomron,* Samaria's Guilt.

Marx, Karl (1818–1883) German–Jewish philosopher, economist, and historian, and the father of revolutionary socialism. He taught that human history was the history of the change in productive relationships, characterized by the permanent conflict of the working and exploiting classes. For him, a classless society free of exploitation would only come about by a socialist revolution, the outcome of capitalism's internal contradictions.

Mendelsohn, Eric (1887–1953) German–Jewish architect who played a crucial part in the development of modern architecture. Built in Germany, Palestine, and the United States.

Mendelssohn, Moses (Ben Menachem) (1729–1786) Philosopher and founder of the Haskalah in Germany. He was rationalist even in matters of religion. Taught the separation of the spheres of faith and of practical life, as practical social life must be subject to some degree of state coercion, whereas in matters of faith no coercion was possible.

Mendelssohn, Felix (1809–1847) German composer whose Jewish father had converted the family to Christianity. Grandson of M. Moses. Among his most famous works are the overtures *A Midsummer Night's Dream* and *The Hebrides*, and the *Italian* and *Scottish* symphonies. Having attained great celebrity in his lifetime, his reputation declined after his death, partly because of the anti-Semitic climate in Europe.

Mendes-France, Pierre (1907–1982) French–Jewish politician and leader of the French Socialist Party. A minister in de Gaulle's Free French government and in 1954 prime minister, when he introduced economic reforms and supported decolonialization.

Michelangelo Buonarroti (1475–1564) Sculptor, painter, architect, and poet of Renaissance Italy, a colossus of art in any era. His most renowned works include, in painting the ceiling of the Vatican's Sistine Chapel, in architecture St. Peter's in Rome, and in sculpture Moses and David.

Miller, Arthur (1910–2005) American–Jewish playwright, among the most important of the twentieth century. He uses drama to protest against the values of capitalism in *Death of a Salesman, All My Sons, View From the Bridge,* and *The Crucible.*

Miller, Glenn (1904–1944) American master of jazz, composer, conductor, and clarinettist. The first to take a white big band into jazz.

Miró, Joan (1893–1983) Prominent Spanish painter of the Surrealist school.

Modigliani, Amadeo (1884–1920) Italian–Jewish painter of unique style. His portrait subjects, with their elongated necks and dulled eyes, exude a feeling of an essential unhappiness and gentleness.

Molière, Jean-Baptiste Poquelin (1622–1673) French actor-playwright. Giant of social comedy. His plays include *L'Avare, The Miser,* and *Tartuffe.*

Montesquieu, Charles-Louis (1689–1755) French philosopher of socio-political issues. Advocated the separation of powers of legislative, judicial, and executive authorities.

Morpurgo, Rachel (1790–1871) Hebrew-language poet of the *Haskalah* era who lived in Trieste, Italy. In correspondence with many of the leading *maskilim* of her time.

Moses de Leon (1240–1305?) Kabbalist who lived in Spain, author of the *Zohar.*

Mozart, Wolfgang Amadeus (1756–1791) Austrian composer, one of the supreme artists in music of any age. Composed in all genres, including dozens of symphonies, concerti, and operas. The latter include *The Magic Flute* and *Don Giovanni.*

Munch, Edvard (1863–1944) Norwegian painter, a precursor of the Expressionists whose work expressed an existential dread. His most celebrated painting is *The Scream.*

Niemeyer, Oscar (1907–) Brazilian–Jewish architect and a prominent modernist. Best known for the center of the new city of Brasilia. In Israel designed Haifa University, *Kikar HaMedina,* State Square, in Tel Aviv, and other projects.

Nietzsche, Friedrich (1844–1900) German philosopher. Declared the death of God, and the need for new ethics. Influenced by Darwin's theory of evolution, perceived struggle for survival, and drive for power to be ethical standards of universal validity.

Owen, Robert (1771–1858) English socialist and industrial reformer. Pioneer of co-operative societies and trade unions.

Oz, Amos (1939-) Israeli novelist and essayist, one of the most important of the "post-1948 generation." His list of novels includes *Artzot HaTan,* Where the Jackal Howls; *Makom Akher,* Elsewhere Perhaps; *Mikhael Sheli,* My Michael; *Ad Mavet,* Unto Death; *Har HaEtza HaRa'a,* The Hill of Evil Counsel; *Menukha Nekhona,* A Perfect Peace; *Sipur al Ahava VeHoshekh,* A Story of Love and Darkness. Among his essay collections are *BeOr HaTkhelet Ha'Aza,* Under This Blazing Light; *Po VeSham be'Eretz Yisrael,* In the Land of Israel.

Pascal, Blaise (1623–1662) French religious philosopher, physicist, and mathematician. In physics he worked in the field of hydraulics, in mathematics in probability theory, while in philosophy he defended Christianity.

Peretz, Isaac Leib (1852–1915) Author, poet, and playwright in Yiddish and in Hebrew; in Yiddish one of the greatest. His stories depict the poverty-stricken lives of the Jewish masses cut off from the wider society, and their struggle to maintain existence. Also reworked Hasidic tales in the spirit of new contemporary ideas.

Petronius (first century CE) Roman author of *Satyricon.*

Philo of Alexandria (Judaeus—Yedidya) (15–10 BCE.–45–50 CE) Greek-speaking Jewish philosopher, the most important representative of Helennistic Judaism. His writings provide the clearest view of the development of Judaism in the Diaspora. As the first to attempt to synthesize revealed faith and philosophical reason, he occupies a unique position in the history of philosophy. He is also regarded by Christians as a forerunner of Christian theology.

Picasso, Pablo (1881–1973) Spanish painter and sculptor, who lived and worked most of his life in France in protest against the fascism ruling Spain. A key figure in twentieth-century art, a fertile innovator in every genre he set his hand to: Cubism, Expressionism, Surrealism, Symbolism, and more.

Pinsker, Leon (1821–1891) Physician and one of the leaders of the *Khibbat Tzion* movement. An activist of *Haskalah* ideas among the Jews of Russia, his mind was changed by the 1881 pogroms against Ukrainian Jews which caused him to compose and publish the pamphlet "Auto-Emancipation," calling for Jewish autonomy on the Jews' own territory.

Pukhachevski, Nechama (1869–1934) Author and pioneer of First Aliya (1882–1903). Her novellas described life in the early settlements.

Protagoras (485–420 BCE) Greek Sophist philosopher who argued that absolute truth did not exist; "Man is the measure of all things" is his famous dictum.

Proust, Marcel (1871–1922) French–Jewish author, one of the luminaries of French literature. His magnum opus, *Remembrance of things Past,* is autobiographically based, the point of observation located in the hero's own mind.

Raab, Esther (1899–1981) Hebrew poet born in the newly founded settlement of Petakh Tikva. A leading poet of the interwar period.

Rabbina (fifth century CE) fifth-generation Babylonian *amora,* by tradition one of those who formally closed the talmudic canon.

Rakhel (Bluvstein) (1890–1931) Leading Hebrew lyric poet of the Third Aliyah (1919–23). She voiced the pain of the individual in the context of building the land and the panoramas of the Sea of Galilee.

RaSHI (Rabbi Solomon ben Isaac) (1040–1105) The pre-eminent commentator on Bible and Talmud and one of the most respected halachic authorities of Ashkenazic

Jewry in the Middle Ages. He preferred the *pshatt* approach to biblical interpretation.

Ratosh, Yonatan (Uriel Halperin) (1909–1981) Poet and thinker, one of the greatest exponents of modern Hebrew poetry and founder and leader of the "Canaanite" group. The Canaanite doctrine was that the Hebrew people now being created in the Land of Israel was unrelated to the Jews living in *Galut: its land was the broad Eretz HaKedem*, The Land of the East, and Ratosh's verse hymned its roots in the Hebrew people's pre-biblical civilization.

Rauschenberg, Robert (1925–2008) American artist. Staged one-off "happenings" as performances of art, worked in different combinations of media. Emphasized spontaneity and the use of everyday materials.

Ravikovitz, Dalia (1936–2005) Hebrew poet and story writer, one of the best known of the "post-1948 generation." Her books include *Ahavat Tapuakh haZahav*, Love of an Orange; *Khoref Kasheh*, Hard Winter; *Tehom Koreh*, Sounding Depths; *Mavet beMishpakha*, Death in the Family; *Ahava Amitit*, True Love; *Kvutzat haKaduregel shel Vinni Mandela*, Winnie Mandela's Football Team.

Reines, Isaac Jacob (1839–1915) Rabbi, founded and led the *Mizrakhi* movement of religious Zionism. Regarding Zionism as a political movement, he supported Herzl's concept of political Zionism.

Rembrandt van Rijn (1606–1669) Dutch painter and one of the greatest artists. A master of light and shadow. Painted many biblical subjects and Jewish characters.

Renoir, Pierre-Auguste (1841–1919) French painter, a founder of the Impressionist school.

Rilke, Rainer Maria (1875–1926) German poet, one of the greatest of modern times. His collections include *The Book of Hours, The Duino Elegies, Sonnets to Orpheus*.

Rosenzweig, Franz (1886–1929) German–Jewish philosopher, a religious existentialist. Out of exploration of the question of the individual and death he became more deeply religious. He regarded reality and history as aspects of a constant divine revelation. The three elements of the universe, God, the world, humankind, are interlinked by the power of creation, revelation, and redemption. These two triangles, placed one on the other, form "The Star of Redemption," the title of Rosenzweig's main work.

Rousseau, Jean-Jaques (1712–1778) French philosopher who concerned himself with educational, social, and political systems. Defended the rights of the people against authority and preached a return to nature.

Saadiah Gaon (882–942) Philosopher and halachic authority, *gaon* of the leading Babylonian yeshivas (first Pumbedita, then Sura) and a pre-eminent leader of Jewry. Compiled the first alphabetical dictionary of Hebrew, *Sefer haAgron*. His philosophy was rationalist, perceiving no opposition between faith and logic.

Saint-Simon, Claude-Henri (1760–1825) French founder of Utopian Socialism. Volunteered to fight for the rebel side in the American Revolution. Called for an atheist state governed by engineers and industrialists.

Sartre, Jean-Paul (1905–1980) French philosopher, playwright, and author. Active in the French Resistance during World War II. A leading Existentialist. Among his works are the trilogy *The Paths of Liberty*, the plays *No Exit, Flies*, and *The Condemned of Altona*.

Schechter, Solomon (1847–1915) Philosopher and cultural researcher who discovered the Cairo *geniza*, which had preserved hundreds of thousands of medieval Jewish manuscripts. One of the founders and mentors of Conservative Judaism in the United States.

Schiller, Friedrich (1759–1805) German poet, playwright, and essayist, whose great theme is longing for national liberty. Many of his poems have been set to music and entered the German folksong treasury. His plays include the historical trilogy *Wallenstein* and the historical drama *William Tell*.

Schoenberg, Arnold (1874–1951) German–Jewish composer, one of the most influential innovators and path-breakers of the twentieth century. His opera, *Moses and Aaron*, is counted among his best work.

Scholem, Gershom (1897–1982) One of the foremost Kabbala scholars and researchers. His books include *Shabtai Tzvi and the Sabbatean Movement*, *Major Trends in Jewish Mysticism*, *On the Kabbala and its Symbolism*.

Shabbatai Zevi (1626–1676) The leader of the largest Jewish messianic movement following the 1648–49 pogroms against Eastern European Jewry and the religious wars afflicting Europe. Arrested by the Turkish Sultan, Shabbatai Zevi capitulated and converted to Islam but remains of the movement persisted for decades after his death.

Shabzi, Shalom (sixteenth–seventeenth century) Yemenite composer of *piyyut* , a giant of the genre.

Shakhar, David (1926–1997) Hebrew novelist. His great work: eight-volume series, *Hekhal haKelim haShevurim*, The Palace of the Broken Vessels.

Shakespeare, William (1564–1616) English dramatist and poet, perhaps the greatest playwright of all. Among his most famous creations are *Hamlet, King Lear, Romeo and Juliet*, and *A Midsummer Night's Dream*.

Shelley, Percy Bysshe (1792–1822) English lyric poet whose work occupies a central place in Romanticism. Expelled from Oxford University for atheism.

Shemaya and Avtalyon (first century BCE) One of five pairs (*zugot*) of sages who occupied the positions of president of the Sanhedrin and chief justice of the High Court. According to tradition they were proselytes.

Shimon Bar Yokhai (second century CE) fourth-generation *tanna*, a disciple of Rabbi Akiva. By tradition, after the collapse of the Bar Kokhba revolt, he and his son, R. Eliezer fled the Romans and hid for twelve years in a cave in the Galilee. A late tradition credits him with composing the Zohar.

Shmuel (second–third century CE) A leading first-generation *amora* in the Babylonian Diaspora and head of the great Nehardea academy. A physician, astronomer, and mathematician who was familiar with the science of his time. His counterpart at the Sura Academy and in the leadership of Babylonian Jewry was Rav.

Schneersohn, Menachem Mendel (1902–1996) Rebbe of the Chabad Hasidim. Towards the end of his life was acclaimed by his followers as the Messiah.

Shneur Zalman of Lyady (1745–1813) Founder of the Chabad sect of Hasidim. With an essentially intellectual approach to Hasidism, he was a much more committed advocate of Torah study and *mitzva*-observance than other Hasidic *rebbes*. In his view, the bearer of Hasidism was the simple middling Jew, whose aspiration was a middling perfection. The *tzaddik*, on the other hand, was endowed with exceptional inborn gifts.

Silver, Abba Hillel (1893–1963) Rabbi and leader of American Reform Jewry. One of the first leaders of Reform to join the Zionist movement, he rose to become an important leader. Active in the diplomatic struggle for the new State of Israel.

Sirkin, Nakhman (1868–1924) Ideologue and leader of Socialist Zionism who taught that only constructive socialism could succeed in making the Zionist vision a reality.

Smolenskin, Peretz (1840–1885) Author, essayist, and editor; leading figure of the later stages of the Haskalah. Edited and published a literary monthly, *HaShakhar*, The Dawn, which, while it lasted, was the most important of its kind. Late in life joined the *Khovevei Tzion*, Lovers of Zion, movement. A sharp critic of contemporary Jewish society, particularly the rabbinic establishment, but also saw the weaknesses in Haskalah teachings.

Socrates (469–399 BCE) Greek philosopher, whose work we know only from the writings of his pupil, Plato. He taught that the truth was to be uncovered by freeing ourselves from prejudices and undertaking a process of logically constructed debate.

Sofer, Moses (*Khatam Sofer*) (1762–1839) nineteenth-century European Orthodoxy's most forceful leader, in the forefront of the battle against Emancipation and the Haskalah. His nickname, *Khatam Sofer*, comes from the initials of his book, **Khiddushei Torat Moshe**, Novelties of the Teachings of Moses. He laid down that R. Joseph Caro's halachic codification, *Shulkhan Arukh*, The Laid Table, was the last word on halacha and not open to further change, in so doing endorsing the attempt of rabbis in the late eighteenth-century to halt the development of Judaism. His famous dictum is "Torah forbids innovation."

Soloveitchik, Joseph Dov Halevi (1903–1993) Rabbi and theologian, a leading authority in Modern Orthodoxy in the United States. A supporter of Zionism, he had close links to the *Mizrakhi* Religious Zionist movement. His teaching on *halacha* is that it liberates the individual and brings him closer to God.

Soutine, Chaim (1893–1943) Jewish painter who lived and worked in Paris. A prominent Expressionist.

Spinoza, Baruch (1632–1677) Dutch–Jewish philosopher who laid the intellectual foundations of modern humanism. Born into a family of conversed Jews who had returned to Judaism. His teaching offered a substitute for established religion, Pantheism, according to which God and the natural world are one and the laws of nature are the laws of God. A sharp critic of religious dogma and the temporal powers of men of religion, he favored freedom of conscience and thought. Voiced rational doubts about the holiness of Holy Writ and so opened the way for biblical criticism. The heads of the Amsterdam Jewish community responded by labeling him an atheist and proclaiming a decree of ostracism against him.

Teitelbaum, Yoel (1888–1979) *Rebbe* of the Satmar sect of Hasidim. An implacable enemy of Zionism and the State of Israel, which he blamed for preventing redemption and causing the disaster of the Holocaust.

Tolstoy, Lev Nikolayevitch (1828–1910) Russian novelist and thinker. One of the greatest European writers. His most famous works are the novels *War and Peace, Anna Karenina,* and his short story, *The Death of Ivan Ilyich*. In his practical philosophy he preached the simple life and love of one's fellow men.

Toulouse-Lautrec, Henri (1864–1901) French post-Impressionist painter of Parisian nightlife and the creator of striking posters for nightclubs.

Trotsky, Leon (Lev Davidovitch Bronstein) (1879–1940) Russian–Jewish revolutionary activist, ideologue, and writer. One of the leaders of the 1917 Bolshevik Revolution and the architect of the Red Army. Accused of treason by Stalin, he emigrated to Mexico where he was murdered.

van der Rohe, Mies (1886–1969) Dutch architect who did most of his work in Germany and the United States. A key figure in developing the International Style of the Bauhaus school.

Van Gogh, Vincent (1853–1890) Dutch post-Impressionist painter and a key precursor of Expressionism. Alongside his own mental disturbance and emotional turmoil, his paintings display the suffering of humanity as a whole.

Voltaire (François-Marie Arouet) (1694–1778) French author and thinker, a principal figure of the French Enlightenment. His output embraces history, philosophy, essays on scientific themes, political tracts, plays, poetry, and satirical parables. Renowned for his superb wit.

Wagner, Richard (1813–1883) German composer, one of the foremost of the nineteenth century, who devised a new type of opera, a musical drama conceived as a total art form. The inspiration for many of his operas came from German mythology. An extreme anti-Semite.

Wallach, Yona (1944–1985) Israeli poet and important influence on the younger Israeli generation of poets, in contrast to the pre-State generation. *Tat-Hakara Niftakhat Kemo Menifa*, The Subconscious Opens Like a Fan, is a collection of her work.

Wilde, Oscar (1854–1900) Irish novelist, playwright, and poet. His style is brilliant, entertaining, and sparkles with wit. His oeuvre includes the novel, *The Picture of Dorian Grey* and the plays *Lady Windermere's Fan, The Importance of Being Earnest,* and *Salome.*

Wise, Isaac Mayer (1819–1900) One of the first Reform rabbis in the United States. Promoted a moderate reform of Judaism. Directed Hebrew Union College, the Reform movement's rabbinic seminary.

Wise, Stephen (1874–1949) Reform rabbi and leader of American Jewry. Active in the World Zionist Federation and in 1936 elected president of the Zionist Organization of America. An important figure in the diplomatic measures and negotiations that brought about the establishment of the State of Israel.

Woolf, Virginia (1882–1941) English novelist and essayist who constructed her novels using the stream of consciousness technique. Argued for women's financial independence and other causes. Among her works are *Orlando, To the Lighthouse,* and *Mrs. Dalloway.*

Wright, Frank Lloyd (1867–1959) American architect, an inspiration to modern architecture. His architectural thinking was called Organic because he called for structures to be integrated into their natural surroundings. He was influenced by Japanese art. Among his celebrated buildings are the Kaufmann Falling Water house, the Guggenheim Museum in New York, and the Bet Shalom synagogue in Philadelphia.

Yehoshua, Avraham B. (1935–) Novelist and essayist, a leading figure of the "post-1948" literary generation. Author of short stories, novels and plays. His fiction includes *Kol haSippurim,* All the Stories; *Hame'ahev,* The Lover; *Gerushim Me'ukh-*

arim, A Late Divorce; *Molkho,* Five Seasons; *Mar Mani,* Mr. Mani; *HaShiva miHodu,* The Return From India; *Masa el Tom ha'Elef,* A Journey to the End of the Millennium; *HaKala haMeshahreret,* The Liberating Bride; *Shlihuto shel HaMemune al Mashabei Enosh,* A Woman in Jerusalem. Among his essay collections are *Bizkhut haNormaliut,* Between Right and Right; *Hakir vehaHar,* The Wall and the Mountain; *Kokha haNora shel Ashma Ktana,* The Terrible Power of a Minor Guilt; *Ahizat Moledet,* Homeland Grasp.

Yehoshua ben Khananya (first century CE) Tanna, disciple of Rabbi Yokhanan ben Zakai.

Yehuda Halevi (1075–1142) Poet and philosopher, one of those who made Spain in the Middle Ages a golden age of Jewish art. His religious verse comprises hymns to the glory of God and songs of lamentation; his secular verse covers nature poems, love songs, drinking songs, as well as poems of yearning for Zion. Advocated Jews returning to the Land of Israel and as an old man set out to do so, but probably died before reaching his goal. His philosophical work, *The Kuzari,* probes the deepest issues in Judaism, prophesy, revelation, divine law, and Israel's election.

Yehuda Hanasi (135?–220) Known also as "Rabi." Editor of the Mishna and one of the greatest of *tannaim.* Spiritual and political leader of Palestinian Jewry in the second century CE.

Yizhar, S. (Smilansky) (1916–2006) One of the best Israeli novelists and leading figure of the "1948 literary generation." His books include *HaKhursha beGiva,* The Grove on the Hill; *Shayara shel Khatzot,* Midnight Convoy; *Yemei Tziklag,* The Days of Tziklag. From recent years are *Mikdamot, Tzalhavim,* Shining Lights; *Etzel haYam,* By the Sea; *Tzdadiim,* Marginal People; *Milkomiya Yefefiya,* Milkomiya the Beautiful.

Zach, Natan (1930–) Israeli poet and essayist, a star of the "post-1948 literary generation." His books of poetry include *Shirim Shonim,* Miscellaneous Poems; *Kol haKhalav vehaDvash,* All the Milk and Honey; *Bimkom Khalom,* In Place of a Dream; *Kaivan she'Ani baSviva,* Since I'm Nearby. He also wrote the essay *Time and Rhythm in Bergson and Other Modern Poets.*

Further Reading

REFERENCE

Encyclopedia Judaica (26 volumes), Cecil Roth and Geoffrey Wigoden, eds. Jerusalem: Keter, 1971–74.

Shaham, David, Yovel Yirmiyahu, and Tzaban Yair, chief eds. Zman Yehudi Hadash *New Jewish Times: Jewish Culture in a Secular Age—An Encyclopedic View*, Jerusalem: Keter, 2007. Essays by more than 230 scholars that focus on the progress of Jewish secularization through the last two hundred years, and its impact upon Jewish life and history. Includes sections on Jewish cultures, arts and literatures, Jewish languages, society, and historiography.

Werblowsky, R. J., and Geoffrey Wigoder, chief eds. *The Oxford Dictionary of the Jewish Religion*, New York: Oxford University Press; 1997. A comprehensive dictionary of the Jewish religion, includes many entries on Jewish culture.

JUDAISM AS A CULTURE

Biale, David, ed. *Cultures of the Jews*, New York: Schocken, 2002 A collection of essays, written by twenty-three scholars, that addresses the cultural interactions among different groups of Jews, as well as between Jews and the surrounding world; and discusses the changes that took place in Jewish traditions and identities through the ages. The authors raise questions central to the understanding of Judaism and Jewish life and propose answers that reconcile ideas with their historical relativities. Among the contributors are E. S. Greun, Y. Kaplan, I. G. Marcus, E. M. Meyers, A. Rodrigue, E. Yassif, S. J. Whitfeld, and others.

Cohn, Haim H., Lihyot Yehudi. *Being Jewish—Culture, Law, Religion, State,* Tel Aviv: Dvir, 2006 (Hebrew). A very important collection of essays, lectures, court verdicts, and letters by the late Israeli Supreme Court Judge Haim Cohn, that deal with cultural, philosophical, and juridical problems of Judaism in the contemporary reality of Israel. The first part of the book is "Judaism, God, *Halakha*, Culture, Humanism, Zionism." The second part deals with the question of "who is a Jew," The third is about the Hebrew Law, (*Halacha*) and the laws of the state, and the last is about the Jewishness of the State of Israel.

Evron, Boaz. *Jewish State or Israeli Nation?* Bloomington: Indiana University Press, 1995. Evron suggests a new perspective on the history and the tradition of the Jewish people, showing that in the Diaspora, the religious community replaced the nationality of the Jews. The national revival in the nineteenth century should have been a total disconnection from traditional Judaism. The most severe problem in Israel now

249

is the return of the religious component of Jewish existence into Israeli nationality. His book is a wide and deep survey of Jewish history and of the situation of nationality and religion in the State of Israel.

Feiner, Shmuel, *Jewish Enlightenment*. Philadelphia: University of Pennsylvania Press, 2003. A most important research in the history of the Jewish Enlightenment, which is described as a revolution that took place in Central and Eastern Europe in the eighteenth century. It shows how the republic of letters of European Jewry provided an avenue of secularization for Jewish society and culture, sowing the seeds of Jewish liberalism and modern ideology and sparking the Orthodox counter-reaction that culminated in a clash of cultures within the Jewish community.

Funkenstein, Amos. *Perceptions of Jewish History—From Antiquity to the Present*, Berkeley: University of California Press, 1993. Essays on Jewish culture through the ages, as perceived, interpreted and retained in the historical collective memories of the Jewish people. Funkenstein shows that Jewish culture was always interpreted in the context of time and place, and in a very creative understanding. The book surveys the many layers of Jewish culture, from its early beginnings to the present day. Includes an essay entitled "Theological interpretations of the Holocaust."

Kahanoff, Ezer. *National Identity versus Religious Identity within Sefaradi Jewry*, Achva Academic College, 2002. This book focuses on the origins of the process that separated the consciousness of Jewish nationalism from the consciousness of Jewish religion among the Sefaradi Jewish communities in Western Europe, especially in The Netherlands, in the sixteenth and seventeenth centuries. This separation is at the root of the secularization process in Judaism, from that time until today.

Kogel, Renee, and Zeev Katz, eds. *Judaism in a Secular Age*, Jersey City, NJ: Ktav, 1995. An anthology of secular humanistic Jewish thought, contains excerpts from the writings of more than fifty thinkers, writers, and poets, examining the nature of Jewish culture from a humanistic secular point of view, starting with Spinoza ("the precursor"), preceding thinkers such as Herzl, Gordon, Kaplan, Bialik, and then to Dubnov, Ahad Haam, Brener, Arendt, and finally to the latest writers and thinkers, such as Isaiah Berlin, Albert Memmi, Yehuda Bauer, Oz, Yehoshua, and others.

Livneh-Freudenthal, Rachel, and Elchanan Reiner, eds. *Streams Into the Sea, Studies in Jewish Culture and its Context*, Tel Aviv: Alma College, 2001. A collection of articles, essays, and literary excerpts, discusses various aspects of Jewish culture. The first section deals with diverse aspects of political culture in Israel, the second is a selection of articles on various representations of Jewish culture from a critical perspective, and the third section contains essays relating to general culture, which is the major reference for Jewish culture through the ages. Among the contributors are R. Calderon, Y. Schwartz, U. Simon, Y. Zakovitch, and G. Zoran.

Malkin, Yaakov. *Secular Judaism: Faith, Values and Spirituality*, London: Vallentine Mitchell, 2004. An articulation of the beliefs and the practices of secular Judaism, discussing the values of secular Humanism versus the values of the religion and "Relativism." It examines Judaism as a pluralistic culture, rather than as a religion. It describes the classic Jewish texts from a secular point of view, showing that the Bible is the common source of Judaism and the foundation of Jewish culture and civilization.

———, ed. *Secular Jewish Culture—New Thinking in Israel*, Jerusalem: Keter, 2003. A collection of essays, written by twenty-six well-known scholars and writers, that gives expression to sources and contributions in secular Jewish thought in Israel today. The essays in the book deal with the development of secularity, Jewish identity, humanism in Judaism, philosophical influences on Jewish thinking, and the status of women in Judaism. It includes S. Yizhar's essay "The Courage to be Secular," and Malkin's research on "The Influence of the Greek Epicurus and Jewish 'Apikorsim' on Judaism" (English translation, Detroit: Milan, 2009). Among the other contributors are: Shulamit Aloni, Yehuda Bauer, Haim Beer, Manachem Brinker, Rachel Elior.

Memmi, Albert. *The Liberation of the Jew*. New York: Orion, 1966. This French-Jewish writer examines the condition of Jewish existence in twentieth-century reality. He rejects self-denials of Jewish identity, but he does not see a way out of the acceptance of it. He thinks that oppressed people do not have any culture, they have tradition. He argues that the liberation of the Jews must be a national liberation, culture must replace tradition.

Schweid, Eliezer. *The Idea of Modern Jewish Culture*, Brighton, MA: Academic Studies, 2008. A synoptic view of the intellectual, religious, and national developments in modern Judaism, revolving around the central idea of Jewish culture. According to Schweid, the conception of Judaism-as-culture took two main forms: an integrative, vernacular Jewish culture that developed in western central Europe and America, and a national Hebrew culture that found expression in the revival of the Jewish homeland and the State of Israel. The book describes the contributions of Mendelssohn, Wessely, Krochmal, Zunz, Ahad Ha-Am, Bialik, A. D. Gordon, Kook, Kaplan, and Dubnow to the formulation of the various versions of modern Jewish cultural ideal.

Silver, Mitchell. *Respecting the Wicked Child—a Philosophy of Secular Jewish Identity and Education*. Amherst: University of Massachusetts Press, 1998. A philosophical rationale and a description of how Jewish identity in the materialist, multicultural, Christian-dominated American society can be maintained without compromising one's liberal and secular values, reconciling the imperatives and values of tradition and the ideas of modernity. "The Wicked Child" refers to one of the 'four sons' in the Passover *Haggada*.

Wine, Sherwin T. *Judaism Beyond God*. Jersey City, NJ: Ktav, 1995. The "Credo" of the founder of the first Humanistic secular Jewish congregation in America. In his book Rabbi Wine presents a secular and humanistic alternative to conventional Judaism. He answers questions about Jewish identity, the meaning of Jewish history, and Jewish ethics. He provides new, secular ways of celebrating holidays and ceremonies of the Jewish life cycle.

RELIGION AND SECULARITY IN ISRAEL

Brinker, Menachem. *Mahshavot Israeliot. Israeli Thoughts*, Jerusalem: Carmel, 2007. A selection of essays and articles, written by a leading Israeli philosopher, discussing Jewish culture, identity, nationality, and secularity from an Israeli point of view. Includes also essays on Nietzsche, Heidegger, Sartre, "The Jewish Question," and some other issues.

Cohen, Asher, and Bernhard Susser. *Israel and the Politics of Jewish Identity: The Secular—Religious Impasse*, Baltimore: The Johns Hopkins University Press, 2000. A survey of the history of political relationships between the secular and the religious communities in Israel, showing a transformation from co-existence to a conflict that goes from bad to worse. The book ties this transformation to the structural changes in Israeli politics, from a dominant-party system to a balanced two camps system, and to the growing connecion of the political right wing in Israel with religiosity. It also examines the effect of the massive immigration of secular Jews from the former Soviet Union on Israeli society.

Oz, Amos. *Kol Hatikvot. All Our Hopes—Essays on the Israeli Condition,* Jerusalem: Keter, 1998. A collection of essays written by one of the best-known Hebrew writers, dealing with problems of Jewish secular identity in Israel today, the splits in Israeli society, and the part they play in the current cultural and political situation, the past and future of Israel and other issues. The essay "Full Cart—Empty Cart" is included in this volume.

Ravitzky Aviezer. *Herut al Ha-Luhot. Freedom Inscribed, Diverse Voices of the Jewish Religious Thoughts,* Tel Aviv: Am Oved, 1999. A collection of essays written by a leading religious Israeli philosopher that discusses the problem of Israeli existence from a religious Zionism point of view. It includes essays on modernism and secularity as perceived in Orthodox thought, and on the dispute between secular and religious Zionism in Israel.

Yehoshua, Avraham B. *Homeland Grasp—20 Articles and One Story,* Tel Aviv: Hakibbutz Hameuchad, 2008. This book of reflections on Jewish identity and culture in Israel and in the Diaspora by a leading Hebrew writer contains the essay, "An attempt to identify the root cause of Anti-Semitism" (Azure 32, spring 2008), and Yehoshua's May 2006 controversial lecture in Washington. A short story, "Bosom Friend," concludes the book.

GREAT MINDS ON RELIGION AND RELIGIOUSNESS

Dawkins, Richard, *The God Delusion.* New York: Bantam Books, 2006. The famous biologist claims that the existence of God is scientifically and logically not reasonable, and that a personal God is a delusion. He argues that evolution is the explanation for the creation of the world and everything in it.

Gay, Peter. *A Godless Jew—Freud, Atheism, and the Making of Psychoanalysis,* New Haven: Yale University Press, 1987. A research book discussing the long-running controversy about the relationship between psychoanalysis and religion, Judaism in particular, provide new insight into Freud's views on religion and how they did and did not affect the development of psychoanalysis. It argues that Freud was a particular kind of atheist, a Jewish atheist, and that enabled him to make his discoveries.

Jammer, Max. *Einstein and Religion,* Princeton: Princeton University Press, 1999. The author of this book, a distinguished physicist and philosopher, offers a well-documented answer to the question about Einstein's religiosity. Einstein was most influenced by Spinoza's thesis of an unrestricted determinism and the belief in the existence of a superior intelligence that reveals itself in the harmony and beauty of nature. The book includes a rare 1920 poem by Einstein that refers to Spinoza.

Index